DATE DUE

MEXICAN FINANCIAL DEVELOPMENT

*Published with the assistance of a grant
from the Ford Foundation
under its program for the support of publications
in the humanities and social sciences*

MEXICAN
FINANCIAL
DEVELOPMENT

By **Dwight S. Brothers,** *Rice University*

and **Leopoldo Solís M.,** *El Colegio de México*

AUSTIN
LONDON   UNIVERSITY OF TEXAS PRESS

The sections of this book originally drafted in Spanish
were translated into English by Marian Berdecio.

Printed by The University of Texas Printing Division, Austin
Bound by Universal Bookbindery, Inc., San Antonio

PREFACE

This book contains the results of our efforts to establish and analyze the record of recent Mexican financial development. We have attempted not only to prepare an accurate and detailed chronicle of the course this development has taken but also (and more importantly) to establish relationships between the operation of the financial system and the stability and growth of the Mexican economy.

The study consists of four main parts. The first part contains a summary description of Mexican financial development prior to 1940, with emphasis on postrevolutionary experience and the factors accounting for changes in the country's financial structure during this period. The various institutions and instruments—as well as markets and policies—which characterized the Mexican financial system and its operation at the end of the 1930s are described in some detail in order to establish a bench mark against which subsequent development can be measured and appraised. The second part of the study consists of detailed accounts of the development of the various components of the financial system during the period 1940–1960. Separate sections describe the development of the money and capital market, the formulation and execution of monetary and financial policies, the nature of Mexican monetary and financial experience, and the outstanding characteristics of public and private finance during this period. In the third part of the study an attempt is made to formulate a satisfactory theoretical explanation of the record of Mexican experience as revealed in the first two parts of the study. Relationships between monetary policy, domestic stability, and external equilibrium are analyzed as well as factors governing the growth of domestic indebtedness, the development of financial intermediation, and the operation of the market for loanable funds. The fourth and final part of the study contains a review of experience since 1960 and speculation with respect to the future course of Mexican financial development. Specific proposals for future monetary and financial policies are offered.

In general, our procedure is to establish on the basis of empirical evidence the course of the Mexican financial development and then to analyze the course of this development with the aid of hypotheses suggested by recent theoretical literature. By means of this procedure we believe we have been able to identify the principal forces which account for the remarkable financial development which has occurred. Also, we believe that this procedure has enabled us to achieve a deeper understanding of some of the country's current financial problems and, perhaps, has afforded a sound basis for suggesting policies consistent with a future course of financial development appropriate to Mexico's requirements.

We are acutely aware of the limitations of our study, and believe the reader should be forewarned. Specifically, because of deficiencies in the available statistical data, we have not been able to develop a clear picture of financial processes in the private sector, particularly at the level of the individual household and business enterprise. Furthermore, we have not undertaken to explain Mexican financial markets and market instruments in terms which are likely to be of the greatest interest to those concerned with the mechanics of financial practice. Instead, we have focused on the process of financial change as viewed in aggregative and, at times, fairly abstract terms—in an effort to devise a satisfactory theoretical explanation of the phenomena under investigation and also to provide a basis for appraising the appropriateness of public policies.

Our empirical work has been greatly assisted by earlier path-breaking efforts of others. Of particular importance has been the pioneering statistical study covering the period 1939–1951 prepared by the Combined Mexican Working Party.[1] The historical studies prepared by various experts for publication in the volume commemorating the semicentennial of the Mexican revolution have also been very helpful.[2] We have been assisted also by O. Ernest Moore's historical study of Mexican financial institutions[3] and by access to an unpublished study of Mexican financial markets prepared by the staff of the Departa-

[1] Combined Mexican Working Party, *The Economic Development of Mexico*. International Bank for Reconstruction and Development (Baltimore: Johns Hopkins Press, 1953).

[2] *México: Cincuenta Años de Revolución*. Volume I: "La Economía" (México: Fondo de Cultura Económica, 1960).

[3] O. Ernest Moore, *Evolución de las Instituciones Financieras en México* (México: Centro de Estudios Monetarios Latinoamericanos, 1963).

mento de Estudios Económicos of Banco de México.[4] A recent study by Santillán López and Rosas Fígueroa[5] has been a particularly valuable source of information, as has Robert Bennett's doctoral dissertation.[6] And finally, we have been assisted in our work by the statistical publications and other studies prepared by the International Monetary Fund,[7] the Economic Commission for Latin America,[8] and various agencies of the Mexican Government.[9]

Our understanding of specific financial institutions and processes has been assisted by the numerous detailed studies which have recently been made. The studies by Antonio Campos[10] and Gustavo Petricioli and Miguel de la Madrid[11] of the private financieras have been particularly valuable, as have Calvin Blair's study of Nacional Financiera[12] and Arturo García-Torres' study of insurance companies.[13]

[4] "El Mercado Dinero y Capitales en México." Prepared under the direction of Professor Frank M. Tamagna and Lic. Leopoldo Solís M., 1961.

[5] Roberto Santillán López and Aniceto Rosas Figueroa, *Teoría General de las Finanzas Públicas y el Caso de México* (México: Universidad Nacional Autónoma de México, 1962).

[6] Robert L. Bennett, *Financial Intermediaries in Mexican Economic Development, 1944–1960* (doctoral dissertation, University of Texas, 1963). Unfortunately, Bennett's book based on this work (*The Financial Sector and Economic Development: The Mexican Case* [Baltimore: Johns Hopkins Press, 1965]) was not available prior to the time our manuscript was completed and in the hands of our publisher.

[7] Especially International Monetary Fund, *International Financial Statistics.*

[8] Of the numerous ECLA studies, *External Disequilibrium in the Economic Development of Latin America: The Case of Mexico* (2 vols., 1957) and *La Inflación en México* (1962)—both in mimeograph form—are those we have found most useful.

[9] Principally those issued by Banco de México, Nacional Financiera, and the Secretaría de Industria y Comercio.

[10] Antonio Campos Andapia, *Las Sociedades Financieras Privadas en México* (México: Centro de Estudios Monetarios Latinoamericanos, 1963).

[11] Gustavo Petricioli and Miguel de la Madrid, *Evolución y Control de las Sociedades Financieras Privadas en México* (Brazil: VII Reuniao de Técnicos dos Bancos Centrais do Continente Americano, 1963).

[12] Calvin P. Blair, "Nacional Financiera: Entrepreneurship in a Mixed Economy," *Public Policy and Private Enterprise in Mexico*, ed. Raymond Vernon (Cambridge: Harvard University Press, 1964).

[13] Arturo García-Torres Hassey, *Las Instituciones de Seguros en México: Su Contribución al Ahorro y al Financiamiento del Desarrollo Económico* (México: Universidad Nacional Autónoma de México, Escuela Nacional de Economía, 1964).

We believe that a study of the sort we have attempted is especially appropriate at this time not only because of recent improvements in Mexican financial statistics but also because of recent advances in financial theory and techniques of financial analysis. In particular, our analytical framework is closely modeled, on the one hand, on Gurley and Shaw's important theoretical work[14] and, on the other hand, on the massive empirical studies of United States financial development made by Goldsmith,[15] Kuznets,[16] and Friedman,[17] among others.

In addition to the empirical and theoretical works already referred to, we have of course studied the accumulated literature which pertains in one way or another to the Mexican monetary and financial system. We have not borrowed heavily from this literature, however, largely because its relevance to our approach to the study of Mexican financial development is, in most instances, tangential at best. For this reason we have taken the liberty of writing without footnotes—except in the case of our statistical tables and charts, in which we attempt to provide the necessary documentation and explanation of procedures employed. A bibliography containing the major Spanish- and English-language works concerned with various aspects of Mexican financial development is appended as a guide to further reading.

Finally, a few words about the objectives of this study. Actually, we have two objectives in mind. First, we hope to contribute to understanding of Mexican financial development. We believe that better understanding of the past will permit a more accurate appraisal of contemporary problems and facilitate the choice of intelligent policies in the future. Second, we also are hopeful that our analysis of

[14] John G. Gurley and Edward S. Shaw, *Money in a Theory of Finance* (Washington: Brookings Institution, 1960); also numerous articles by the same authors in various professional journals.

[15] Raymond W. Goldsmith, *Financial Intermediaries in the American Economy since 1900* (Princeton: National Bureau of Economic Research, 1958). A preliminary draft of Goldsmith's forthcoming study of the financial development of Mexico was made available to us just at the time final revisions of our manuscript were being made. Consequently, while we were not able to build on Goldsmith's findings, we benefited from the opportunity to check our findings against his.

[16] Simon Kuznets, *Capital in the American Economy: Its Formation and Financing* (Princeton: National Bureau of Economic Research, 1961).

[17] Milton Friedman and Anna Jacobson Schwartz, *A Monetary History of the United States* (Princeton: National Bureau of Economic Research, 1963).

the record of Mexican experience might make some contribution to general understanding of the phenomenon of financial development and its relation to overall economic development. We believe that the Mexican record of financial development contains much that should be of interest to others engaged in related theoretical and empirical studies and, furthermore, that this record contains many lessons for those countries presently confronted with circumstances and problems not too unlike those encountered in Mexico.

Dwight S. Brothers

Leopoldo Solís M.

ACKNOWLEDGMENTS

We are indebted to numerous individuals who have encouraged and assisted us in the preparation of this book. Especially to Sergio Ghigliazza, whose ideas and criticisms are reflected throughout the book, we wish to acknowledge our gratitude. For their service as research assistants, we want to express our appreciation to Arturo García-Torres, Carlos Ammler, Luis Sánchez Lugo, Roberto Gatica, and Alan Rufus Waters. Marian Berdecio's translation of drafts of various chapters originally written in Spanish facilitated our progress, and our thanks go to her for her conscientious service in this capacity. The uncomplaining service of Vera Wallis and Florence Fulton in typing and retyping various drafts is greatly appreciated. And, finally, we wish to acknowledge the encouragement and many courtesies extended by Gustavo Petricioli of Banco de México and by the personnel of the University of Texas Press.

CONTENTS

Part III. The 1940–1960 Period—Analysis

Part IV. Developments since 1960

TABLES

CHARTS and DIAGRAMS

PART I · · · THE EARLY STAGES

CHAPTER I

DEVELOPMENT OF FINANCIAL SYSTEM PRIOR TO 1940

Introduction

THE HISTORY OF Mexican financial development since the achievement of independence from Spain is one of fitful progression from the most rudimentary of systems to a system which today in many respects is the most advanced and sophisticated in all of Latin America. It is a history of continual adjustment to the changing financial requirements of a developing economy as well as to changes in domestic political conditions and to forces emanating from outside the country—particularly from the United States. Especially in recent years has the evolution of the Mexican financial system been closely related to the ambitious program of economic development to which the country is committed, and to attempts on the part of the federal government to utilize the financial system as a vehicle for implementation of developmental policies.

On numerous occasions in the past the performance of the Mexican monetary and banking system has generated dissatisfaction and clamor for reform. In some instances this has resulted because of abuses and mistakes by those in positions of responsibility for the conduct of the financial affairs of the country; in other instances the existing financial system has been the object of criticism because of its failure to withstand the pressure of events such as internal civil disorders or international crises. In recent times, because of its central role in the country's program of economic development, when the Mexican economy has failed to perform up to expectations the financial system has often been blamed and various changes in institutional structure, instruments of control, and policies have ensued.

Not only is the present-day Mexican financial system expected to provide an institutional framework for the mobilization of savings and the channeling of these savings into productive investment, but also it is supposed to promote continuous augmentation of the aggregate volume of savings and capital formation while at the same time serving as a principal vehicle for exercise of control over resource allocation. The system also bears primary responsibility for maintenance of stability in the domestic economy and in the country's international financial relations. These latter responsibilities are made particularly onerous, on the one hand, by the fact that there exists neither the sensitive money market nor the broad capital market generally considered as prerequisites of successful stabilization policies and, on the other hand, by the absence of an effective fiscal system. The difficulty of the assignment is compounded by the vulnerability of the financial system to pressures emanating from outside the country as well as by the susceptibility of policy decisions to influences growing out of calculations of a political nature.

In spite of the handicaps under which it operates, the Mexican financial system has performed remarkably well in recent years. The managers of the system have demonstrated a high degree of ingenuity in devising (and in borrowing from abroad) institutions and instruments of policy appropriate to the Mexican environment. Despite whatever political and other differences in viewpoint may divide them, managers of both public and private financial institutions evidence a high degree of sophistication and appear to share a common understanding of interrelationships between money and credit, the domestic price level and the international balance of payments, and resource allocation and income distribution.

As a prelude to discussion of the development of the Mexican financial system since 1940, and also in order to better understand the course which this development has taken, this chapter contains a brief history of Mexican financial development prior to 1940. The financial experience and institutional development of the prerevolutionary period is reviewed first, and this is followed by a description of events during the revolution and the extremely difficult period which followed. The postrevolutionary reconstruction of the financial system during the 1920s and 1930s is described in somewhat greater detail than are earlier developments. The chapter ends with a fairly detailed inventory of the Mexican financial system as it existed in the latter part of the 1930s, which is intended to serve as something of a bench mark against which developments since 1940—those with which this book is principally concerned—can be gauged and appraised.

Prerevolutionary System

THE EARLY STAGES

Upon the achievement of independence in 1821, and for nearly fifty years thereafter, the inadequacy of the financial system—both in terms of institutional organization and resources—was a fundamental factor limiting Mexican economic development. The sole financial institutions left as a legacy of the Spanish colonial rule were the mint (Casa de Moneda) and a national pawn shop (Nacional Monte de Piedad), neither of which was of much economic significance. Silver and gold, the bases of the monetary circulation and also principal commodity exports, were in short supply and both domestic and foreign credits for financing either public or private ventures were virtually unavailable. The new government was dependent upon tariff revenues but the inherent limitations on the yield that could be obtained from this source, combined with the financial burden imposed by a series of internal disorders and external attacks, kept the public finances in a deplorable state. In short, the Mexican financial system in the immediate post-independence period was grossly inadequate and constituted a serious impediment to economic improvement.

The extreme financial stringency which prevailed explains early attempts to promote the development of a more adequate monetary and banking system. In 1830 the government established the country's first development banking institution—Banco de Avío. This institution was intended to facilitate industrial development, especially the development of a Mexican cotton-textile industry, by making credit available to importers of the necessary equipment. In 1837 Banco Nacional de Amortización de Moneda de Cobre was established with the purpose of retiring copper coinage which had become excessive and threatened to bring about a collapse of the existing rudimentary monetary system. These two institutions—the first created to increase the availability of credit for financing investment and the second to assist the government in its efforts at monetary reform—proved to be ineffective and both were terminated in the early 1840s. They are evidence of attempts by the young government to cope with the monetary and credit problems with which it was confronted, but amount to little more than curiosities in Mexican financial history. Their significance in the present context is that they represent the earliest examples of the Mexican propensity to devise financial expediencies in efforts to overcome fundamental economic difficulties.

In the ensuing twenty years or so various proposals were made for establishing other sorts of governmental financial institutions, but for numerous reasons (e.g., insufficient resources, political instability, etc.) no action was taken. Following the French invasion in 1864, in accordance with an arrangement negotiated with Maximilian, the first Mexican commercial banking institution was established—Banco de Londres, México y Sudamérica. This British-financed institution received deposits and made loans, issued notes which quickly achieved general acceptability as a means of payment, and otherwise provided banking services for merchants engaged in foreign commerce. Subsequently, after Maximilian had been deposed and Porfirio Díaz had assumed the presidency, several other private commercial banks were established, the most notable of which was Banco Nacional Mexicano established by French financial interests in 1884. Both Banco de Londres (now officially named Banco de Londres y México) and Banco Nacional (now officially named Banco Nacional de México) continue to operate in Mexico to this day, but not without a record of harrowing financial and political experiences. Most other commercial banks established in Mexico during the nineteenth century have now disappeared as a consequence of financial failure, public disfavor, or merger.

It was inevitable that commercial banking be initiated by foreigners not only because the capital necessary for such activities was unavailable in Mexico but also because the Mexicans had little knowledge of the banking function and no banking experience. Furthermore, the establishment of foreign-owned banking facilities was related to opportunities afforded foreign capital for investment in Mexico, especially in mining and in agricultural and other commercial ventures oriented toward export markets. Finally, an essential aspect of the development of commercial banking in Mexico during the nineteenth century was inducement in the form of so-called concessions granted foreign financial interests by the government.

THE DÍAZ ERA

As the number of private commercial banks issuing their own notes increased the question of public regulation was raised. Pressure for governmental control over the issuance of bank notes was intensified in 1884 when, during a financial crisis, several banks were forced to suspend payment. As a consequence corrective legislation was enacted (Código de Comercio, 1884) which was intended to restrict the note-issuing authority of all but Banco Nacional Mexicano and, in effect, to confer on this French-owned institution the powers of a central bank. The attempt to favor Banco Nacional at the expense of other banks (especially Banco de Londres) resulted in much debate, legal maneuvering, and political compromise— with the result that the intent of the original legislation was thwarted. The issue of plurality of note issue versus monopoly of note issue under the control of the federal government was not to be finally resolved in favor of the latter position until many years later.

As a consequence of these events the banking system and various underlying governmental concessions became highly confused, if not chaotic, during the latter part of the 1880s and the first half of the 1890s. Monetary difficulties were intensified by the tendency of the gold value of silver to decline, a tendency which began in the 1870s as first the United States and then other countries demonetized silver. One consequence of the declining external value of the peso was provision of protection for domestic economic activities from foreign competition. Gold practically disappeared from circulation and, although Mexico was to be legally a bimetallic country until 1905, the de facto standard became silver. Throughout this period the vagaries of United States silver policy had severe repercussions in Mexico and were largely responsible for the financial panic and ensuing depression of 1893–1894. The principal factor working to sustain the Mexican monetary and financial system and to promote economic development during this period was a substantial flow of foreign capital into railroad construction, mining activities, and other ventures related to international commerce.

In an effort to overcome the deficiencies of the country's financial system, new legislation was enacted (Ley General de Instituciones de Crédito, 1897) which placed limitations in the form of reserve requirements on the commercial banks' authority to issue notes, provided for a nationwide system of branch banking, and otherwise thoroughly reorganized the banking system. This law is particularly noteworthy because of the provision which classified credit institutions as either banks of issue (commercial banks), mortgage banks (institutions engaged in supplying long-term credits), and *bancos refaccionarios* (institutions supposed to meet the intermediate-term credit needs of agriculture, mining, and manufacturing industry). Here is evidence of an early concern with the allocation of the total credit resources of the country as between short- and longer-term commitments and as between various types of applicants and applications. Extensive reliance upon selective credit controls continues to characterize Mexican monetary and financial policies to the present day.

The 1897 law stimulated an expansion of banking activities, particularly in the number of note-issuing banks. However, the monetary problems of the country became increasingly severe as the value of silver and the peso continued to depreciate vis-à-vis gold and gold-standard currencies. The adverse effects of this devaluation of the Mexican currency were numerous. The burden of the foreign-held gold debt was increased; inasmuch as Mexico's international trade was conducted largely with the gold-standard countries, the terms of trade moved against Mexico; and because of a reduction in Mexico's ability to import, tariff revenues were curtailed. It was in response to these circumstances that further reforms were made in 1905 which suspended free coinage of silver pesos and switched the currency system to a gold basis (without, however, completely discarding the bimetallic character of the previous system).

In spite of the monetary and banking reforms of 1897 and 1905, another severe financial crisis occurred in 1907 (the same year, coincidentally, in which the Mexico City stock exchange was organized). The difficulty this time was associated with depressed prices for Mexico's export commodities (especially cotton and henequen) which in turn caused widespread bankruptcy among producers and heavy bad-debt losses on the part of commercial banks. Because the banks maintained inadequate reserves against such a contingency, many became illiquid and failed despite efforts on the part of the government to support them. The banking system was subjected to mounting criticism, not only on the grounds that it had abused the note-issue privilege but also that it had failed to meet the country's need for intermediate- and long-term credit and had discriminated between credit applicants for political and other unjustified reasons. In 1908 some additional amendments were made to the banking code and plans were drafted for the creation of an official institution which would facilitate the flow of credit to the agricultural sector of the economy. But the revolution intervened.

Destruction and Reconstruction

REVOLUTION AND ITS AFTERMATH

With the revolution the difficulties of the Mexican financial system were compounded by excessive issuance of paper money by each of the various contesting forces, and this in turn gave impetus to hoarding and exportation of gold and silver. The currency and banking system did not break down immediately upon establishment of the revolutionary government under Madero, however, and most banks remained open and most bank notes continued to circulate at par for nearly two years after Díaz' resignation. The breakdown of the system began around the middle of 1913 following Madero's assassination and was reflected in rapid depreciation of paper money, extreme price inflation, widespread falsification of money, and defaults by the government, the banks, and other debtors. In short, beginning in 1913 the prerevolutionary financial system collapsed and ceased to function.

Following the destructive contests with the revolutionary armies of Villa and Zapata the revolutionary government under Carranza was forced to give immediate consideration to the re-establishment of a workable financial system. The circumstances, of course, were very difficult—not only because the country was physically exhausted but also because debtor-creditor relationships were hopelessly distorted and Mexico's international relations, particularly with the United States, were at the point of rupture. Nevertheless, various attempts were made at financial reconstruction between 1914 and 1916. The issuance of new bank notes was halted, efforts were made to weed out counterfeit notes, and a substantial portion of the outstanding issues of paper money was retired from circulation by decree, surtaxes, and other means. These actions greatly reduced the amount of money in circulation, and what little commerce there was became almost solely dependent upon metallic money—which slowly returned from hoards into circulation.

In 1917, in accordance with the provisions of the new constitution adopted in that year, preparations were begun for establishment of a new monetary system based on gold and a new banking system based on governmental monopoly of the note issue. Return to the gold standard at the prerevolutionary gold parity (75 centigrams of gold per peso) was assisted by a substantial gold inflow during the period 1917–1920 as a result of the changed international conditions occasioned by the outbreak of World War I as well as by the resumption of Mexico's silver and other exports. However, establishment of the banking system called for in the new constitution was hampered by the very shaky economic condition of the country and by the distrust of banking and bank notes which had been instilled in the mind of the public. The Mexican monetary system continued to be largely dependent upon metallic money until 1925.

RECONSTRUCTION AND DEVELOPMENT IN NEW DIRECTIONS

In 1925 a most significant step toward the establishment of the modern banking system called for in the 1917 constitution was taken with the organization of Banco de México, S.A., under the jurisdiction of the Secretaría de Hacienda y Crédito Público. This institution as an agency of the government was endowed with the powers and responsibilities of a central bank. It was granted a monopoly over the issuance of paper money and authority to establish the rates of exchange between the peso and foreign currencies. But while Banco de México was granted statutory authority to act as the central bank beginning in 1925 (actually some of the original provisions governing the activities of Banco de México were first included in the Ley General de Instituciones de Crédito y Establecimientos Bancarios enacted in 1926), it was unable to gain immediate control over either the money supply or private commercial banks because of an initial period of near financial impotence. In fact, it was not until 1931 that Banco de México was able to exercise much influence except in so far as its competition with the private commercial banks affected their behavior. Between 1925 and 1931 the practice of plural emission of bank notes was not significantly altered, nor was Banco de México able to control the domestic money supply or to exercise any significant influence on the value of the peso vis-à-vis other currencies.

Throughout the 1920s Mexico lost substantial amounts of gold partly as a consequence of large issues of silver money and a resulting depreciation of silver relative to gold and the U.S. dollar, and partly as a consequence of a sharp decline in export earnings and foreign investment in Mexico relative to the 1917–1920 period. World economic conditions and the decline in commodity prices in 1930 and 1931 compounded the country's financial difficulties, and in mid-1931 Mexico was forced to officially abandon the gold standard in favor of what was in effect an inconvertible bimetallic standard. The statutory basis for demonetization of gold and for reformulation of Banco de México was the Ley Monetaria enacted in July of 1931—the so-called "Ley Calles." This law stipulated that the gold parity of the peso was to remain unchanged (75 centigrams), that while gold was demonetized it would continue to be used to settle international accounts, and that thereafter silver coinage would be reduced to fiduciary status with the exception that the silver peso was to continue to be the standard coin.

Also contained in this legislation were significant changes in the statutory provisions governing the activities of Banco de México. The law strengthened Banco de México control over the issuance of bank notes and provided that the country's monetary reserves were subject to the control of the central bank. The law also required that all commercial banking institutions associate with Banco de México by purchasing stock equal to 6 per cent of their capital, by maintaining reserve deposits with Banco de México, and, in general, by meeting its requirements with respect to reserves, capitalization, investments, etc. As a consequence of these provisions, Banco de México acquired both the authority and financial resources necessary to begin functioning as a central bank.

With its newly acquired powers, and in response to worsening economic conditions attributable, in part at least, to the depression in the United States and elsewhere, Banco de México moved in 1932 to halt the decline in the money supply and the internal price level. Substantial amounts of notes were issued on the basis of silver, free coinage of silver was recommenced, and the rate of exchange between the peso and the dollar was forced downward by means of sizable purchases of dollars. While the pursuit of certain economic policy goals through central banking actions was now clearly possible, the activities of Banco de México were still severely handicapped, especially because of the virtual absence of a domestic money and capital market. Furthermore, it was not until 1935 that Banco de México was able fully to achieve a monopoly of note issue and effectively to implement the controls over the commercial banks called for in the 1931 legislation.

The law governing the activities of Banco de México was again revised in 1936, further strengthening its position and defining more clearly than had the 1931 law the powers and responsibilities assigned to it. The functions of Banco de México as stipulated in this law can be summarized as follows: regulation of the domestic money supply and of the foreign exchange market; service as a reserve bank and discount house for private deposit banks and other designated financial institutions; establishment and administration of the reserve requirements of associated institutions; establishment of policies governing the activities of Comisión Nacional Bancaria (the official bank-examining agency which was originally established in 1925 as an adjunct of Banco de México); and service as the fiscal agent of the federal government. These are essentially the same functions and responsibilities assigned Banco de México to the present day.

The 1930s witnessed a substantial increase in the number of commerical banks and other types of private financial institutions. Also, numerous government-sponsored institutions were established. The most significant of the latter type were Banco Nacional Hipotecario Urbano y de Obras Públicas (established in 1933), Nacional Financiera (established in 1934), Banco Nacional de Crédito Ejidal (established in 1935), and Banco Nacional de Comercio Exterior (established in 1937). Previously, in 1926, Banco Nacional de Crédito Agricola had been established. These publicly-owned investment or development banks, each of which was associated in its operations with Banco de México, were intended to channel credits into sectors of the economy deemed not to have sufficient access to needed financing from private institutions. None of these public financial institutions was very successful during the thirties (the most successful were the agricultural credit banks), but in subsequent years several became quite important components of the financial system.

The Mexican financial scene in the 1930s, especially under the Cárdenas Administration, was dominated by the government's agricultural development and public works programs. The substantial deficits incurred by the government were largely financed by Banco de México, with a resulting sizable increase in the money supply. The effects, of course, were highly inflationary, particularly so because the projects being financed in this fashion in most instances were of a long-term, slow pay-out nature and made little immediate contribution to production. Especially during 1935, 1936, and 1937 did the money supply and prices increase at a rapid rate as a consequence of the manner in which the public works program was financed.

Banco de México had supported the peso at around 3.6 to the dollar since the time of the U.S. devaluation in 1933. However, the inflationary financing of the government's budgetary deficits served to make maintenance of this rate of exchange difficult. Furthermore, the demand for Mexico's commodity exports dropped sharply in 1937 and 1938 in response to the depression in the United States. At about the same time also, the Mexican expropriation of foreign-owned petroleum properties initiated a movement of both domestic and foreign capital from the country which further depleted gold and dollar reserves. In these circumstances Banco de México was forced in 1938 to abandon its support for the peso at the 1933 rate. An official rate of 4.85 pesos to the dollar was then announced, but Banco de México was unable to lend much support to it, as inflationary financing of government deficits and unfavorable payments balances continued throughout 1938 and 1939. Speculation against the peso further depleted Banco de México's gold and dollar reserves and the exchange rate continued to deteriorate as the country's reserves approached exhaustion.

In September of 1939 war was declared in Europe and the Mexican financial picture began to change dramatically. In the following months a large increase in the demand for Mexican raw materials in international markets coincided with a sizable capital inflow—a combination of repatriated Mexican capital and of flight capital from Europe. As a consequence Mexican foreign exchange holdings began to be replenished and the official exchange rate of 4.85 pesos to the dollar was gradually re-established.

Table I-A contains the available statistical indexes of Mexican financial experience and institutional development during the 1930s. The data in the table permit comparison of the financial circumstances of the country during the 1930s with those which prevailed in the period immediately preceding the revolution. It is evident that during the first twenty years following the overthrow of Díaz very little change occurred in the various parameters of Mexican financial development. Between 1930 and 1940, however, quite substantial changes in the country's financial system were registered.

TABLE I-A

INDEXES OF FINANCIAL DEVELOPMENT PRIOR TO 1940

Year	Monetary Circulation[a]			Resources of Credit Institutions[b]	Number of Private Credit Institutions[c]	Wholesale Price Index[d]	Exchange Rate[e]
	Total	Coin and Currency	Checking Deposits			(1935=100)	(Pesos per dollar)
		(Millions of pesos)					
1907	300	261	39	764	98		2.01
1930	......	......	......	535	102		2.26
1931	316	188	128	436			2.65
1932	295	187	108	462			3.17
1933	391	218	173	625			3.53
1934	482	266	216	657			3.60
1935	538	301	237	640		100.0	3.58
1936	596	359	237	953		106.7	3.60
1937	716	442	274	1,072		125.9	3.60
1938	702	477	225	1,069		133.5	4.50
1939	840	545	295	1,295		134.3	5.18
1940	943	614	329	1,622	204	137.7	5.50

Source: Presidencia de la República, Secretaría Privada, and Nacional Financiera, S.A., Subgerencia de Investigaciones Económicas, *50 Años de Revolución Mexicana in Cifras* (México, 1963).

[a] Figures are averages for the year.

[b] End-of-year figures.

[c] Banking system institutions and auxiliary institutions; figures include branches and agencies.

[d] Based on prices in Mexico City.

[e] Figures are averages for the year.

Circumstances at the End of the 1930s

HERITAGE OF PAST EXPERIENCE

As the foregoing account indicates, by the end of the 1930s post-independence Mexico had experienced a variety of financial difficulties and, in response to these difficulties, had attempted several sorts of financial policies. The first fifty years was a period of extreme financial stringency during which neither significant financial nor economic development occurred; the period between 1870 and 1910 witnessed the establishment in collaboration with foreign financial interests of a rudimentary but semimodern monetary and banking system; in the twenty years following Díaz' resignation the pre-revolutionary financial system was largely destroyed and a beginning was made at reconstruction along lines deemed appropriate by the revolutionary government; and, finally, between 1930 and 1940 a functioning central bank and a number of other official financial institutions were established to control and supplement private banking institutions and to promote economic development.

Also, by the end of the 1930s Mexico had accumulated experience with a wide variety of monetary systems ranging from a silver coin standard through bimetallism and a gold standard to inconvertible paper and finally, to a modern form of managed money. Four currency depreciations had occurred, all for different reasons. At the end of the nineteenth century the difficulty was attributable to a decline in the world price of silver. During the revolution the virtual cessation of domestic economic activity coupled with uncontrolled issuance of paper money was the cause. During the worldwide depression of the early 1930s Mexico was forced to devalue because of inability to market export commodities at adequate prices. Finally, the depreciation in the latter half of the 1930s was occasioned by inflationary financing of government sector deficits, in combination with capital flight motivated, in part at least, by government policies which adversely affected foreign investors.

Thus by the end of the 1930s Mexico and Mexicans had had a good deal of unhappy financial experience. Bank failures, inflations, and currency devaluations had induced widespread distrust of financial institutions and processes. Likewise, by the end of the 1930s Mexico knew from experience about the disadvantages which can result from external disequilibrium, heavy dependence upon foreign investment, and capricious international capital movements. And, finally, Mexico had acquired some experience with inflationary central-bank financing of governmental deficits and with the use of development banks as means for promoting the growth of selected sectors of the economy. It was with this heritage of experience and insight that Mexico emerged from the 1930s.

LEGISLATION GOVERNING BANKING AND FINANCE

The legal foundation of the Mexican financial system as it existed at the end of the 1930s was incorporated in a series of legislative acts which extended and modified the principles relating to money and banking written into the 1917 constitution. We have previously referred to the original legislation underlying the establishment of Banco de México and to the most significant amendments enacted in subsequent years. The principal statutes governing the operations of this institution in the latter part of the 1930s were the Ley Orgánica del Banco de México and the Ley Monetaria, both as amended in 1936.

In addition to these statutes the financial system at the end of the 1930s was governed by the Ley General de Instituciones de Crédito and the Ley General de Títulos y Operaciones de Crédito. The former law had a long history, but a significant revision was enacted in 1932. It prescribed in detail the proper functions of the different types of financial institutions, and in particular provided for the regulation of auxiliary institutions engaged in financial activities which differed from those carried out by traditional types of banking institutions. As shown in Table I-B, which follows, included in this latter category were a diversity of national and private credit institutions ranging from a pawnshop and public warehouses on the one hand to the Mexico City stock exchange and credit unions on the other. Also specifically provided for in this legislation were the various specialized national development banks which, as we have seen, became numerous during the 1930s.

The Ley General de Títulos y Operaciones de Crédito, which was enacted in 1932, provided for complementary regulation of banking and credit operations—especially of the creation and circulation of credit instruments. This legislation was intended not only to assure that desirable credit practices and instruments were developed, but also (and perhaps primarily) to promote the expanded employment of credit instruments other than money in commercial transactions.

It is clear from the legislative record that those responsible for public policy during the 1930s were acutely aware of the limitations imposed on the economic development of Mexico by the inadequacies of the existing financial system. Equally apparent, however, is an insistence that the development of the country's financial system be closely supervised to assure consistency with the country's constitution and the government's development program.

FINANCIAL INSTITUTIONS AND INSTRUMENTS

The financial structure which had evolved by the end of the 1930s, while still fairly rudimentary, was a good deal more sophisticated than was the case ten years earlier. Most importantly, the authority of Banco de México was firmly established and was sufficient, in spite of a very limited money and capital market, to exercise a substantial degree of control over the volume and allocation of credit. The ability of Banco de México to control the latter was bolstered by the various specialized development banks which facilitated the flow of credit into sectors of the economy not well served by private financial institutions—notably agriculture, construction, and foreign commerce. Furthermore, the fiscal strength of the federal government was increased as a consequence of access to the growing credit resources of the central bank, a fact which was reflected in the large-scale public works program initiated in the mid-1930s. And finally, the commercial banking system was better able to finance a growing volume of trade, if not an extensive program of industrial development, as private banks were afforded recourse to discounting and other accommodations by the central bank.

The institutional structure of the financial system at the end of the 1930s is indicated in Table I-B. As shown, the system consisted of

TABLE I-B

FINANCIAL INSTITUTIONS AT END OF 1930s

BANKING SYSTEM INSTITUTIONS	
National[a]	Private[b]
Banco de México (1925)	Deposit Banks (61)
National Agricultural Credit Bank (1926)	Savings Banks (6)[c]
National Urban Mortgage and Public Works Bank (1933)	Trust Institutions (8)[c]
Nacional Financiera (1934)	Financial Societies (29)[d]
National Ejido Credit Bank (1935)	Capitalization Banks (8)
National Foreign Commerce Bank (1937)	Mortgage Loan Banks (2)
National Workers' Bank for Industrial Promotion (1937)[e]	
OTHER INSTITUTIONS	
National Pawnshop and Savings Institution (1775)[f]	Stock Exchange (1)
Governing Board of Civilian Pensions (1925)[g]	General Deposit Warehouses (13)
National Deposit Warehouses (1936)	Clearing House Associations (5)
National Union of Sugar Producers (1938)[h]	Credit Unions (9)

SOURCE: Moore, *Evolución de las Instituciones Financieras en México*.
  [a] Figures in parentheses indicate date institutions originally established.
  [b] Figures in parentheses indicate number of institutions operating in 1940. Branches and agencies are excluded.
  [c] Includes departments of deposit banks.
  [d] Officially classified as banking system institutions in 1941.
  [e] Incorporated into the National Cooperative Promotion Bank when this institution was established in 1944.
  [f] Nationalized in 1949.
  [g] Replaced in 1959 by Institute of Security and Social Services for Public Employees.
  [h] Nationalized in 1953.

Banco de México and various other national financial institutions and a larger number of private institutions—including a sizable number of deposit and savings banks (some with numerous branches) and several each of fiduciary, investment, and mortgage-lending institutions. All of the official financial institutions with the exception of the national pawnshop and savings institution (Nacional Monte de Piedad) had been established during the previous fifteen years. And similarly, most of the private financial institutions operating at the end of the 1930s were either not operating a few years earlier or, if operating, were engaged in quite different types of activities.

Another aspect of the Mexican financial structure as it existed at the end of the 1930s is evident from an examination of the assets and liabilities of the institutions comprising the banking system. As shown in Table I-C, money (i.e., coin, currency, and checking-deposit liabilities of the monetary system) was the most important type of financial instrument, amounting to nearly half of all claims held against banking system institutions. Coin and currency in circulation (the monetary liabilities of Banco de México) amounted to more than twice the outstanding volume of checking-deposit liabilities of the privately owned commercial banks. A substantial portion of the indebtedness of the banking system also consisted of various quasi-monetary obligations, especially those of national institutions other than Banco de México. Of the total assets held by banking system institutions, roughly 25 per cent consisted of holdings of foreign exchange and claims on government, these two items being about equal in amount. Claims on enterprises and individuals represented upwards of 40 per cent of total banking system assets, and about half of these were held by nonmonetary institutions.

Neither insurance arrangements nor transactions between private borrowers and lenders in the money and capital market were of much financial significance. Trade credits and intrafamily loans presumably were common but evidence of the quantitative importance of these sorts of financing is not available. The domestic debt obligations of government were owed almost exclusively to the central bank, there being little interest in government securities on the part of either private financial institutions or noninstitutional investors. Mexican foreign indebtedness was fairly large, but its economic and financial significance was clouded by the fact that it was in default and heavily discounted by holders.

TABLE 1-C

ASSETS AND LIABILITIES OF BANKING SYSTEM INSTITUTIONS AT END OF 1930s

(Millions of pesos)

	Banking System	Monetary System		Nonmonetary Institutions	
		Banco de México	Deposit Banks	National	Private
Assets					
Foreign Exchange[a]	243.2	209.8	30.6	2.5	0.3
Claims on Government	247.7	223.0	9.2	11.4	4.1
Claims of Enterprises and Individuals	782.0	93.1	301.6	281.1	106.2
Claims on Credit Institutions	241.4	38.9	144.0	36.8	21.7
Other Assets	374.5	297.1	34.0	21.1	22.3
Liabilities					
Money[b]	882.1	616.5	264.0	1.6	‒‒‒
Quasi-Money[c]	368.3	3.9	95.7	225.4	43.3
Obligations of Other Credit Institutions	244.7	147.4	62.2	23.2	11.9
Other Liabilities	393.7	94.1	97.5	102.7	99.4

SOURCE: Annual reports of Banco de México, S.A.

[a] Holdings of gold, silver, and foreign currencies.
[b] Coin, currency, and checking deposit liabilities to enterprises and individuals.
[c] All domestic and foreign currency obligations to enterprises and individuals except monetary liabilities and capital account items.

FINANCIAL POLICIES AND INSTRUMENTS OF CONTROL

As previously indicated, Mexican financial policies under the Cárdenas Administration (1935–1940) were dictated by the requirements of the government's agricultural development and public works programs and, in the last several years, by a combination of external factors. The essential character of financial policy under Cárdenas is evident from the fact that in every year except 1935 the federal government incurred budgetary deficits which for the most part were directly monetized by means of purchases of government securities by Banco de México. Thus, in an effort to counter the deflationary tendencies prevalent at the time and to promote recovery and economic development, the money supply was nearly doubled. The resulting substantial increase in the level of prices served, on the one hand, to divert resources from private consumption and investment to the public sector and, on the other hand, to produce an adverse balance of international payments. As previously noted, this latter development was accentuated by renewed depression in the United States in 1937 and 1938 and by repercussions from the Mexican expropriation of foreign-owned petroleum properties in 1938. While the financial policies of the Cárdenas Administration did work to support a greatly expanded volume of public expenditures, it seems clear that had it not been for the advent of World War II these policies would have necessitated a painful financial readjustment in the last months of 1939 or the early 1940s.

Financial policy during much of the 1930s was crudely inflationary. But, given the circumstances, it is difficult to conceive of a satisfactory alternative course of action. Neither the federal treasury nor the central bank had the financial strength or the instruments of financial control to proceed otherwise. There existed little possibility of financing the increased public expenditures by means of either taxation or selective credit controls. To some extent, of course, the various official development banks served to influence the allocation of loanable funds, but their significance was principally as a means of channeling central bank credit to designated projects rather than as a device for mobilizing additional financial resources in the domestic and foreign capital markets. Indeed, for all practical purposes there was no domestic capital market and foreign capital was virtually unavailable to Mexico until the last months of 1939. Under these circumstances neither sophisticated financial policies nor sensitive financial controls were either desirable or feasible.

Conclusion

We have reviewed the course of Mexican financial development up to 1940 with the purpose of providing the background necessary for comprehending the remarkable financial development which has occurred since 1940—the record of which occupies the remainder of this book. We have seen that, in spite of an eventful financial history, Mexico at the end of the 1930s was greatly handicapped in its efforts to achieve more rapid economic growth and greater economic stability by the rudimentary stage of financial development then achieved. In subsequent chapters we shall describe and analyze the various dimensions of Mexican financial development since 1940—not only in order to better understand what has occurred but also to better anticipate fruitful possibilities for further financial development.

PART II . . . THE 1940–1960 PERIOD—HISTORY

CHAPTER II

MONEY AND CAPITAL MARKET

Introduction

ONE MEASURE of the effect of financial development on overall economic development is the extent to which savings are encouraged and capital formation is facilitated by financial processes. Indeed, among the best indexes of the effectiveness of a country's financial system are the rates of domestic saving and capital formation. Another important gauge of the effectiveness of a financial system is its contribution to maintenance of price stability and an appropriate balance in international payments—and thereby to a country's ability to sustain a satisfactory rate of output growth over time. A third way in which the operation of a financial system contributes to economic development is by affording an institutional framework within which savers and investors may deal with one another, rationing the distribution of loanable funds as between alternative employments, and thereby contributing to a more efficient allocation of productive resources. Market processes in the financial sphere serve not only to reduce disparities in the productivity of labor and capital employed in various activities but also to facilitate the movement of goods from producers to consumers upon which both subsequent production and the general economic well-being of any society depend.

In this chapter we shall describe the development of the Mexican money and capital market as it occurred during the 1940–1960 period. Our purpose is to familiarize the reader with the various institutions and instruments around which market activities were organized as well as with the practices and procedures which characterized the behavior of market participants. Relationships between the operation of the money and capital market and the record of savings, capital formation, financial stability, and growth of output during this period —which are explored in subsequent chapters—can be understood only after one achieves an understanding of the factors governing the operation of the financial market.

Institutional Development

The principal participants in the money and capital market throughout the period were, in addition to ultimate savers and investors, the various financial institutions comprising the banking system. Of these, the most significant among the national institutions were Banco de México and Nacional Financiera and, among the private institutions, the deposit and savings banks and, during the latter part of the period, the financieras and various fiduciary institutions. While the primary function of the money and capital market was to provide a linkage between ultimate savers and ultimate borrowers, the operation of this market was dominated by the institutions which served as intermediaries in the saving-investment process. Therefore, the development of the money and capital market was closely bound up with the development of these institutions.

NATIONAL CREDIT INSTITUTIONS

In the previous chapter we indicated that a number of specialized national institutions were established during the 1930s in an effort to facilitate the movement of loan funds to sectors of the economy and specific activities for which the market did not voluntarily provide an adequate supply of credit and in which the government had a special interest—for reasons of economic development and, to a lesser degree, social welfare. This practice continued during the 1940s and 1950s with the establishment of several additional such institutions. More significant from the point of view of the operation of the money and capital market, however, was the increased importance of certain of the national institutions established prior to 1940—most notably Banco de México and Nacional Financiera. As will be evident at various points throughout the remainder of this chapter and the book as a whole, these latter two institutions have come to exercise a dominant influence in the financial market.

In Table II-A is shown a complete listing of all national banking

TABLE II-A

NATIONAL CREDIT INSTITUTIONS, 1940–1960

BANKING SYSTEM INSTITUTIONS

Established Prior to 1940	*Established Subsequent to 1940*[a]
Banco de México, S.A.	National Bank for Small Business (1943)
National Agricultural Credit Bank	National Cooperative Promotion Bank (1944)
National Urban Mortgage and Public	National Army and Navy Bank (1946)
Works Bank	National Motion Picture Bank (1947)
Nacional Financiera, S.A.	National Transport Bank (1953)
National Ejido Credit Bank	National Sugar Producers' Financiera (1953)
National Foreign Commerce Bank	

OTHER INSTITUTIONS

National Pawnshop and Savings Institution	Guaranty and Promotion Fund for Agricul-
National Deposit Warehouses	ture, Cattle Raising, and Chicken Farming
National Union of Sugar Producers	(1954)
Mexican Institute of Social Security (1942)	Guaranty and Promotion Fund for Tourism
National Saving Association (1950)	(1957)
Guaranty and Promotion Fund for Medium	Institute of Security and Social Services
and Small Industry (1954)	for Public Employees (1959)

ASSETS OF NATIONAL BANKING SYSTEM INSTITUTIONS[b]
(Millions of pesos)

	1940	1950	1955	1960
Banco de México	1,075.4	5,620.7	9,009.4	13,204.6
Nacional Financiera	18.2	1,203.9	2,491.7	⎰
Other	329.9	2,753.8	7,083.2	⎱ 19,544.7[c]
Totals	1,423.5	9,578.4	18,584.3	32,749.3

SOURCE: Moore, *Evolución de las Instituciones Financieras en México;* also, annual reports of Banco de México, S.A., and Nacional Financiera, S.A.

  [a] Figures in parentheses indicate date institutions originally established.

  [b] End-of-year figures; intrasystem claims included.

  [c] Includes Nacional Financiera and other national institutions. Year-end figure for Nacional Financiera not available, but assets of this institution as reported for June 30, 1960, amounted to 5,886.8 million pesos.

system institutions operating in 1960, along with figures indicating the growth in the assets of these institutions during the period 1940–1960. As shown, only six additional national banking institutions were established between 1940 and 1960, and these were designed to serve the needs of special groups of borrowers. Several additional auxiliary institutions were established during the period, and the operations of several others were substantially altered, but these institutions as a group continued to be relatively insignificant. The major share of the growth in total assets of national banking institutions between 1940 and 1960 was accounted for by Banco de México and Nacional Financiera, the figures being about 40 per cent and 20 per cent respectively, as shown in Table II-A. For the most part the resources of the national credit institutions as a whole were devoted to financing industrial and agricultural activities, although the loans granted in support of small businesses, foreign trade, residential construction, and the extension of public services were not inconsiderable.

Throughout the period Banco de México became increasingly effective in carrying out its duties as central bank. As a result of modifications in its powers and instruments of control, as well as of changes in the significance of institutions and practices subject to its jurisdiction, the influence of Banco de México in the money and capital market became progressively more important. However, as shown in Table II-A, the proportion held by Banco de México of the total assets of national banking system institutions tended to decline as the number and volume of credits extended by other national institutions increased. It should be pointed out that this decline reflects special circumstances (e.g., the nationalization in 1953 of the previously established sugar producers' financiera) and changed practices (e.g., greater reliance on foreign credits which were channeled through Nacional Financiera and other specialized official lending agencies) rather than diminution of the power and influence of Banco de México.

The major share of the resources at the disposal of the specialized national institutions was derived from federal funds, foreign credits, and Banco de México rediscounts. The role of Nacional Financiera in particular became increasingly important throughout the period, not only because of growth in its own resources but also because of progressive enlargement of various public trust funds subject to its administration and also because of extension of its capacity as guarantor of the domestic and foreign indebtedness of a variety of public and private enterprises. Only a relatively small proportion of the resources of the specialized national credit institutions was obtained by competition for funds in the domestic market, although Nacional Financiera (and to a lesser extent the National Urban Mortgage and Public Works Bank and the National Sugar Producers' Financiera) raised funds by means of securities issues.

PRIVATE CREDIT INSTITUTIONS

The types of private credit institutions operating in 1960 were the same as those operating in 1940 with the single exception of savings and loan associations, several of which were established in the early 1950s. However, the number of private credit institutions of various sorts increased greatly over the period, especially between 1940 and 1950, and the activities in which the established types of institutions were engaged changed in response to changes in policies governing their operations as well as a result of new opportunities for profit-making. Also, the rates of growth of the different types of private institutions varied over the period, with the deposit and savings banks making the most substantial gains in the 1940s while the financieras and certain other nonmonetary banking system institutions registered the highest rates of growth during the 1950s.

Table II-B contains data showing the increase which occurred in the number of the various types of private credit institutions as well as the growth of their assets. As shown, while the number of private credit institutions increased substantially during the period, even more significant was the increase in branches and agencies. By 1960 the number and variety, as well as geographic distribution, of private credit institutions was such that most borrowers and lenders throughout the country had access via intermediaries to the money and capital market—although output growth in some sectors of the economy, most notably agriculture, continued to be inhibited by limited credit availability.

The resources of private credit institutions were mobilized almost entirely in the domestic market with only a relatively small proportion being derived from Banco de México credits and from foreign sources. In contrast with the national banks, the activities of the private institutions were profit-motivated, and consequently changes in supply and demand conditions in the market influenced both the sources and uses of funds moving through private institutions and

TABLE II-B

PRIVATE CREDIT INSTITUTIONS, 1940–1960

| | NUMBER OF INSTITUTIONS[a] | | | |
	1940	1950	1955	1960
Banking System				
Deposit Banks	61	106	106	102
Savings Banks	6	85	100	108
Financial Societies	29	96	92	98
Trust Institutions	8	91	99	113
Mortgage Loan Banks	2	20	24	26
Capitalization Banks	8	16	16	12
Savings and Loan Associations			4	3
Branches and Agencies	61	846	1,146	2,346
Other Institutions				
Stock Exchanges	1	2	2	3
General Deposit Warehouses	13	23	27	29
Clearing House Associations	5	8	10	11
Credit Unions	9	67	94	72

| | ASSETS OF PRIVATE BANKING SYSTEM INSTITUTIONS[b] | | | |
| | (Millions of pesos) | | | |
	1940	1950	1955	1960
Deposit Banks	659.8	4,524.0	8,552.6	13,350.8
Savings Banks	37.9	523.2	1,467.5	2,902.9
Financial Societies	8.3	916.5	1,994.6	9,057.8
Mortgage Loan Banks	80.4	491.2	1,138.6	2,167.5
Other	59.4	487.5	698.4	933.9
Totals	845.8	6,942.4	13,851.7	28,412.9

SOURCE: Moore, *Evolución de las Instituciones Financieras en México;* also annual reports of Banco de México, S.A.

[a] End-of-year figures.
[b] End-of-year figures; intrasystem claims included.

also the relative rates of growth of the various types of such institutions. During the period between 1940 and 1950 the deposit and savings banks made the most substantial gains, reflecting the need of the economy for the relatively simple instruments which these institutions were capable of supplying. The spectacular growth of the resources made available to the private financieras during the 1950s relative to those made available to deposit and savings banks and other private institutions demonstrated the competitive advantage achieved by the financieras in the loanable funds market. On the one hand the financieras were able to offer highly liquid and high-yielding paper which was well suited to savers' preferences and on the other hand, these institutions were freer from the profit-restricting limitations on fund utilization imposed by Banco de México than were most other private credit institutions. Furthermore, most financieras were operated in association with deposit and savings banks and also often with fiduciary institutions, and thereby were recipients of large amounts of funds which were able to be employed in the purchase of claims on industrial and consumer borrowers not suitable for direct holding by the financial intermediaries making the funds available.

Mortgage banks were able to maintain their relative position among the private credit institutions, reflecting the fact that their obligations continued to be well regarded by certain types of investors. Savings and loan associations and so-called capitalization banks, however, were unable to compete effectively for funds, and as a consequence both the number and assets of these institutions remained virtually constant throughout the 1950s. In general, the financial intermediaries expanding their operations during the 1950s relative to private credit institutions as a whole were those which were capable of issuing liquid claims at attractive rates and which were otherwise sufficiently flexible in their operations to satisfy the changing preferences of savers and other lenders as well as of investors and other borrowers.

OTHER FINANCIAL INSTITUTIONS

In Mexico most credit-granting institutions are called "banks," and consequently the "banking system" as we shall use the term throughout the book includes not only deposit and savings banks but also the various specialized national and private credit institutions indicated in Table II-A and Table II-B. In addition to the banking system institutions there exist a number of financial institutions such as insurance companies, social security trust funds, and other auxiliary institutions (e.g., credit unions, producers' cooperatives, public warehouses, and the organized securities exchanges) which either issue financial claims or in one way or another facilitate the flow of financial resources between the various sectors of the economy.

With the exception of the organized securities exchanges, about which more will be said later in the chapter, most of these auxiliary institutions do not play a very significant role in financial processes.

The insurance companies and the social security system appear to be gaining greater significance, although the full extent of their involvement in the money and capital market is difficult to ascertain. For present purposes it will be sufficient to restrict our discussion of these latter two institutions to a few remarks regarding the nature and scope of their activities.

A sizable number of private insurance companies operate in Mexico. In the past these institutions engaged principally in issuance of fire and other casualty contracts, the growth of life insurance being limited by the prevailing inequality in income distribution and the relatively small size of the middle class. Furthermore, long-term saving contracts of the sort generally employed as a basis for life insurance were not attractive in the inflationary environment which prevailed in Mexico throughout most of the period under discussion. While there is evidence of some acceleration in the rate of growth of insurance company assets in recent years, the resources of these institutions have continued to be small relative to those of the banking system institutions, the ratio at the end of 1960 being 5.6 per cent.

The social security system originated in the early 1940s, and over the years coverage has been extended so that by 1960 virtually all employees of government and of organized labor were eligible for benefits. Provisions for medical services and retirement income have been liberalized as time has passed, but substantial disparities exist as between different groups. Little is known about the financial aspects of the social security system since the various trust funds do not make regular public disclosures. Apparently, however, trust fund reserves are not channeled into the financial markets in any large amounts but instead are employed principally for financing physical facilities relating to the interests of beneficiaries or to the broader political interests of those who exercise authority over the management of the trust funds.

Financial Instruments

Paralleling the changes which occurred in the institutional structure of the financial system were changes in the types of financial instruments employed in the money and capital market. During the 1940s, when commercial banks were the most important private institutions operating in the market, demand deposits and savings accounts were the principal means for capturing funds from the nonbank public while banking system credits were largely in the form of commercial loans and discounts. The vigorous growth of other private credit institutions during the 1950s was associated with increased reliance on debt instruments such as financial bonds, mortgages, and term obligations (these latter often possessing the character of deposits) as means for capturing funds, while assets of financial intermediaries consisted increasingly of secured working capital and equipment loans and other fixed-term credits. In the latter period there also occurred an increase in the use of debt instruments such as acceptances, *cédulas hipotecarias,* and various sorts of trust instruments which were not ultimate obligations of credit institutions but rather were contingent liabilities, being supported by the guarantees of these institutions.

Throughout the whole period private financial institutions were the main source of instruments employed to capture loanable funds in the domestic market. These institutions accounted for practically all checking and savings deposits and for more than half of the sight and time obligations of all banking system institutions. With the growth in the number and variety of private institutions, and also with the expansion of the network of branches and agencies of these institutions, the mobilization of funds in the domestic market became increasingly dependent upon their operations. While the national institutions were not unimportant, their liabilities were to a large extent denominated in foreign currencies, reflecting an increasingly heavy reliance on loans from foreign credit institutions as well as a strong preference on the part of domestic lenders for claims denominated in foreign currencies.

FACTORS GOVERNING CHARACTERISTICS OF FINANCIAL INSTRUMENTS

The most outstanding characteristic of financial instruments employed in the money and capital market throughout the whole period under consideration was the high degree of liquidity which many of these instruments possessed. Lenders evidenced a strong preference for liquid financial assets and consequently financial institutions and other borrowers found it necessary to accommodate this preference in order to mobilize the funds necessary for financing deficit spending in the public and private sectors. The liquidity of the obligations of financial institutions, as well as those of selected enterprises, was underwritten throughout the period by Banco de México and Nacional Financiera, and ultimately by the federal government, in an effort to increase the competiveness of financial instruments vis-à-vis other assets and thereby to contribute to the flow of savings into the money and capital market. Another reason for official support of a wide range of financial instruments was to bolster public confidence in these instruments and the issuing institutions and thereby to foster development of the money and capital market.

The preference for liquid financial assets on the part of lenders is explained in part by the relatively low level of income received by the bulk of the population in association with a high propensity to spend for consumer goods. Such savings as were made were usually earmarked for purchases of durable consumer goods (e.g., household appliances, automobiles, or housing) and therefore these savings were generally accumulated in a form readily available for spending. The fact that per capita income increased regularly and that further future increases in income were widely anticipated served to diminish saving which might otherwise have been motivated by security considerations.

Market preference for liquid financial assets was intensified by the long period of inflation which lasted from the 1930s until the mid-1950s. Households and businesses alike learned that ownership of goods provided the best means of protection against a rising level of prices, and consequently only financial assets readily available for the purchase of goods were deemed to be desirable. Large savers in particular—those who were generally the most sophisticated investors—reacted to the prospect of continued inflation by maintaining financial assets at minimum levels and in the most liquid forms in an effort to protect the real value of their wealth against erosion from price increases, while at the same time maintaining the necessary funds available for transactions purposes and for purposes of assuring the desired degree of flexibility in their operations.

Of course liquidity preference was not absolute nor was it insensitive to yield differentials. As we shall see, the volume of the various types of claims against financial institutions and other borrowers increased regularly over the period. Furthermore, money balances appear to have been held at minimum levels reflecting recognition of the opportunity cost of holding this type of liquid asset instead of other, interest-bearing claims which were close money substitutes. Thus, while a strong preference for liquidity characterized the money and capital market throughout the period, this was manifested principally in the growth of nonmonetary claims—most of which were highly liquid and were in fact a form of quasi-money—relative to money balances.

A final significant characteristic of financial instruments employed to mobilize funds in the money and capital market was the sizable proportion of these instruments which over the period under consideration came to be denominated in foreign currencies. Investors were induced by the devaluations of the peso which occurred in 1948 and 1949, and especially the further devaluation in 1954, to demand financial instruments which would eliminate risk of loss in value caused by depreciation of the peso. In an effort to avoid the full force of this demand from being reflected in movements of capital from the country into foreign financial markets, the Mexican authorities condoned the assumption of foreign currency obligations by financial institutions operating in the domestic money and capital market. This afforded an opportunity for investors to hedge against devaluation to the extent desired without withdrawing their funds from the domestic market, and also obviated the drain on the country's foreign exchange reserves which the latter course of action would have entailed. During the 1940–1960 period foreign currency obligations of banking system institutions (whether in the form of demand or time deposits or other types of liabilities) increased at a much faster rate than did obligations denominated in pesos.

The liquidity preference of savers was thus reflected in liabilities of intermediary institutions, and the character of these liabilities in turn governed in substantial degree the types of credits extended to borrowers. The bulk of the funds mobilized from private domestic savers which were channeled through the banking system went into short-term loans, and consequently a large part of capital formation was necessarily financed from the internal funds of the investing unit —or from public funds or foreign credits. However, while the principal limitation on long-term credit was on the side of supply rather than on the side of demand, nevertheless the labor-intensive structure of production was such that a relatively large volume of short-term financing was required by manufacturing enterprises. Furthermore, industrial and commercial enterprises were not hampered by short-term financing of inventories and receivables, especially since regular renewal was assured in most cases. The sectors principally disadvantaged by the short-term nature of the credit market were agriculture and construction, and special steps were taken to ease the situation through the operations of specialized national credit institutions.

BANKING SYSTEM INDEBTEDNESS

Monetary obligations of banking system institutions (i.e., coin, currency, and checking deposit liabilities of Banco de México and the deposit banks) maintained a virtually constant relationship to the current value of gross national product throughout the 1940–1960 period—both growing at an average annual rate of approximately 6.1 per cent. Total banking system liabilities, however, represented a constantly increasing proportion of gross national product, due largely to the rapid growth of the outstanding volume of the various quasi-monetary debt obligations which assumed increasing importance in the money and capital market.

As shown in Table II-C, checking deposits constituted a relatively constant proportion of the total liabilities of banking system institutions during the period under consideration, although a slight tendency for this proportion to fall is evident in the latter part of the 1950s. However, the proportion of the total money supply represented by

TABLE II-C

OBLIGATIONS OF BANKING SYSTEM INSTITUTIONS, 1940–1960[a]
(Per cent of total)

	1940	1950	1955	1960
Denominated in Pesos				
Coin and Currency	41.9	27.4	22.7	18.4
Checking Deposits	25.3	28.9	24.2	21.2
Saving Deposits	2.2	5.0	5.4	5.4
Demand and Time Obligations	9.6	6.7	11.9	15.6
Securities[b]	14.8	18.2	16.5	13.5
Other	2.7	3.6	2.6	1.9
Denominated in Foreign Currencies				
Demand Deposits	2.6	2.1	4.7	3.3
Saving Deposits	0.1	0.1	1.9	1.4
Other Obligations	0.8	8.0	10.1	19.3
Totals	100.0	100.0	100.0	100.0

Source: Annual reports of Banco de México, S.A.

[a] End-of-year figures; intrasystem obligations excluded.
[b] Includes small amount of securities denominated in dollars issued by Nacional Financiera, S.A.

checking deposits increased from 37.6 per cent in 1940 to 53.4 per cent in 1960. The growth in the relative importance of checking deposits as a component of the money supply was associated with a steady increase in the use of this instrument for effecting commercial transactions—a development which in turn was related to increasing public confidence in banking processes and to the increased number and greater geographic dispersion of commercial banks and branches. The growth of checking deposits reflected the superiority of this instrument—both in terms of safety and convenience—as a means of payment. Checking deposits, and all forms of money for that matter, were demanded principally for transactions purposes. Speculative considerations were manifested largely by the behavior of holdings of quasi-money—especially claims denominated in foreign currencies.

The proportion of banking system indebtedness represented by savings deposits increased throughout the period, rising from 2.2 per cent of the total in 1940 to 5.4 per cent in 1960. Although the interest rate payable on savings deposits was maintained at a quite low rate (the permissible rate set by the National Banking Commission was 4.5 per cent for national currency deposits and 3 per cent for foreign currency deposits during most of the period), nevertheless it was sufficient to attract the surplus funds of certain types of savers. The main source of savings deposits appears to have been small savers to whom other higher-yielding instruments were either unfamiliar or unavailable. Savings deposits were a particularly effective means of mobilizing funds from small savers in the provinces where the main access to the money and capital market was afforded by deposit and savings banks and their branches. Because there was no minimum deposit requirement, a large number of small accounts existed, with the result that the banks incurred quite high administrative costs. In general, savings deposits were not attractive to large savers familiar with alternative opportunities in the financial market. A high degree of liquidity for savings deposits existed as a result of the customary banking practice of granting collateral loans secured by deposit balances to depositors who desired to withdraw upon demand more than the legally permissible percentage of their deposits. As a consequence of this practice, savings deposits and checking deposits were equally liquid, with the exception that it was necessary to make withdrawals of the former in person.

Various types of demand and time liabilities of private banking system institutions other than checking and savings deposits were also effective instruments for mobilizing loanable funds, especially during the 1950s. The most important of these were loans by enterprises and individuals to financial institutions and acceptances issued with guarantees of financial institutions. In addition, of course, there were various intrasystem debt claims representing either temporary loans or a systematic channeling of funds from one type of institution to another, but discussion of the role of intrasystem transactions is deferred until a later chapter.

Loans received from enterprises and individuals in return for promissory notes were a principal means employed by the private financieras to attract funds, accounting for 13 per cent of the remarkable growth in the funds at the disposal of these institutions during the period 1950–1960. These loans were nominally repayable only after a specified term, usually from three to six months, although in practice they were usually recoverable by lenders upon demand. Loans to financieras were denominated in both pesos and foreign currencies, with those stated in terms of the former generally yielding between 8 and 12 per cent and those stated in terms of the latter yielding between 7 and 9 per cent. Acceptances bearing the guarantees of private financieras also became quite significant, although these liabilities were of a contingent or indirect sort and were matched by assets in the form of promissory notes of ultimate borrowers. The commission charged by financieras for handling these instruments ranged from 2.5 per cent to around 4.0 per cent. Yields to the holders fell within the same range as those for financiera loans. Other private financial institutions also showed loans and acceptances in their liability accounts, but the majority of the outstanding volume of these instruments throughout the whole period was reflected in the accounts of the financieras.

Another instrument which achieved some importance as a means of mobilizing funds was the investment trust, a special form of time-deposit obligation of fiduciary departments of deposit and savings banks. Investment trusts offered savers yields competitive with those obtainable from financiera promissory notes and acceptances and also were of comparable liquidity. Trust obligations were not subject to reserve requirements, and furthermore they carried certain guarantees not usually associated with other types of financial instruments. Thus the period of growth in the volume of funds channeled into investment trusts coincided with the period of rapid expansion of financiera assets, reflecting the fact that both developments were motivated by the increasingly severe reserve requirements imposed on deposit and savings banks which had the effect of reducing the yields obtainable from funds subject to these requirements. Indeed, the growth of investment trusts and that of financieras appears to have been related in another way in that a sizable proportion of the funds going into the trusts were probably subsequently channeled to the financieras in the form of loans, rediscounts, or deposits. Again, however, we prefer to defer discussion of intrasystem movements of funds until later.

The principal instruments employed by banking system institutions as means for mobilizing long-term funds in the market were bonds and *cédulas hipotecarias.* The latter are a form of mortgage secured not only by real estate but also by the guarantees of issuing mortgage banking institutions. These instruments offered a combination of liquidity and yield (averaging around 8 per cent) which was attractive to certain investors, generally those of a conservative bent. The features of financial bonds and other similar long-term instruments issued by banking system institutions varied widely, but generally the yields on these instruments were competitive with those obtainable on *cédulas hipotecarias.* In addition, of course, banking system institutions raised funds by retaining earnings and by issuing new shares, but funds from these sources as reflected in the capital accounts of banking system institutions were relatively insignificant. Altogether, the proportion of banking system indebtedness represented by long-term obligations (i.e., by bonds, mortgages, shares, and other capital account items) constituted from between about 15 per cent to 22 per cent of total banking system obligations during the period 1940–1960.

BANKING SYSTEM CREDIT

The growth of commercial banks and other banking system institutions and extension of the services of these institutions to all regions of the country not only increased their ability to mobilize funds but also facilitated the extension of loans and other credits. Not only was the growth of banking system claims on borrowers commensurate with that of obligations to lenders, but also there was a fairly close correspondence between the character of banking system liabilities and banking system assets. Thus while the major share of banking system obligations was short term, so also was the greater part of the loanable funds of the system channeled into short-term loans and credits. What intermediate and long-term credit was available came principally from national institutions and mortgage transactions, and consequently those enterprises requiring long-term funds beyond what they were capable of generating through their own operations were largely dependent upon these sources of deficit financing.

Table II-D contains a breakdown of banking system credits, security holdings, and other claims for the period 1940–1960. We see that while the major share of bank lending took the form of relatively short-term credits, the proportion of total banking system claims represented by holdings of securities increased somewhat during the 1940s and then declined during the 1950s. The most common sort of short-term credit took the form of loans and discounts, the balance consisting of collateral- and working-capital loans and lines of credit. Intermediate-term credits consisted principally of equipment loans with maturities up to five years while long-term credits were based principally on mortgages.

In general commercial and industrial enterprises were not seriously disadvantaged by unsuitable credit maturities. For one thing the structure of production in Mexico is especially suited to heavy reliance on short-term credit arrangements. Labor is abundant and relatively low in cost so that productive processes tend to be labor-intensive and

TABLE II-D

CLAIMS OF BANKING SYSTEM INSTITUTIONS, 1940–1960[a]
(Per cent of total)

	1940	1950	1955	1960
Credits[b]				
Less than One Year	25.5	25.5	29.4	35.2
More than One Year	14.1	19.8	21.5	27.5
Credits to Government	0.6	0.1	—[c]	—[c]
Securities[b]				
Mortgages	0.1	3.0	2.4	0.8
Shares and other Securities	2.1	5.3	3.8	5.7
Government Securities	17.1	17.7	11.0	10.8
Other Claims				
Gold and Foreign Exchange	17.6	20.8	22.0	11.7
Other Assets	22.8	7.8	9.9	8.2
Totals	100.0	100.0	100.0	100.0

Source: Annual reports of Banco de México, S.A.

[a] End-of-year figures; intrasystem claims excluded.
[b] Figures indicate claims against enterprises and individuals and against government.
[c] Less than one-half of one per cent.

to require considerable short-term financing. Likewise the requirements of commercial enterprises are well satisfied by short-term financing of inventories and installment credits. Investment expenditures for plant and equipment beyond what could be supported with internal funds were probably curtailed to some extent by the limited availability of long-term credits, but this inhibition was minimized by the various procedures which evolved for extending nominally short-term credits into longer terms. For instance, the needs of some borrowers for longer-term financing were met by revolving credits and bank assurances of automatic renewals of maturing obligations.

But while industrial and commercial enterprises were not seriously hampered by insufficient and inappropriate credit, the agricultural sector of the economy clearly was adversely affected by limited access to the credit resources of the country. Not only was the ability of the agricultural sector to adopt more capital-intensive techniques of production limited by the unavailability of suitable long-term credits, but increased productivity was inhibited by insufficient short-term credits as well. The risky nature of much of Mexico's agriculture, as well as the system of land tenure, has served to make agricultural loans relatively unattractive to private lending institutions. Efforts were made to force commercial banks and certain other private institutions to increase their agricultural credits (as explained in the following chapter), but with limited success. By 1960 only about 16.7 per cent of the total amount of credit made available in support of agricultural and stock-raising activities came from private banking institutions, and most of this was concentrated on the highly commercialized agriculture of the northwest. The balance of agricultural credits was provided by various of the national banking institutions, but again these credits favored market-oriented activities, especially those directed toward export markets, to the neglect of more traditional agricultural ventures.

Securities Market

We have previously indicated that operation of the money and capital market was dominated by the activities of various national and private banking system institutions. However, the several organized securities exchanges also played a role in the market for loan funds and it is appropriate to say a few words about these organizations before proceeding to an examination of market behavior.

ORGANIZED EXCHANGES

By 1960 there existed three organized securities exchanges in Mexico: the Bolsa de Valores de México, established in Mexico City in 1907; the Bolsa de Valores de Monterrey, established in 1950; and the Bolsa de Valores de Occidente, established in Guadalajara in 1960. Of the three, the Mexico City exchange is by far the most significant, accounting for well above 90 per cent of the total volume of transactions in stocks and bonds conducted through the exchanges in 1960. However, the proportion of total recorded transactions in securities effected through the organized exchanges is quite small, amounting to only about 5 per cent in 1960. Furthermore, of these transactions only about 3 per cent involved equity securities, the balance consisting of transactions involving bonds and other fixed-yield securities.

The principal explanation of the relatively insignificant role played by the organized exchanges in the money and capital market is that Banco de México, Nacional Financiera, and other national and private banking system institutions generally conduct their transactions directly with purchasers and sellers of securities, these generally being other banking system institutions and related to the market support operations of Banco de México and Nacional Financiera on the one hand and to the security-reserve requirements of Banco de México (as explained in the next chapter) on the other. The small importance of equity securities was due principally to three factors: first, the desire on the part of those who control industrial and other enterprises to retain control and avoid the risk of attempts by outsiders to interfere with their management prerogatives (especially decisions regarding the reporting of profits and the declaration of dividends which would affect taxation); second, the treatment of interest as a tax-deductible cost while dividends afford no tax advantage; and third, the high cost of this means of financing, given the prospect of inflation. Thus the limitation on the growth of equity financing during the period under study lay principally on the side of supply since industrial groups persistently refused to issue shares and thereby suffer loss of control over policies and profits as well as loss of secrecy as a result of being required to disclose their financial positions. Furthermore, it appears that under the circumstances which prevailed during the period, the cost of financing expansion by means of equity issues instead of by means of internal funds or issues of fixed-interest securities or bank loans would generally have been more expensive.

Thus, for various reasons enterprises tended to utilize their own funds for financing investment in fixed capital and to depend upon external financing principally for working capital purposes. As a consequence, of course, little possibility existed for the majority of savers and wealth holders to protect themselves from inflation and devaluation by means of equity shares—even when industrial expansion was financed by new issues, the securities were usually restricted to the group already holding control—with the result that many were led to seek safeguards by purchasing real estate and other inflation hedges as well as by holding deposits denominated in foreign currencies and financial assets in foreign financial markets.

OTHER CHARACTERISTICS OF THE SECURITIES MARKET

The importance of the securities market is not commensurate with the low volume of transactions effected in the organized exchanges nor should it be obscured by the relatively insignificant role of equity financing. We have previously shown that the volume of loan funds mobilized by securities issues was quite significant, and that government, public enterprises, and financial institutions in particular depended heavily upon issuance of various securities as a principal means of raising funds in the market. However, in order to understand how the securities market performed its important function without a significant volume of transactions on the organized exchanges and with very little trading in equity issues, it is necessary to make some additional observations concerning characteristics of the market.

As previously explained, market quotations of all fixed-yield securities except corporate bonds were maintained at the nominal or par value of these instruments regardless of changes in basic supply and demand conditions or in monetary and financial policies. In 1960 over 80 per cent of the outstanding volume of fixed-yield securities consisted of government bonds, *cédulas hipotecarias*, mortgage bonds, financial bonds, *certificados de participación*, and other such instruments whose prices were supported at par—the balance consisting of industrial obligations, and even certain of these were maintained at market prices equal to their nominal values.

The constancy of market prices was due to the willingness of the various issuing institutions to buy or sell their securities at any given time, which in turn had the effect of conferring upon these instruments a high degree of liquidity independent of stated maturities. By supporting, and in fact establishing, security prices the various financial institutions assumed to some extent the function fulfilled by securities exchanges in the United States and other countries. This practice also helps explain why the bulk of securities transactions are not effected through the organized exchanges in Mexico.

We previously stated that the reason prices of fixed-yield securities were supported by the issuing institutions was to increase the competitiveness of financial instruments vis-à-vis other assets and also to bolster public confidence in the financial market, thereby contributing to its development. While these considerations explain the general policy of supporting security prices in the market, from the viewpoint of the various groups of issuing institutions the practice was also made necessary in order to compete for funds in a market characterized by a high-liquidity preference on the part of savers and other lenders. Only by insuring lenders against the risk of capital losses, and by offsetting variations in supply and demand by adjustments in their own holdings, were institutions issuing fixed-yield securities able to compete effectively with other totally liquid claims available in the market which did not require claimants to bear any risk of capital loss.

FIXED-YIELD SECURITIES

The amount of funds channeled through the money and capital market by means of issues of fixed-yield securities was considerable in spite of the relatively low volume of transactions effected through the organized exchanges. Thus, for example, at the end of 1960 government and other securities issued by entities in the public sector valued at 13.9 billion pesos and private securities valued at 4.4 billion pesos were outstanding, making a total equal to nearly 30 per cent of the total resources of all banking system institutions. Furthermore, between 1942 and 1960 outstanding fixed-yield securities increased by 17.6 billion pesos, evidencing that these instruments were very important as a means of facilitating the movement of loan funds from lenders to borrowers.

In Table II-E are shown the type and distribution of outstanding fixed-yield securities during the period under study. Securities issued by government and governmental agencies comprised the major proportion of all outstanding issues over the period, but issues by various decentralized agencies increased substantially relative to securities issued directly by governmental units. Outstanding private indebtedness represented by fixed-yield securities increased relative to outstanding fixed-yield public obligations during the 1940s, but some relative decline was registered during the 1950s.

TABLE II-E

TYPE AND DISTRIBUTION OF FIXED-YIELD SECURITIES, 1942–1960
(Per cent of total)

	1942	1950	1955	1960
Type				
Public Debt	83.7	71.9	74.1	76.2
Government	77.5	45.7	37.0	38.2
Decentralized Agencies[a]	6.2	26.2	37.1	38.0
Private Debt	16.3	28.1	25.9	23.8
Totals	100.0	100.0	100.0	100.0
Distribution				
Banco de México	51.5	43.3	23.5	10.6
Other National Banking System Institutions	11.1	4.4	13.1	6.5
Private Banking System Institutions	5.3	15.1	21.7	28.3
Insurance Companies	3.1	3.7	5.8	5.2
Enterprises, Individuals, and Other Public Sector Investors[b]	29.0	33.5	35.9	49.3
Totals	100.0	100.0	100.0	100.0

Source: Annual reports of Comisión Nacional de Valores.

[a] Includes official financial institutions.
[b] Other public sector investors include the federal, state, and local governments, social security trust funds, and public enterprises.

Also shown in Table II-E is the distribution of holdings of fixed-yield securities as between various types of holders or investors. It is noteworthy that Banco de México holdings decreased from 51.5 per cent of the total outstanding amount of fixed-yield securities in 1942 to 10.6 per cent of this amount in 1960. The proportionate share of total fixed-yield securities held by other national credit institutions also declined, but not so dramatically. Corresponding increases occurred in the holdings of private credit institutions and various other investors in both the public and private sector. We shall have more to say about the motivations and processes underlying the shift in ownership of outstanding fixed-yield securities in a later chapter.

MARKET RATES OF INTEREST

Security yields varied from the low rates paid on government securities and savings deposits to the high rates required to be paid by issuers whose securities were not supported in the market and by borrowers with poor credit ratings. The structure of yields which prevailed in selected years is indicated in Table II-F. As shown, government securities yielded between 3 and 6 per cent. These securities were obligatory components of the portfolios of deposit and savings banks, financieras, and insurance companies (under the provisions of the reserve requirements imposed by Banco de México and other regulatory agencies); also a sizable volume of government securities was held by public enterprises and official agencies. The relatively low rate on government securities was able to be maintained only as a result of policies which forced various investors to hold these securities at yields substantially below prevailing market rates. There existed virtually no voluntary demand for government securities on the part of private enterprises and individuals. We shall demonstrate in a later chapter how Banco de México, during the latter part of the period, was able to dispose of a significant portion of its holdings of government securities to other credit institutions.

TABLE II-F

INTEREST RATES, 1940–1960
(Annual averages—per cent per annum)

	1940	1950	1955	1960
Peso Obligations				
Official Discount Rate	3.0	4.5	4.5	4.5
Mexican Government Bonds	3.0	6.0	5.0	6.0
Savings Deposits	4.0	4.5	4.5	4.5
Commercial Loans	n.a.	10.9	10.2	11.5
Mortgage Loans	n.a.	10.3	10.3	12.0
Cédulas Hipotecarias	8.0	8.0	8.0	8.0
Financial Bonds	n.a.	8.0	8.0	8.2
Industrial Bonds	8.0	8.0	8.5	10.0
Financiera Loans	n.a.	n.a.	11.5	12.0
Composite Index[a]	n.a.	10.7	11.4	14.0
Foreign Currency Obligations				
Savings Deposits	2.5	2.5	3.0	3.0
Financial Bonds	n.a.	n.a.	3.0	3.5
Financiera Loans	n.a.	n.a.	7.5	9.0

Source: International Monetary Fund, *International Financial Statistics*; Sidney Homer, *A History of Interest Rates* (New Brunswick, New Jersey: Rutgers University Press, 1963); also, annual reports of Banco de México, S.A.

[a] Estimated as yield realized by private financial institutions on assets not subject to requirements imposed by Banco de México.

We have previously referred to rates which were in effect for savings deposits (4.5 per cent for national-currency deposits and 3 per cent for foreign-currency deposits in 1960), these rates being only slightly higher than those in effect in 1940. Nominal rates on commercial and mortgage loans during the 1950s were in excess of 10 per cent, with the true rate being somewhat higher. The yield on *cédulas hipotecarias*, whose real estate backing coupled with an implied liquidity guarantee on the part of issuing mortgage banks made them especially attractive, averaged around 8 per cent throughout the period. Financial bonds issued by national credit institutions yielded from 6 per cent to 10 per cent depending upon date of issue, while those issued by private credit institutions ranged from 7 per cent to upwards of 10 per cent. Financial bonds denominated in foreign currencies (principally issued by Nacional Financiera) yielded between 3 and 4 per cent during the latter part of the 1950s. The nominal yield on industrial obligations ranged from 8 per cent to 10 per cent over the 1940–1960 period, although the true yield on most of these obligations had risen to around 12 per cent by 1960 because of the discounts at which they were available in the market and also as a result of profit-sharing provisions incorporated in the terms of some of these obligations. Finally, the rates in effect in 1960 for loans to financieras averaged around 12 per cent for pesos and 9 per cent for foreign currencies.

There exists no satisfactory overall index of lending rates. The nominal rates quoted by lending institutions do not accurately indicate the cost of borrowing because of commissions, charges for opening credit accounts (usually equal to a minimum of 1 per cent of the amount involved), and discount of interest in advance. Furthermore it was customary practice to require borrowers to maintain reciprocal balances with the lending institution equal to a specified proportion (usually around 20 per cent) of the amount of their indebtedness, which had the effect of increasing the effective, or real, rate of interest. Perhaps the best composite index of market rates is given by the yield obtained by private financial institutions on that portion of their portfolio not subject to the requirements of the selective credit control program administered by Banco de México. Such an index for the period 1950–1960 is shown in Table II-F, and it indicates that market rates rose slowly but continuously throughout this period from 10.7 per cent in 1950 to 14 per cent in 1960. Of course the fact that the annual rate of increase in wholesale prices between 1950 and

1955 averaged 9.4 per cent while it was reduced to only 3.1 per cent during the period 1956–1960 means that the real rate of interest during the former period was quite low and that it increased greatly during the latter period.

We shall have more to say about these and related matters in subsequent chapters, but perhaps it is appropriate here to indicate that the sharply higher real or adjusted level of yields obtainable in the market after 1955 was the result of the stabilization program carried out by the monetary and financial authorities coupled with continued strong liquidity preference motivated, in part at least, by expectation of further inflation and devaluation. Other factors were the relatively high rates which private banks were able to earn on their free funds and the increased fixed costs of commercial banks—brought about by the expansion of the number of branches and services offered customers—both of which served to introduce a downward inflexibility into the structure of market yields.

Conclusion

The development of the money and capital market described in this chapter reflects the increased role played by financial processes in the economic life of the country. With the institutional development which occurred, and also with the greater sophistication of financial instruments and market practices, transactions of all sorts were facilitated. Not only were investable resources augmented as a result of the development of the financial system, but also because these resources were given greater mobility they were able to contribute more to the efficiency and growth of the overall economy. Furthermore, the easier movement of goods from producers to consumers also contributed to economic growth. Of course it is not possible to precisely determine the contribution of the development of the domestic money and capital market to overall economic development of Mexico (or, for that matter, the cause-and-effect relationships of these two complementary types of development), but nevertheless it seems clear that as the financial system developed, and as the volume of financial resources channeled through the market increased, the development of the Mexican economy was progressively less inhibited by an inadequate financial structure. Whether the performance of the financial system was as efficient as it might have been in promoting economic growth is another matter, however, and we shall consider this question in more detail in later chapters.

Of course the development of the money and capital market was influenced by various actions of the government and its agencies charged with responsibility for monetary and financial policies. Thus in order to understand the course of this development, and the associated monetary and financial experience of Mexico during the period under consideration, it is necessary to familiarize ourselves with the manner in which these policies were formulated and executed. This is the objective of the chapter which follows.

CHAPTER III

MONETARY AND FINANCIAL POLICY

Introduction

THE MONETARY and fiscal authorities attempt to influence the volume and allocation of loanable funds as well as the development of the institutional structure of the banking and overall financial system. In general, the objective of monetary and financial policy is to further economic development by exercising a stabilizing influence within a dynamic growth context while at the same time inducing desired changes in the amount and allocation of the credit resources of the country. Since financial instruments are competitive with other types of assets (e.g., with commodities, real estate, gold and jewelry, etc.), the volume of resources channeled into the financial market is affected by policy measures which alter the quantity and characteristics of these instruments. Furthermore, because differences exist in the composition of financial claims and obligations of various types of creditors and debtors, monetary and financial policy measures which affect differentially either the supply of or demand for the various types of financial instruments also exercise an influence on the sources and uses of loanable funds. To the extent that the amount and allocation of savings flowing into the money and capital market are modified by policy actions, both a short- and long-term influence may be exercised on the process of economic development.

It is usually the case that authority and responsibility for controlling development and operation of the monetary and financial system of a country is entrusted to various agencies of government so that much attention to the problem of coordination is essential if public policies are to be effective. Furthermore, since circumstances change and since financial markets are constantly in the process of adaptation to the impact of actions on the part of the authorities as well as to changes in practices and circumstances in other sectors of the economy, what constitute appropriate policies and instruments of control at one time might be quite inappropriate at some later date. Also, with increased information, better theory, and improved administrative ability it becomes feasible to employ progressively more sophisticated techniques in an effort to achieve policy objectives. Certainly in the case of Mexico the number of agencies with responsibilities for formulation, execution, and coordination of monetary and financial policy has increased over time, and also policy objectives as well as techniques of control have undergone substantial modification. During the 1940s principal reliance was placed on quantitative controls imposed on the commercial banks while during the 1950s increasing use was made of qualitative controls, with both types of controls being extended to several sorts of nonmonetary financial institutions.

In this chapter we shall examine Mexican monetary and financial policy objectives and policy-making procedures as well as instruments of control as these evolved during the period 1940–1960. Various policy measures and their consequences will also be reviewed. This material, along with that describing the development of the money and capital market already presented, is employed in the following chapter as a basis for a detailed examination of the record of recent Mexican monetary and financial experience.

Objectives and Procedures

The goals of monetary and financial policy, and the procedures followed in establishing these goals, have evolved along with the development of the Mexican money and capital market and changes in the country's economic circumstances. In general, the goals of policy are maintenance of domestic stability and external equilibrium and promotion of rapid economic growth. The principal means employed in pursuit of these goals are those of monetary and fiscal policy. However, the apparent similarity in these regards between Mexico and advanced industrialized countries such as the United States is misleading. In fact, neither the priorities placed on these various goals nor the techniques employed by those in positions of policy-making responsibility are those commonly found in the more advanced countries. As a prelude to our description of the situation in Mexico, it is appropriate that we examine some of the reasons for these differences in objectives and techniques of monetary and financial policy.

MEXICO AND THE MORE ADVANCED COUNTRIES

In advanced industrialized countries such as the United States, the principal objectives of monetary policy are those of domestic full employment and price stability and maintenance of orderly conditions in financial markets. It is expected that external stability and economic growth will be facilitated by general, quantitative monetary measures of a stabilizing sort, but main reliance is placed on the operation of market forces as modified by fiscal policy and various ad hoc interventions to achieve these ends. In contrast, in Mexico monetary policy is oriented to a much greater extent to the objective of growth promotion, and fiscal policy is a less important technique of control.

The main reason for the greater reliance on monetary control techniques in Mexico is that the country's fiscal system is weaker than those of advanced countries. Tax revenues of the federal government have ranged between 8 per cent and 12 per cent of gross national product in recent years as compared with a range of 20 per cent to 30 per cent for advanced industrialized countries such as the United States and those of Western Europe. Furthermore, the Mexican fiscal system is less effective as an instrument of policy because the responsiveness of tax revenues to increases in gross national product is markedly lower than in the wealthier countries whose systems of taxation are more progressive. Therefore, pending substantial reform of the fiscal system, Mexico must of necessity rely principally upon monetary measures in pursuing economic policy objectives.

Monetary policy measures of a conventional sort are also of limited effectiveness in Mexico. In the Mexican circumstances it is not possible to rely on such tools as open-market operations and variations in the discount rate because the market for government and other securities is not well developed and also because the overall credit market is not sufficiently well integrated to permit pressures introduced in one part to be transmitted to all other parts. Another limiting factor is that the demand for credit is governed more by shifts in consumer preferences and expectations regarding the prospects for profits (whether as a result of productive activity or speculation) than by changes in the cost of borrowed funds, and consequently marginal adjustments in interest rates introduced by means of open-market operations or traditional rediscounting procedures would not be very effective in controlling the aggregate volume of expenditures. Attempts to exercise control through induced adjustments in the general level of interest rates would require changes of such magnitudes as to be inconsistent with the need to promote lending and development of a market for long-term securities. Furthermore, exclusive reliance on interest-rate adjustments would probably work to inhibit investment expenditures more than it would spending for consumption goods, and thereby would hamper economic growth.

For all these reasons, monetary policy is directed primarily toward limitation of credit availability rather than alteration of the cost of borrowed funds. This is not to say that measures of a quantitative sort designed to influence the terms of borrowing are unimportant. The point is, however, that the peculiarities of the Mexican circumstances dictate greater reliance on qualitative credit controls than is common in countries with more fully developed financial markets and fiscal systems.

Actually, certain characteristics of the Mexican monetary and financial system are such as to permit controls exercised by the monetary authorities to be particularly effective. Money is demanded almost solely for transactions purposes, the velocity of monetary circulation is already quite high, and monetary policies are not greatly hampered by a wide variety of money substitutes. For these reasons it is more feasible to influence the performance of the Mexican economy by means of various monetary measures, and especially by selective credit controls, than, for example, is the case in the United States where all sorts of offsetting adjustments to monetary changes are possible.

Because monetary policies do afford the most effective available means of exercising control, and because promotion of economic growth and development are of such overriding importance, it is not surprising to find that monetary control techniques of various sorts

are the principal instruments employed in efforts to maintain a high
level of economic activity. While domestic stability and external equilibrium are recognized as important goals of policy, the priority they
are accorded is at all times dependent upon the assumption that these
goals are not inconsistent with rapid growth and, indeed, that they
are necessary prerequisites for the rapid and sustained growth which
Mexico is determined to achieve.

POLICY-MAKING PROCEDURES

The Ministry of Finance (Secretaría de Hacienda y Crédito Publico)
is the highest authority in matters pertaining to monetary and credit
policy. Operating under its jurisdiction are Banco de México, the
National Banking Commission, the National Securities Commission,
the National Insurance Commission, and (to some extent) the various
nationalized credit institutions. Banco de México, as central bank, has
primary responsibility for both formulation and execution of monetary and financial policy as determined in consultation and close coordination with the Ministry of Finance. The functions of the National Banking Commission and the National Securities Commission
are, respectively, to supervise activities of banking system institutions and to insure compliance with legal requirements on the part of
all participants in the money and capital market. The function of the
National Insurance Commission is to regulate practices of the private
insurance companies. These supervisory and regulatory agencies do
not participate in policy formulation except in an advisory capacity.

The relationships between the Ministry of Finance, Banco de México, and the other official financial agencies of the government—as
well as the membership of the governing boards of these agencies as
of the end of 1964—is shown in Chapter VII (see Table VII-A).
The reader may find it useful to consult this guide to the organizational structure of the Mexican financial system in connection with
his reading of the following paragraphs.

The various national credit institutions are governed principally by
directives from the ministries specifically concerned with the area of
their activities, but to the extent that the operations of these institutions are capable of exercising a significant influence on the behavior
of the money and capital market (either directly or indirectly through
competition with private credit institutions) the Ministry of Finance
maintains close supervision. For example, the Agrarian Credit Bank
and the Ejido Bank are subject to the authority of both the Ministry

of Finance and the Ministry of Agriculture. In the case of Nacional Financiera, by far the most important of the national credit institutions, a relationship with the Ministry of Finance has developed which in most respects is similar to that between Banco de México and the Ministry of Finance. Furthermore, because of their dominant positions in the money and capital market, Nacional Financiera and Banco de México of necessity must maintain close coordination of their activities.

POSITION OF BANCO DE MÉXICO

Banco de México is owned jointly by the federal government (which holds 51 per cent of outstanding ownership shares) and by the various "associated institutions" (which hold the remaining shares in proportion to their respective capitalizations). The director of Banco de México is appointed by the President of the Republic, the term of his appointment usually corresponding with the six-year length of a presidential administration. However, the incumbent, Rodrigo Gómez, is now serving his third six-year term as general director, having been initially appointed in 1952 after many years of prior service in various capacities as an official of Banco de México. Several past presidents made more than one appointment to the position; for example, in General Lázaro Cárdenas' Administration (1934–1940) there were three different directors.

Relations between Banco de México and the Ministry of Finance are generally amicable. Banco de México adapts its operations to the requirements of government policy directives, and within this framework pursues by means of the instruments available to it the traditional central bank objectives of domestic stability and external equilibrium and the promotion of the overall growth and development of the national economy. Proposals for specific monetary policy measures usually originate with Banco de México, but before other than routine measures are taken, the director consults with the Minister of Finance. As this arrangement works out in practice, the success of Banco de México proposals in government councils is dependent upon their technical quality, the respect they command in various quarters throughout the public sector, and, of course, the persuasiveness of and general esteem enjoyed by the director.

The director of Banco de México also consults regularly with the chairman of the National Banking Commission in order to insure common objectives and coordination in the activities of these two agencies of government. Banco de México is also represented on the executive board of the National Securities Commission, and through this channel is able to assure that the actions of the Commission conform to the requirements of governmental credit policy. While from an organizational viewpoint the National Banking Commission and the National Securities Commission are not subordinates of Banco de México, the power and influence of the latter is such that it is capable of exercising a dominant influence over the activities of these other regulatory bodies.

Viewed historically, the development of Banco de México powers may be divided into three stages. As already described in Chapter I, the period from 1925 to 1936 was the formative stage during which Banco de México gradually increased its ability to influence the operation of the monetary system. The second stage, which occupied roughly the period 1936–1948, was characterized by extension of Banco de México authority to impose reserve requirements on commercial banks and by increased flexibility in monetary policy which reliance on this traditional instrument of control permitted. During this period it became possible for Banco de México to require cash reserves up to 50 per cent of total commercial bank demand deposits and 100 per cent reserves against marginal or incremental deposits when deemed necessary for achievement of the traditional objectives of monetary policy. Beginning in 1948 a third phase was initiated during which Banco de México's powers and responsibilities were both extended. During this latter phase, which has extended to the present day, various nonmonetary financial institutions such as savings banks and financieras have been subjected to Banco de México reserve requirements, and also Banco de México has undertaken, by means of various types of selective credit controls, to direct financial resources into activities judged to be most conducive to promotion of overall economic development. As a result, the authority of Banco de México extends well beyond that of the traditional central bank concerned only with regulation of commercial bank contributions to the money supply.

NACIONAL FINANCIERA AND OTHER NATIONAL CREDIT INSTITUTIONS

The basic law governing credit institutions (Ley General de Instituciones de Crédito y Organizaciones Auxiliares, 1941) defines national institutions as those "established with participation of the Federal government or in which the government reserves the right to appoint the majority of the board of directors or veto agreements adopted by the assembly or the board" (Article 1). While under the provisions of this law the federal government is empowered to designate any credit institution as a national institution for reasons of the public interest, normally nationalized institutions are those in which the government has provided the majority share of the capitalization. There are exceptions, however, such as the Financiera Nacional Azucarera, S.A., and the Banco Nacional Cinematográfico, S.A., both of which are capitalized principally with private funds. Also, there have been instances, not anticipated in the law, in which private credit institutions have become a part of the national banking system because an established national institution has become majority stockholder as a result of supporting operations.

Generally speaking, national credit institutions other than Banco de México do not have regulatory or supervisory powers. Nevertheless, because they control a large proportion of the total resources of the banking system as a whole, and because the loans they are capable of making are generally for longer terms and their lending rates are generally lower than those offered by private credit agencies, the operations of the national credit institutions often exercise a decisive influence in the money and capital market.

The activities of the various national credit institutions are closely prescribed by governing statutes and by directives emanating from the Ministry of Finance. Coordination of their activities both with one another and with overall monetary and financial policy is achieved by frequent consultations between the various agency administrators and the director of Banco de México. The objectives outlined in official directives are adapted to accommodate changing circumstances, and Banco de México frequently revises the volume and terms of its lending to and purchases from these agencies in order to facilitate achievement of these objectives. Overall responsibility for coordination is vested in a credit-coordinating committee which operates under the direction of the Ministry of Finance (Comité Coordinador de las Instituciones Nacionales de Crédito), whose function it is to maintain consistency between the programs of the various individual institutions and the resources available to the national banking system as a whole.

Nacional Financiera is the most important national institution other than Banco de México. It functions principally as a development bank and is the major supplier of funds for financing industrial investment expenditures as well as being a major issuer of securities. Nacional

Financiera also acts as the principal agent of the government in arranging and administering foreign loans and is responsible for exercising overall control of foreign credits to both public and private borrowers. Nacional Financiera is also responsible for promoting the development of the securities market, and the terms on which its own securities are offered to the public tend to govern the structure of rates and maturities for the market as a whole. Finally, Nacional Financiera serves as federal fiscal agent in the marketing of government securities.

As in the case of Banco de México, Nacional Financiera development may be divided into stages. The institution was originally established in 1934 with the principal purpose of promoting development of the domestic capital market. In the early years it was relatively insignificant and unsuccessful, and toward the end of 1940 its charter was amended in an effort to increase its effectiveness. In essence the statutory change converted Nacional Financiera into the national development bank, and in subsequent years the scope of its activities as well as its overall importance in the financial and industrial affairs of the country has greatly increased. With the support of Banco de México credits and loans from the Export-Import Bank, Nacional Financiera became the major source of financing for industrial investment during the 1940s. Beginning in 1947 Nacional Financiera was designated as the institution through which all foreign loans requiring governmental guarantees were to be channeled and also was directed to concentrate its resources in support of infrastructure investment and establishment and/or expansion of industries deemed basic to economic development. In this latter connection, Nacional Financiera's activities during the 1950s came to be closely related to the government's import-substitution program. The importance of Nacional Financiera's combined financial and entrepreneurial role in promoting industrialization and overall economic development in recent years can hardly be overestimated.

With the exception of Nacional Financiera, whose vast and varied activities in both the public and private sectors cover a wide spectrum, national credit institutions are specialized organizations whose resources are earmarked for application in support of specific activities or sectors of the economy. For example, the Agrarian Credit Bank (Banco Nacional de Crédito Agrícola y Ganadero) specializes in loans to small farmers and the Ejido Bank (Banco Nacional de Crédito Ejidal) specializes in providing credit to farmers organized in *ejidos.* Both of these institutions have access to federal funds which by discounting and other procedures are loaned out through regional branches located throughout the country. Likewise the Mortgage and Public Works Bank (Banco Nacional Hipotecario Urbano y de Obras Públicas) provides loans to contractors engaged in federal construction projects, extends credits to states and municipalities in support of public works, and is an important source of financing for residential construction in competition with private banking institutions and insurance companies. This agency depends for its funds principally upon issues of mortgage bonds and foreign loans. The activities of the various other national credit institutions are similarly specialized in accordance with the purposes for which they were established.

Instruments of Control

Over the years the practice of central banking and the means of influencing the overall financial policies of the country have changed in response to development of the money and capital market and to underlying changes in the structure of production and the distribution of income. The period 1940–1960 witnessed a series of successive changes in the instruments of monetary and financial control. These changes were motivated by the necessity to adapt the credit system to meet new requirements of borrowers and lenders and to accommodate novel forms of financial intermediation. Legal sanction for these changes is evidenced in the modifications made in the statutory powers and responsibilities of the various types of credit institutions. Monetary and financial policy in Mexico has evolved out of a process of interaction between market forces and private initiative on the one hand and between statutory authority and discretionary management on the other.

RESERVE REQUIREMENTS

The basic instrument governing the availability of credit and the size of the money supply is the reserve requirement. Private banks are legally required to maintain reserves with Banco de México in cash and securities in amounts equal to specified percentages of their deposit and other selected liabilities. By means of this requirement the central bank can either prevent or encourage money creation and credit expansion.

Legal reserve requirements are based on both total deposit obligations at any given time and on increments in these obligations. For example, a commercial bank may be required to maintain cash and security reserves equal to 50 per cent of existing obligations and also be informed that for subsequent marginal increases in its obligations beyond a specified date the applicable requirement will be 75 per cent. This latter form of reserve requirement has proven to be a highly useful technique, not only because it permits tight control to be exercised over credit expansion but also because it permits the reserve requirement to be revised without forcing banks to adjust their reserve positions at the moment revisions are introduced. Furthermore, the marginal reserve requirement penalizes those banks which increase credits most rapidly during periods of restrictive policy while favoring these same banks during periods in which policy is directed toward the promotion of credit expansion. The technique creates certain administrative problems, however, the most serious of which is that the central bank must be able to diagnose promptly any changes in market conditions so that undesired expansions or contractions of deposits can be subjected to appropriate marginal reserve requirements before substantial changes occur.

Table III-A contains a summary of the record of changes in reserve requirements imposed on various banking system institutions during the years 1940–1960. Initially (i.e., beginning in 1936) deposit and savings banks were required to maintain a cash reserve equal to the sum of 7 per cent of their deposit obligations and 50 per cent of the average daily volume of check clearings during the previous week. In mid-1940 the reserve requirement based on checking-account activity was abandoned and the percentage required with respect to deposits was increased to 10 per cent. Subsequently during the 1940's the requirements imposed on the deposit banks became both more stringent (cash reserves equal to 50 per cent of deposits were required for a period) and more complicated (a distinction was made between deposits denominated in domestic currencies and those denominated in foreign currencies and also between banks operating in the Federal District and those operating in other parts of the country). Furthermore, separate requirements were imposed on the deposit liabilities of deposit banks and those of savings banks, and, also, the distinction between existing and incremental deposits was introduced into the regulations.

Beginning in 1948 and 1949, cash-reserve requirements were supplemented by requirements governing the division of bank assets as between various types of securities and other credits. This action constituted initiation of selective credit controls, and by means of its power to regulate the character of bank assets Banco de México was able to influence directly the allocation of the credit resources of the banking system as between competing employments.

The supplementary security-reserve requirement was first devised as a means of forcing deposit and savings banks (and subsequently private financieras) to acquire securities or grant credits which otherwise would not have been attractive. Generally the securities required were government bonds or issues of public enterprises, and normally they were purchased from Banco de México. For the most part these securities—whose prices were supported at fixed levels by Banco de México—did not offer yields competitive with those realized by the banks on other investments. However, reserves in this form did provide an interest return, and in this respect were preferable from the banks' viewpoint to an equal amount of non-earning cash reserves. From Banco de México's viewpoint, on the other hand, the security-reserve requirement had much the same effect in neutralizing excess reserves as would have been produced by increases in the cash-reserve requirement while also affording a means of shifting public securities from the central bank portfolio to portfolios of the private banks.

In addition to the cash- and security-reserve requirements, Banco de México was able to direct the private banks to employ a specified percentage of funds at their disposal in support of credits to certain types of activities. This directed credit requirement left the banks free to choose between loan applicants so long as the claims acquired related to activities which Banco de México wished to support. In general, Banco de México employed the directed-credit device to stimulate the flow of credits to the agricultural sector and other selected, nonspeculative lines of activity.

The security-reserve and directed-credit techniques were applied in conjunction with the marginal cash-reserve requirement. In effect banks were given the option either of maintaining 100 per cent cash reserves with respect to increments in deposit obligations or of meeting a lower marginal cash-reserve requirement while fulfilling the security- and directed-credit requirements. A penalty levy of 2 per cent of any cash-reserve deficiency was imposed on banks which failed to satisfy the requirement. When banks elected to meet the security- and directed-credit requirements, some portion of funds which became available to them through incremental deposits was usually free for use as they saw fit.

TABLE III-A

RESERVE REQUIREMENTS, 1940–1960

Initial Date	Institution	Federal District	Outside Federal District	Currency — Mexican	Currency — Foreign	Required Reserves[a] — Cash	Directed Investments — Securities	Directed Investments — Credits
Sept. 23, 1936	Deposit and Savings Banks	X	X	X	X	7 %		
July 17, 1940	" " "	X	X	X	X	10		
July 14, 1941	Deposit Banks	X	X	X	X	20		
" " "	" "	X	X		X	25		
" " "	" "	X	X		X	50		
Jan. 19, 1944	" "		X	X		37		
May 18, 1944	" "		X	X	X	50		
Aug. 7, 1946	" "	X				30		
March 22, 1948	" "	X		X	X	25	10 %	
Oct. 13, 1948	" "	X		X		20		
" " "	" "		X		X	25	25	10 %
Sept. 30, 1949	" "	X	X	X		30	20	50
" " "	" "		X	X		20	15	65
" " "	" "	X	X		X	20	5	
Jan. 12, 1951	Savings Banks	X	X	X		20		

Date	Institution								
June 15, 1951	Deposit Banks	X	X				100		
Jan. 8, 1955	" " "b	X	X		X		25	75	
Jan. 10, 1955	" " "		X	X		X	20	10	45
" " "	" " "	X	X	X		X	30	20	35
Aug. 31, 1955	Savings Banksc		X	X		X	10	37.5	52.5
July 1, 1957	Deposit Banks	X	X	X			25	30	20
" " "	" " "	X	X	X			15	13	42
Jan. 15, 1958	Financieras	X	X	X			1	19	
" " "	" " "	X	X	X	X		1	24	
March 6, 1959	"	X	X	X	X		25	75	
July 15, 1959	Deposit Banks	X	X		X		15	30	30
" " "	" " "	X	X		X		15	10	45
May 4, 1960	Financierasd	X	X		X		1	19	80
May 20, 1960	Deposit Banks and Financierase	X	X		X		15 %	15 %	70 %

SOURCE: Annual reports of Banco de México, S. A.

a Percentages relate to demand-deposit and savings-deposit liabilities of the deposit and savings banks and short-term obligations of financieras, except where otherwise indicated.
b On additions to deposits as of January 8, 1955.
c On additions to deposits as of August 31, 1955.
d For financieras with total domestic currency obligations ranging between 20 and 50 million pesos, increases in these obligations exceeding 1 per cent per month are subject to a 100-per-cent cash reserve requirement.
e For fixed-term deposits of no less than ninety days.

As already indicated, reserve requirements are based on the deposit obligations of the banking institutions to which the regulations are applicable. However, in the regulations an attempt is made to discriminate between demand deposits and savings deposits as well as between deposits denominated in domestic and foreign currencies. Furthermore, an attempt is made to discriminate between different types of banking institutions as evidenced by the different reserve requirements imposed on ordinary deposit banks, savings banks, and investment banks of the sort represented by the private financieras. One problem in this connection is that similar financial operations may be carried out by nominally different institutions, and consequently Banco de México attempts to accord more or less equal treatment to comparable activities regardless of the institutional environment in which they are carried on. For example, fixed-term deposits for not less than ninety days are subject to the same reserve requirements whether maintained with deposit and savings banks or with financieras. In practice, however, the legal reserve requirements have been more onerous for the deposit banks than for the savings banks, and more onerous for both of these types of institutions than for the private financieras.

As shown in Table III-A, numerous adjustments in reserve requirements were made between 1940 and 1960, while during the same period the tendency was for the requirements to become both more complicated and more severe. These developments, particularly during the 1950s, are indicative of the restrictive measures Banco de México was compelled to take in response to balance-of-payments pressures and in an effort to counter the inflationary effects of mounting deficits in the public sector. Another factor in this connection was the continuous decline throughout the whole period in the ratio of currency to the money supply, which in the absence of higher reserve requirements would have permitted an increase in the ability of the banking system to produce a multiple expansion of the money supply on the basis of a given increment in reserves.

SECURITIES TRANSACTIONS AND REDISCOUNTING

Banco de México's use of the reserve requirement permits it to control the composition of claims acquired by the deposit and savings banks and the private financieras and thereby to influence the allocation of credit resources as between alternative applications. This qualitative or selective credit-control scheme is complemented by Banco de

México's ability to determine what types and amounts of securities to add to its own portfolio and also what types and amounts of rediscounts or credits are to be made available to various banking system institutions.

Actually, the initial and most significant impact of Banco de México operations on both the volume and allocation of the credit resources of the country is made at the time it purchases securities. This action makes funds available to issuers of the securities and also introduces reserves into the banking system. Subsequent security sales by Banco de México from its securities portfolio to banks in fulfillment of their reserve requirements is significant primarily because these transactions permit excess reserves to be absorbed. There need not be close correlation between the types of securities Banco de México is currently acquiring from issuers and the types it is currently disposing of to banks—although there may be, and over any long-run period there is almost certain to be. The fact that the majority of Banco de México sales under the stimulus of the security-reserve requirement have involved securities issued either by the federal government or by various national credit institutions indicates that Banco de México has served as a significant source of funds for these borrowers.

In the case of rediscounts, Banco de México is able to exercise an influence on the allocation of credit resources by determining which types of borrowers and which types of collateral are eligible. The rediscounting privilege is restricted primarily to other national credit institutions, although private banks are occasionally supported by this means in instances in which relief from temporary distress is required. But regardless of whether rediscounting operations involve national or private institutions, the majority of claims acquired by Banco de México are based on credits originally made available to enterprises and individuals.

Table III-B contains data showing the net results of Banco de México's securities transactions and rediscounting operations during the 1940–1960 period. During the 1940s and into the 1950s through 1955, Banco de México security holdings consisted principally of claims on the government. During these years rediscounts were relatively small as compared to securities holdings. Between 1955 and 1960, however, holdings of government securities declined while holdings of securities issued by banking system institutions increased sharply. During this same five-year period rediscounts increased rapidly, so that by the end of 1960 Banco de México's rediscount

TABLE III-B

BANCO DE MÉXICO HOLDINGS OF REDISCOUNTS AND SECURITIES, 1940–1960
(Millions of Pesos)

	1940	1950	1955	1960
Enterprises and Individuals				
Rediscounts	82.0	195.1	306.7	2,740.2
Securities	1.1	228.6	116.0	480.8
Banking System				
Rediscounts	3.3	18.2	37.6	207.6
Securities	16.9	217.1	375.8	1,014.5
Government				
Rediscounts	12.4	7.8	69.4	517.3
Securities	296.0	1,718.0	1,989.3	1,383.2

SOURCE: Annual Reports of Banco de México, S.A.

credits exceeded its holdings of securities. We shall examine these developments in greater detail in subsequent chapters, but it seems appropriate in the present context to make two additional points with reference to the data shown in Table III-B.

First, it is clear that the change in the relative sizes of Banco de México holdings of securities and rediscounts reflects the sizable transfers of securities to other banking system institutions in connection with the security-reserve requirement scheme. However, Banco de México also reduced its security holdings by selling at competitive yields large amounts of government bonds to various decentralized government agencies and enterprises with state participation which were required to employ their excess funds for this purpose. By means of this latter procedure Banco de México was able to gain command of savings which could be directed to investment projects whose noninflationary financing was deemed to be especially crucial to the country's program of economic development.

The second point has to do with rediscounting. We have already indicated that the rediscounting procedure is employed as a means of affording central bank support to various kinds of bank lending practices, particularly to certain practices carried out by national credit institutions. In the early part of the period under study, the agricultural credit banks were heavily supported in their operations by the rediscount technique. More recently Banco de México rediscount operations have been integrated with the government's price support policies for basic agricultural products. The procedure was as follows. Large amounts of commercial paper (actually, warehouse receipts) based on purchases of agricultural products by CEIMSA (Compañía Exportadora e Importadora Mexicana, S.A., the government agency employed to administer price-support programs for basic agricultural commodities) were rediscounted by Banco de México and subsequently sold to banking system institutions. The details of the process are somewhat complicated, but the essence of what happened is that Banco de México rediscounted the CEIMSA paper at 4.5 per cent and then marketed the paper to the banks at the very attractive yield of 13.5 per cent. Thus, rediscounting was combined with a form of open-market sales in such a manner as to provide low-cost financing for the government price-support agency while preventing a corresponding increase in the liquidity of the banking system. Banco de México, in effect, was engaged in subsidization of the price-support program, but in such a manner as to minimize the inflationary impact of the practice.

GROWTH RATE LIMITATIONS

We have seen that one of the results of the supplementary security-reserve and directed-credit schemes is that Banco de México is able to dictate to some degree the structure of bank claims. This power has been employed to force the banks to use a larger portion of their resources for acquiring longer-term securities (especially those issued by the government and other public-sector borrowers) than they would have done on their own volition. A similar but somewhat different device has been employed to induce the banks to extend the maturities of their own obligations with the purpose of reducing the liquidity of banking system obligations and also as a means of controlling the volume of funds made available to various lending institutions. The device consists of maximum limits on the rate of growth of certain types of short-term obligations.

Perhaps the best example of application of the maximum-growth-rate technique is the limitation imposed on the growth of financiera loan obligations. Because of concern that rapid expansion of highly liquid financial obligations of the financieras constituted a growing threat to the stability of the financial system, and also because of the appearance of unsound competitive practices, Banco de México in 1960 decreed that further expansion of these sorts of obligations at a rate in excess of 12 per cent per annum would be subjected to a

penalty levy. The effect of this regulation was to slow the rate of financiera growth and also to induce switching to alternative fund-raising
techniques, namely the issuance of longer-term securities. A similar
maximum limit had earlier been imposed on the rate of growth of
cédulas hipotecarias, in 1958, again for the purpose of modifying the
structure of indebtedness.

RELATION TO FISCAL POLICY

Earlier in this chapter we stated that in Mexico the effectiveness of
fiscal policy as an instrument for promotion of stabilization and
growth is limited because the general level of taxation and government savings is relatively low and the degree of progressivity is such
as to make tax revenues relatively unresponsive to changes in gross
national product. It should be added, however, that variations in governmental and other public spending programs are capable of producing significant changes in the level of aggregate expenditure as well
as in the allocation of resources as between the public and private
sectors of the economy. In general, expenditures in the public sector
exceed receipts so that a characteristic feature of fiscal policy is that
it gives rise to a continuing need for financing public sector deficits.
For this reason, the operations of Banco de México and Nacional Financiera as the agencies responsible for debt management are closely
related to those of the fiscal authorities.

A basic problem relating to fiscal policy is that the public sector
deficits must somehow be financed. In their efforts to arrange the
necessary financing in a manner consistent with the objectives of stability and growth, those entrusted with debt-management responsibilities have attempted to avoid resort to inflationary expansion of the
money supply while at the same time bringing about desired adjustments in the structure of financial claims and the allocation of productive resources. We have already discussed the various instruments
and techniques of control employed in this effort. The success with
which the assignment has been carried out in recent years will be
examined in the next chapter.

Factors Governing Policy Measures

Banco de México and the other agencies charged with
responsibility for carrying out monetary and financial policies of the
government are often confronted with the necessity of attempting to
reconcile essentially inconsistent objectives. For example, the goals of

domestic stability and balance-of-payments equilibrium may be difficult to achieve simultaneously, and neither of these goals in some situations is consistent with the full utilization of productive resources and the high rate of capital formation required for satisfactory economic growth. Consequently, the policy-making authorities are often faced with the dilemma of choosing between these competing objectives, with the knowledge that regardless of the choices made criticism will be forthcoming from one quarter or another.

PRINCIPAL ENVIRONMENTAL FACTORS

For an understanding of the policy measures taken it is necessary to appreciate the environment within which the authorities must operate. First of all, it is important to stress the close relationship between conditions in the domestic economy, the balance of international payments, and especially the dependence of foreign exchange receipts upon raw material exports whose prices in international markets are notoriously unstable. Fluctuations in Mexico's balance of payments are caused principally by variations in receipts from raw material exports, and therefore are largely uncontrollable by monetary and financial policy measures or any other means. Secondly, a sizable proportion (ranging from 35 per cent to nearly 50 per cent in recent years) of total investment expenditures is accounted for by the public sector (i.e., by the federal government, states and municipalities, and decentralized government agencies and enterprises with state participation), and consequently decisions regarding these expenditures are influenced by political as well as economic considerations. Even in the case of investment expenditures in the private sector, there are various reasons for expecting that these expenditures are not very responsive to changes in domestic interest rate levels (e.g., heavy reliance upon self-financing and foreign financing, overwhelming influence of expectations regarding future income and price levels, etc.). The point is that because the main autonomous items in national income and product accounts of the country are not amenable to control by traditional monetary and credit control measures, unconventional control measures have been necessary in order to achieve desired results.

Another important environmental factor is the existence of powerful, unified financial groups which are at the same time the principal savers and the principal investors operating in the private sector. These financial groups not only control important segments of the industrial and financial system, but they also generally react as a bloc to changes in the country's domestic and international financial circumstances. For example, when equilibrium in Mexico's balance of payments is disturbed by fluctuations in prices of raw material exports (which, in turn, are likely to be the product of cyclical fluctuations in the United States) the domestic repercussions tend to be aggravated by responses of the private financial groups. These groups are generally well informed about current and future prospects, especially concerning balance-of-payment matters, and in domestic markets for goods and loanable funds their operations give powerful reinforcement to forces originating in international markets. Any inconsistency between domestic and external balance therefore tends to be quickly accentuated. A second point meriting attention in this connection is that the existence of clearly identifiable private financial groupings makes it possible to exercise some influence on the level of expenditures in those industries controlled by the groups by imposing requirements on the financial institutions through which the groups mainly conduct their operations. Thus, for example, certain of the large financieras are controlled by the same interests controlling sizable shares of the brewing industry, glass-making and packaging, and steel production—so that the imposition of controls on these financieras in effect constitutes either indirect control over the financial resources available to these industries or a means for restricting credits extended by the various financial groups to other borrowers. In short, the existence of large, semiautonomous financial and industrial groups is another reason, in addition to those already stated, why it has proven necessary for the Mexican authorities to adopt unconventional and fairly extreme monetary and financial control measures.

OTHER SPECIAL CIRCUMSTANCES

Because of the vulnerability of Mexican financial and goods markets to destabilizing speculation, it has proven necessary to distinguish between productive and speculative activities and to restrict credit accordingly. Another explanation of the heavy reliance on selective credit control, therefore, is the need to stimulate some types of private expenditures while at the same time guarding against destabilizing speculation. The basis for a further distinction arises in connection with the need for financing high-priority public expenditures of an investment and social welfare sort on relatively favorable terms. In this latter connection the monetary authorities employ their powers to assure credit to the public sector on more favorable terms than those available to private borrowers whose needs for deficit financing are deemed to be of lower priority. In effect, because of the limited usefulness of fiscal policy for this purpose, monetary policy is the most appropriate means for subsidizing the public sector and thereby for influencing the allocation of investable resources in a manner deemed appropriate for promoting the desired rate and type of economic growth and development.

Conclusion

We have seen that the problems of financing economic development in Mexico are in many ways different from the problems of financial policy usually encountered in the more advanced countries, and that as a consequence Mexican monetary and financial policies and instruments of control are somewhat unconventional. In the following chapter we examine the record of Mexican monetary and financial experience during the period 1940–1960, and in so doing we explain in greater detail the nature of the problems confronted by those in positions of policy-making responsibility and also appraise the effectiveness of the various measures and specific instruments of control employed in pursuit of policy objectives.

CHAPTER IV

MONETARY AND FINANCIAL EXPERIENCE

Introduction

IN PREVIOUS CHAPTERS we have described the development of the Mexican money and capital market and the *modus operandi* of Mexican monetary and financial policies. We have seen that substantial changes occurred in market institutions and instruments between 1940 and 1960 as well as in the policies and policy instruments governing market behavior.

In this chapter we proceed to examine in detail Mexican monetary and financial experience during the period 1940–1960, with emphasis on the manner in which the various monetary and financial policies pursued manifested themselves in this experience and also the degree to which the objectives of these policies were realized. More specifically, in this chapter we review the behavior of money, prices, and the balance of payments. We also attempt to probe into the financial processes underlying the capital formation which occurred, and to adduce evidence concerning the pattern of fund flows through the financial system to deficit-spending units in both the public and private sectors. We are concerned not only to formulate an accurate account of Mexican monetary and financial experience, but also to de-

velop an accurate interpretation of the influence various public policies (as well as forces beyond the control of policy makers) had in
conditioning this experience.

Money, Prices, and the Balance of Payments

The behavior of the money supply, the wholesale price
level, and the exchange parity between the peso and the dollar during the period 1940–1960 is summarized in Table IV-A. It is evident
that almost continuous price inflation and periodic devaluation characterized Mexican experience between 1940 and 1955, although it
should be added that the degree of monetary instability was less
marked in Mexico during this period than in most other Latin American countries. As shown in the table, Mexican experience during the
period 1956–1960 differed from that of preceding years in that during this latter period inflation was, relatively speaking, quite mild and
further devaluation of the peso was avoided. Obviously, efforts to
achieve monetary stability were much more successful in this more
recent period than formerly. In the analysis which follows this contrast
is emphasized.

FACTORS AFFECTING THE MONEY SUPPLY

The money supply—i.e., coin, currency, and checking-deposit liabilities of the monetary system to enterprises and individuals—increased
in roughly the same proportion as gross national product over the period 1940–1960. This was reflected in a more or less constant velocity
of monetary circulation, and suggests that money balances were held
principally for transactions purposes. Also, the composition of the
means of payment changed significantly over the period, with checking deposits becoming increasingly important relative to metallic
money and note issues of Banco de México. In 1940 checking deposits
constituted only 37.6 per cent of the money supply, but by 1960 the
proportion had risen to 53.4 per cent. This development evidences increasing public understanding of, and confidence in, banks and banking processes.

The Mexican money supply in its various forms consists of claims
by the non-bank public against the issuing institutions, i.e., claims
held by business enterprises and individuals against Banco de México
and the private deposit banks. Growth in the monetary liabilities of
these institutions is governed by the growth of their assets and of their
other, nonmonetary, liabilities. In order to understand the behavior

TABLE IV-A

INDEXES OF MEXICAN MONETARY AND FINANCIAL EXPERIENCE, 1940–1960

Year	Money Supply[a] Total	Money Supply[a] Coin and Currency	Money Supply[a] Checking Deposits	Velocity of Circulation[b]	Interest Rate[c] (% per annum)	Wholesale Prices[d]	Terms of Trade[e]	Exchange Rate (pesos per $)
	(millions of pesos—end of year)			(yearly avg.)		(1950=100)		(yearly avg.)
1940	1,060.4	661.2	399.2	8.0		33.0	75.3	5.40
1941	1,269.5	797.3	472.2	7.5		35.2	62.7	4.86
1942	1,749.9	1,021.1	728.8	7.4		38.8	69.1	4.85
1943	2,672.9	1,477.5	1,195.4	6.1		46.8	80.7	4.85
1944	3,309.9	1,768.1	1,541.8	5.9		57.4	91.9	4.85
1945	3,539.5	1,657.9	1,881.6	5.8		63.9	99.6	4.85
1946	3,460.8	1,728.6	1,732.2	7.5		73.5	99.9	4.85
1947	3,438.7	1,753.8	1,684.9	8.6		77.8	109.0	4.85
1948	3,916.9	2,121.0	1,795.9	8.9	9.7	83.4	112.2	5.76
1949	4,352.9	2,378.4	1,974.5	8.9	10.6	91.4	105.9	8.02
1950	5,988.5	2,914.2	3,074.3	8.5	10.7	100.0	100.0	8.65
1951	6,800.9	3,457.8	3,343.1	8.2	11.4	124.0	105.6	8.65
1952	7,078.0	3,648.6	3,429.4	8.9	11.3	128.6	108.2	8.65
1953	7,652.9	3,863.6	3,789.3	8.0	10.6	126.1	106.6	8.65
1954	8,723.5	4,637.0	4,086.5	8.5	11.5	137.9	96.3	11.34
1955	10,516.7	5,084.0	5,432.7	8.9	11.4	156.7	93.8	12.50
1956	11,692.2	5,734.2	5,958.0	8.9	12.0	164.0	91.9	12.50
1957	12,493.4	6,093.5	6,399.9	8.9	12.6	171.0	86.4	12.50
1958	13,386.8	6,615.1	6,771.7	9.2	13.0	178.6	75.3	12.50
1959	15,434.4	7,250.5	8,183.9	8.8	13.4	180.7	75.6	12.50
1960	16,909.3	7,871.7	9,037.6	8.6	14.0	189.7	76.1	12.50

SOURCE: Annual reports of Banco de México, S.A., and publications of Banco Nacional de Comercio Exterior and the Economic Commission for Latin America.

a Coin, currency, and checking-deposit liabilities of Banco de México and deposit banks.
b Computed as ratio of annual gross national product to average money supply during year.
c Estimated as the average yield on the assets of private banking institutions, excluding legally required investments.
d Index of prices of 210 articles in Mexico City.
e Computed as ratio of annual index of export prices to annual index of import prices. Data for the years 1940–1954 are taken from publications of Economic Commission for Latin America; data for the years 1955–1960 are taken from publications of Banco Nacional de Comercio Exterior.

of the money supply during the period under consideration it is necessary to examine the nature of changes which occurred in the underlying assets and nonmonetary liabilities of the monetary institutions.

In Table IV-B the behavior of these interrelated items in the combined balance sheet of Banco de México and the deposit banks is indicated. It is apparent from the data shown that the growth in the money supply which occurred was, during some years and some periods, governed by combinations of changes in assets and nonmonetary liabilities of one sort while in other years or periods different combinations of changes in these governing factors were the main determinants of the behavior of the money supply. For example, in 1950 a large increase in the foreign-exchange holdings of the monetary system was the principal change on the asset side associated with the increase in monetary liabilities of the system during that year; in 1960, on the other hand, foreign-exchange holdings were reduced and the increase in monetary system assets which occurred consisted largely of increases in system claims on government, enterprises and individuals, and nonmonetary credit institutions. As a third example, in 1954 the effect on the money supply of increases in the various types of monetary system assets was offset in substantial degree by an increase in nonmonetary but highly liquid liabilities (principally deposits denominated in foreign currencies) which are designated in Table IV-B as "quasi-money."

For present purposes it is sufficient to restrict our analysis to periods rather than to individual years. Considering first the period 1940–1950, it is apparent that during this period the factors accounting for the growth in the money supply which occurred were the almost continuous increases in claims of the monetary system against various sorts of domestic borrowers, coupled with sporadic, but occasionally very large, increases in foreign-exchange reserves (especially during 1949 and 1950 as a consequence of the devaluation of the peso and the stimulus to export demand occasioned by the Korean War). The effect of these increases in monetary system assets on the money supply was not offset to any appreciable extent by increases in the nonmonetary liabilities of the system over the period.

The same factors contributed to a further sizable increase in the money supply during the period 1951–1955. However, the influence of monetary-system credits to enterprises and individuals was, relatively speaking, somewhat greater than that of credits to other borrowers (especially to government) than was the case during the 1940–1950 period. Furthermore, not until after the 1954 devaluation was any further substantial basis for monetary expansion afforded by increases in the peso value of foreign-exchange reserves. Finally, the effect of increases in monetary system assets on the money supply was

TABLE IV-B

CHANGES IN ASSETS AND LIABILITIES OF THE MEXICAN

MONETARY SYSTEM, 1940–1960[a]

(Millions of pesos)

Year	Changes in Monetary Liabilities[b]	Changes in Assets					Changes in Non-Monetary Liabilities	
		Foreign Exchange Reserves[c]	Claims on Government	Claims on Enterprises and Individuals	Claims on Other Credit Institutions[d]	Other Assets	Quasi-Money[e]	Other Liabilities[f]
1940	178.3	94.3	95.5	8.1	-5.5	44.7	51.6	7.2
1941	209.1	3.0	128.5	156.1	-19.3	-2.8	19.1	37.3
1942	480.4	196.2	146.1	123.5	41.0	18.9	17.2	28.1
1943	923.0	681.7	41.2	245.3	-77.1	105.9	41.5	32.5
1944	637.0	241.8	109.2	309.8	10.9	113.7	98.5	49.9
1945	229.6	473.4	106.1	167.2	107.6	-448.4	78.8	97.5
1946	-78.7	-479.8	61.5	381.5	120.0	16.4	28.2	150.1
1947	-22.1	-561.1	241.2	127.6	304.0	91.6	149.0	76.4
1948	478.2	85.2	452.2	242.3	30.6	176.4	171.9	336.6
1949	436.0	599.7	381.5	-238.5	-37.4	2.3	101.6	170.0
1950	1,635.6	1,180.3	74.3	475.8	-313.7	85.2	-105.1	-28.6
1951	812.4	32.9	-311.4	618.8	615.4	167.5	96.7	214.1
1952	277.1	-12.7	103.5	274.4	280.8	63.5	204.6	227.8
1953	574.9	-238.4	290.2	564.3	-9.3	116.3	43.9	104.3
1954	1,070.6	697.0	570.1	519.0	163.5	190.0	635.4	433.6
1955	1,793.2	2,711.6	-19.6	90.4	-384.1	-232.0	46.6	326.5

Year								
1956	1,175.5	733.2	−425.1	1,124.9	18.3	74.1	84.3	265.6
1957	801.2	−286.7	518.7	−0.7	854.3	423.7	440.4	267.7
1958	893.4	−673.9	491.6	1,134.7	−93.1	220.9	423.4	−236.6
1959	2,047.6	666.9	−534.2	1,227.2	813.5	14.6	−278.9	419.3
1960	1,474.9	−495.0	480.0	849.5	601.2	206.3	−111.6	278.7

Source: Annual reports of Banco de México, S.A.

a The monetary system is composed of Banco de México and the private deposit banks; the figures shown in the table represent changes in the combined balance sheets of these two institutions.

b Coin, currency, and checking-deposit liabilities to enterprises and individuals.

c Holdings of gold, silver, and foreign currencies.

d Reflects the net change in the combined balance sheets of Banco de México and the private deposit banks of claims against other credit institutions. That is, the figures show the net result of changes in claims on and obligations to other credit institutions.

e Includes changes in all domestic- and foreign-currency obligations to enterprises and individuals except monetary liabilities and capital-account items.

f Includes changes in capital accounts.

to some extent offset by the growing practice on the part of business enterprises and individuals, especially apparent in 1952 and 1954, of holding liquid assets in the form of quasi-monetary claims against the monetary system rather than in the form of strictly monetary claims.

During the period 1956–1960 not only was the rate of monetary expansion somewhat slower than before, but also the factors underlying this expansion were quite different. Foreign-exchange reserves remained virtually unchanged over the period (although significant short-run variations occurred), and monetary system credits to government, while substantial, were relatively less significant than formerly. Over 80 per cent of the increase in assets of the monetary system was accounted for by the growth that occurred in credits to enterprises and individuals and to other, nonmonetary, credit institutions. The tendency for growth in monetary assets to be offset by growth in quasi-monetary liabilities of the system continued, but to a somewhat lesser degree than in the preceding five years.

It is clear that the most important single factor governing the behavior of the money supply during the period 1940–1955 was the growth in the peso value of foreign-exchange reserves and that this growth, in turn, was largely the result of the currency devaluations of 1948–1949 and 1954. Of course these devaluations were themselves related to preceding monetary expansions based on a growing volume of credits to government and other borrowers—and to the associated increase in the general price level. It is an open question, however, as to whether or not it would have been possible to forestall the necessity for the devaluations by prior monetary restraint. One cannot be certain that monetary restraint within tolerable limits exercised prior to the devaluations would have obviated their necessity, or even that any degree of monetary restraint beyond that actually exercised would have been desirable. It is important to note in this connection that the 1948–1949 devaluation was part of a worldwide readjustment of currencies vis-à-vis the dollar, and that (as argued below) the 1954 devaluation was more closely correlated with the behavior of Mexican export-commodity prices in world markets, and Mexican demand for foreign-produced goods, than with the behavior of the domestic price level. Furthermore, Mexico achieved an enviable increase in output over the period 1940–1955 (the average annual rate of growth in real output averaged above 6 per cent per year) and it is not possible to be sure to what extent, if any, this growth rate would have been lessened by curtailment of the flow of monetary system credit to the public and private sectors of the economy. It cannot be denied, however, that the growth achieved during this period, as well as that realized subsequently, was heavily dependent upon various infrastructure-type investments which were made and which, in lieu of a more effective revenue system or more extensive foreign credits, were necessarily financed by inflationary means.

Following the devaluation in April of 1954 and the period of rapid monetary expansion and inflation which immediately followed, the rate of increase in the money supply was somewhat reduced and the rise in prices was sharply curtailed. We have already noted the changed character of the growth in monetary system assets and liabilities during this period. It is tempting to argue that these changes reflected increased determination or increased ability, or perhaps both, on the part of those responsible for policy to resist repetition of prior inflation-devaluation episodes by means of monetary restraint—and we believe this interpretation possesses considerable validity. However, the fact that the rate of expansion in the money supply during the 1956–1960 period was somewhat greater than that which occurred during the period between the devaluations (i.e., the period 1950–1953) tends to weaken this argument. Furthermore, while it is true that the monetary system did not directly monetize government sector deficits in the 1956–1960 period to nearly the extent that this was done previously, there was substantial indirect support of these deficits by Banco de México (as explained below), and as a consequence it cannot be claimed that the contribution to monetary expansion from this source was really markedly less in the latter period than it was formerly.

We are left with the conclusion, therefore, that the basic difference between the 1956–1960 period and preceding years is to be found not so much in the behavior of the money supply and the extent to which those responsible for monetary policy permitted additions to the money supply, but rather is to be found in the fact that monetary expansion in the more recent period was not manifested in continued inflation and further devaluation of the peso. We are consequently lead to inquire why this was the case.

FACTORS AFFECTING THE PRICE LEVEL

According to the index shown in Table IV-A, wholesale prices were three times higher in 1950 than in 1940, and an additional 50-per-cent increase occurred between 1950 and 1955. Beginning with 1956, however, a sharp break with past experience occurred, and during the period 1956–1960 the rate of increase in wholesale prices was limited to an average of slightly more than 3 per cent per year. How can this behavior of the price level be reconciled with the record of behavior of the money supply just reviewed?

In order to understand the behavior of prices it is necessary to consider not only the degree of utilization of productive capacity and the level of production costs, but also to take into account prevailing expectations and prices received for exports and paid for imports (i.e., Mexico's terms of trade) in world markets. The difficulty is, of course, that very little data on these factors are available, and consequently in the analysis which follows it is necessary to reconstruct Mexican experience in this regard on a more deductive and intuitive basis than we would like.

The government sector during the period 1940–1950 incurred substantial budgetary deficits which were for the most part financed by Banco de México but also to some extent by the deposit banks, and which were thereby directly monetized. By means of this procedure a significant portion of the necessary financial resources was acquired by the government for bidding effectively in domestic markets for the factor inputs needed to carry out its ambitious investment program. This was, in effect, a forced-savings policy carried out by injecting inflationary doses of excess demand into the goods market, and naturally it worked to force prices upward. At the same time attractive investment opportunities abounded in the private sector, and this factor, along with a rising demand for consumer goods associated with rising income levels, added to the upward pressure of demand on prices.

This upward pressure on prices in domestic markets was, of course, related to the behavior of the money supply. Additional amounts of money facilitated an enlarged volume of expenditures, which was the joint product of a rising real volume of transactions and a rising price level. The interrelations between these factors cannot be definitely ascertained, but presumably they were not of a simple cause-and-effect variety. Thus, for example, while increases in the money supply were conducive to a rising price level, the rising price level was also conducive to increases in the money supply. Similarly, while increases in real output presumably would have occurred, to some extent at least, without the increase in the money supply which took place, it is an open question (as already indicated) as to whether or not the same rate of growth in output could have been realized with greater monetary restraint. Furthermore, it is entirely possible that some degree of inflation would have occurred under the circumstances even in the absence of increases in the money supply, supported instead by increased velocity of a fixed stock of money. Perhaps the most defensible summary description of the then-existing situation is that throughout the period 1940–1950 excess demand in the domestic economy which was supported, if not necessarily caused by, monetary expansion produced substantial increases in both output and prices.

Closely related to, and in large measure determining, inflationary pressures in the domestic economy were the strong demand in the world market for Mexican export products and the rapidly rising prices of imported goods. Both the volume and prices of exports and imports increased greatly during World War II and Mexico's relatively favorable wartime terms of trade were further improved during the latter half of the 1940s up until the devaluation of 1948–1949, as indicated in Table IV-A. Following the devaluation and the remobilization and renewed inflation in the United States and elsewhere occasioned by hostilities in Korea, the inflationary stimulus from external factors was resumed and quickly became acute. We have already referred to the behavior of Mexico's foreign-exchange reserves during this episode and to the effect of the large increase in these reserves on the domestic money supply. However, in addition to the strictly monetary aspects, it is necessary to take into account the important contribution to overall excess demand due to the growth in Mexico's exports, including tourist services, in order to fully appreciate the nature of the inflationary stimulus from the foreign sector.

The behavior of prices following the rapid rise during 1949, 1950, and the first half of 1951 was markedly changed. Domestic inflation during the Korean boom had erased the competitive price advantage in international markets obtained from the previous devaluation, and the Mexican price level was consequently more closely linked with that of the United States and other trading partners. Beginning in the latter part of 1951 and continuing through the first several months of 1954 relative price stability prevailed. Nevertheless, a persistent deficit in the balance of payments developed as the demand for Mexican exports declined. While overall demand for consumer and investment goods remained high in the domestic economy during 1951 and 1952, and while monetary expansion continued as monetary system credits to the government and enterprises and individuals continued to increase, excess demand was dissipated and then disappeared in 1953 in the face of continued depression in the export industries. The renewal of price inflation in 1954 and 1955 was clearly a result of the devaluation which occurred in April of 1954, the devaluation in turn being attributable to Mexico's unwillingness to adjust by monetary and other means to the radically altered world market conditions, her own deteriorating terms of trade, and her consequent inability to maintain an adequate level of foreign-exchange reserves.

Immediately following devaluation, prices began rising sharply, evidencing that Mexicans had learned well the lessons of their previous experiences following upon devaluations. Indeed, there were other manifestations of the prevailing inflationary psychology, such as an increasing propensity on the part of wealthowners to maintain deposits in foreign financial markets and in foreign currencies in Mexican banking institutions. Also, in retrospect it becomes evident that a good deal of the investment during the preceding years of excess demand and price inflation had been motivated by speculative considerations—and certainly speculative activities were encouraged by the fact that the pace of inflation was sufficient to keep real interest (i.e., nominal interest after adjustment for price level change) at minimal and, at times, even negative rates during much of the 1940—1955 period.

Beginning in 1956 prices leveled off and a relatively high degree of price stability prevailed in the domestic market during the ensuing five years. This remarkable break with the past was associated with vigorous application of the system of selective credit controls which, as explained in the previous chapter, had first been introduced following the 1948–1949 devaluation but which was not very effective in changing the pattern of financing until 1955. Beginning in that year the selective credit-control scheme permitted the diversion of a portion of the funds flowing through the financial system from the financing of deficit-spending units in the private sector to the financing of public sector deficits occasioned by continued high-level investment expenditures. At the same time the federal government and public enterprises came to rely increasingly on foreign credits. As a result, the necessary deficit financing of the public sector was arranged in a manner which was much less inflationary than that previously employed. These changes in the pattern of fund flows are examined in detail in the next section of this chapter.

Associated with the increasing tightness in the domestic money and capital market, which was brought about by a progressively more vigorous application of the selective credit-control program, was the appearance of excess capacity in certain industries which had previously expanded output rapidly under the stimulus of rising domestic demand (often bolstered by protection from foreign competition) and favorable prices in international markets. Whether this excess capacity was caused by financial tightness or whether it resulted from slackening domestic demand attributable to other causes is, of course, difficult to ascertain. But whatever the reason, expenditures which would further increase productive capacity oriented toward the domestic market clearly became progressively less justifiable in the eyes of private investors. In any case, pressures in the domestic market, which in earlier years had produced upward pressure on the price level, were manifested in rising real rates of interest during the 1956–1960 period. Furthermore, conditions in international markets, more specifically the continued decline in prices of Mexican export commodities and the continued deterioration of Mexico's terms of trade, were not such as to produce any upward pressure on the price level during this period.

FACTORS AFFECTING THE BALANCE OF PAYMENTS AND
THE EXCHANGE RATE

Throughout the foregoing discussion we have occasionally referred to the effect of the international-payments balance on the reserve base of the monetary system and to evidence contained in the balance of payments regarding the changing pressures emanating from outside the Mexican economy and from international financial considerations on the domestic price level. These matters warrant a more careful description and analysis, and it is convenient now to consider this aspect of Mexican monetary and financial experience before proceeding to examine in more detail the pattern of fund flows in the domestic economy.

In Table IV-C is reproduced in summary form the record of Mexico's balance of payments over the period 1940–1960. As shown by the table, during the war years 1940–1945 Mexico achieved a comfortable, if not spectacular, surplus on current account as both receipts and expenditures increased continuously and as foreign capital flowed

TABLE IV-C

MEXICO'S BALANCE OF PAYMENTS, 1940-1960

(Millions of dollars)

| | Current Account | | | | | | | Capital Account | | | | |
| | | Receipts | | | Expenditures | | | | | | Net Errors and Omissions | Variation in Reserves of Banco de México |
Year	Balance	Goods and Services	Tourism and Frontier Transactions	Other	Goods and Services	Debt Service[a]	Other	Balance	Long-Term	Short-Term[b]		
1940	27.1	94.4	50.3	69.3	132.4	20.9	33.6	17.5	7.0	10.5	—22.5	22.1
1941	—25.4	116.7	62.8	63.6	199.5	29.7	39.3	31.2	17.3	13.9	—7.0	—1.2
1942	22.1	144.6	59.2	68.6	172.2	31.6	46.7	24.8	26.8	—2.0	—3.0	43.9
1943	102.6	229.7	73.0	107.4	212.2	43.0	52.3	—8.6	2.4	—11.0	40.2	134.2
1944	25.6	232.3	86.0	114.1	311.0	35.9	59.9	12.0	35.6	—23.6	—0.5	37.1
1945	1.4	271.6	110.7	118.5	372.5	50.7	76.2	11.5	48.8	—37.3	72.6	85.5
1946	—174.1	318.5	151.6	100.1	600.6	60.0	83.7	—7.6	22.2	—29.8	75.2	—106.5
1947	—167.1	423.9	147.3	142.7	720.3	78.1	82.6	61.5	65.0	—3.5	—20.0	—125.6
1948	—59.9	418.8	194.6	102.1	591.4	72.9	111.1	44.3	31.8	12.5	—39.0	—54.6
1949	49.3	406.5	186.4	108.2	514.4	63.8	73.6	10.8	30.4	—19.6	—20.5	39.6
1950	52.6	493.4	238.9	100.4	596.7	77.2	106.2	109.7	66.0	43.7	—30.6	131.5
1951	—199.1	591.6	271.6	63.6	888.8	111.2	125.9	105.8	75.5	30.3	81.6	—11.7
1952	—103.2	625.3	275.1	77.9	828.8	117.4	135.3	73.0	82.1	—9.1	11.3	—18.9
1953	—91.3	559.1	313.4	107.1	807.5	93.8	169.6	96.0	94.8	1.2	—30.7	—26.0
1954	—24.3	615.9	344.9	96.9	788.7	85.7	207.6	81.1	126.5	—45.4	—91.8	—35.1
1955	89.7	738.5	445.3	96.1	883.6	93.1	213.4	215.6	129.2	86.3	—105.2	200.1
1956	—35.6	807.1	508.2	105.1	1,071.6	135.5	248.7	206.8	149.7	57.0	—110.7	60.5
1957	—154.0	706.1	591.4	108.7	1,155.1	134.4	270.8	192.3	191.7	0.5	—66.0	—27.8
1958	—181.6	709.1	541.6	110.2	1,128.6	144.2	269.6	90.3	181.6	—91.2	4.1	—87.0
1959	—31.7	723.0	636.7	97.1	1,006.6	153.1	328.7	150.0	140.7	9.2	—66.4	51.8
1960	—174.0	738.7	669.8	111.7	1,186.4	171.2	336.5	191.4	122.0	69.3	—25.8	—8.6

Source: Annual reports of Banco de México, S.A.

[a] Includes interest on public sector indebtedness and profits on direct private foreign investments.
[b] Exclusive of variation in reserves of Banco de México.

into the country. Following World War II imports increased rapidly and, even though the inflow of capital accelerated, the deficit on current account was such that substantial losses in the foreign-exchange reserves of Banco de México were realized in 1946, 1947, and 1948. It was in this environment that a 45 per cent devaluation of the peso occurred during 1948 and 1949. Actually, of course, this devaluation was a part of the worldwide readjustment of other currencies vis-à-vis the dollar, and the extent to which the peso was devalued was in the middle range of the devaluations that occurred during this period. In consequence, therefore, while the devaluation served to realign the parity between the Mexican and United States price levels, there was relatively little change in this respect in Mexico's position with respect to most European and other Latin American countries.

As a direct result of the devaluation and also of the Korean export boom a current-account surplus was again achieved in 1949 and 1950. This, coupled with a further inflow of foreign capital served to replenish the country's holdings of foreign exchange—and, partly because of the newly established exchange rate, to add very substantially to the peso value of the reserve base of the country's monetary system. Relief from balance-of-payments pressures was only temporary, however, and beginning in 1951 a sizable deficit on current account reappeared and foreign-exchange losses resumed and continued in spite of continued inflowing foreign capital throughout the period prior to the next devaluation in 1954.

The devaluation of the peso from 8.65 to 12.50 to the dollar in April of 1954 marks a significant turning point in Mexican policy and experience and therefore it is appropriate that we examine in some detail the circumstances both before and after the event. This action was apparently instigated by concern on the part of officials over the adverse trend in the country's payments balance, a difficulty which was compounded in the immediately preceding months by unusually large losses in reserves resulting from declines in the volume and prices of exports and an outflow of short-term capital. A principal underlying factor in this situation was, of course, the recession underway in the United States. Rather than responding with policies which would have induced stabilizing adjustments in domestic markets, the authorities decided upon devaluation in an effort to reserve as free a hand as possible to pursue the objectives of the country's program of economic development.

Actually, Mexico's financial difficulties seemed not to be of crisis proportions at the time, and many Mexican and foreign observers alike were quite surprised by and critical of the announcement of devaluation. The action was criticized not only because it appeared to some to have been unnecessary, but also because in the period following the devaluation, i.e., in the ensuing eight to ten months, it failed to produce the improvement in Mexico's foreign-exchange position which had followed previous devaluations. Indeed, reserves declined by almost 50 per cent during the two and a half months immediately following the devaluation as capital outflow accelerated and the dollar value of exports continued to decline while that of imports remained more or less unchanged. Furthermore, the domestic price level increased rapidly under the impetus of widespread expectation of cumulative monetary instability. In short, following the 1954 devaluation it seemed apparent that this action not only had failed to correct Mexico's balance-of-payments weakness, but that it also had served to undermine confidence in the future stability of the peso.

There are various reasons why the 1954 devaluation had consequences different from those associated with the earlier postwar devaluations. We have already referred to the fact that these previous devaluations were a part of a worldwide realignment of currency values vis-à-vis the dollar and, as such, manifested distortions in international financial relationships not mainly attributable to domestic policies which were inconsistent with maintenance of external equilibrium. Another factor explaining the response to the 1954 devaluation is found in the nature of Mexican exports—most of which consisted of commodities whose prices were determined in world markets in competition with more or less identical exports of other countries—so that devaluation of the peso had little or no immediate effect on the ability of export industries to command additional dollars and other hard currencies. Furthermore, by 1954, as a result of past actions designed to substitute domestic production for imports, Mexican imports consisted largely of capital equipment and raw and semifinished materials necessary for continuation of the country's program of industrial development, and therefore the devaluation merely served to increase the peso cost of a more or less unchanged volume of imported goods.

While the 1954 devaluation generated much suspicion and ill will, the situation was temporarily alleviated during the latter half of 1954 and the first part of 1955 by the favorable crop season, quick recovery of the United States from the 1954 recession, and sizable increases in receipts from tourism. These developments, in combination with restrictive monetary policies, produced a small surplus on current account in 1955. Likewise in 1955 a substantial inflow of foreign capital (both long- and short-term) was recorded, which, together with the current account surplus, was sufficient to re-establish a workable level of foreign-exchange reserves.

The pattern of current-account deficits was again re-established in 1956, and in each of the five years 1956–1960 the value of imports exceeded that of exports by sizable amounts. Furthermore, an outflow of short-term capital occurred from time to time (a part of which presumably was reflected in the "errors and omissions" account of the balance of payments), motivated, we must suppose, by uncertainty regarding prospects for the peso. Losses of foreign exchange from this source were especially severe in 1958. While the country's foreign-exchange reserves tended to be bolstered by continued inflow of long-term capital during these years, this factor was offset by mounting debt-service obligations. Indeed, in both 1959 and 1960 the amounts required for foreign-debt service exceeded inflows of long-term capital from abroad. Under these circumstances stand-by credits from the Export-Import Bank and the International Monetary Fund were arranged in an effort to assure maintenance of the established exchange-rate parity.

Thus, even though the Mexican price level remained relatively stable, balance-of-payments pressures during the years 1956–1960 continued to be very serious indeed. Not only was Mexico forced to ration foreign exchange as best she could within the freely convertible framework, but also the country was under constant threat that something would trigger large-scale flight of capital which would drain away the relatively meager official holdings of foreign-exchange reserves.

Balance-of-payments considerations clearly became a more important determinant of monetary and financial policies as there developed in government circles a strong determination to avoid further devaluation. The task was made difficult by adverse developments in international markets, and especially by a heightened sensitivity of wealth holders to any and all developments which could be interpreted as reflecting adversely on prospects for the peso. Much of Mexico's monetary and financial experience during the period since 1954 evidences a concerted effort on the part of the government and the cen-

tral bank to assure exchange-rate stability without unduly throttling
the growth of the economy.

Public and Private Finance

In this section we consider the manner in which the
deficits of the government sector, of public enterprises, and of private
enterprises and individuals were financed during the period under
consideration, emphasizing changes which occurred in the pattern
of this financing which have relevance to the record of domestic monetary stability and external financial equilibrium just reviewed.

At the outset it is necessary to state more precisely than heretofore
the distinction between the public and private sectors of the Mexican
economy, and between the government sector proper and the numerous so-called decentralized and autonomous agencies and enterprises
with state participation—which we shall designate simply as "public
enterprises." The distinction between the public and private sectors
is not easy to establish. The federal government is directly involved
in the management of numerous industrial and commercial enterprises (e.g., those engaged in the production and distribution of
petroleum products and electric power). In addition, price controls,
subsidies, and tax exemptions administered by agencies of the federal government significantly influence the production and consumption of many goods and services (e.g., foodstuffs and transportation).
Also, the central bank, whose legal position is such as to bind it very
closely to the federal government, exercises general credit controls,
and, in conjunction with various other official financial institutions,
facilitates the flow of credits to selected sectors of the economy (e.g.,
agriculture and foreign trade). Furthermore, tariffs and import li-
censing are employed to stimulate and control investment in a wide
range of industries as well as to exercise control over the country's
balance of international payments. In short, the influence of the federal government and of governmental policies pervades the entire
economy, and consequently the distinction between what constitutes
public finance and what constitutes private finance is blurred, to say
the least.

The matter is made more difficult by numerous instances of mixed
public and private financing. Certain of the so-called autonomous
agencies and official enterprises of the federal government are partially capitalized with private funds, as, indeed, are certain official
financial institutions. A similar situation is encountered in the case

of certain privately controlled enterprises which are partially capitalized with public funds. Thus, it is not possible to employ source of capital as the basis for distinguishing between public and private enterprises, since the task of unraveling the numerous instances of joint public and private financial participation would be extremely tedious, if indeed it would be possible at all.

The only feasible procedure is to adopt the same distinction between the public and private sectors of the economy employed in the compilation of official statistics. According to official usage in this connection the public sector of the economy is generally considered to consist of the following: 1) the federal government, including the numerous administrative agencies directly responsible to it (e.g., the Ministry of Communications and Public Works); 2) the federal district and state, territorial, and municipal governments; 3) the various autonomous agencies of the federal government (e.g., Mexican Railways); and 4) the various official business enterprises managed by the federal government (e.g., Altos Hornos, S.A.). In the analysis which follows, the first two of the above are considered to constitute the government sector and are examined separately from the latter two, which are considered to comprise the public-enterprise sector. Accordingly, the private sector of the economy is deemed to incorporate all economic units not included in either of the two major component parts of the public sector so defined, and consequently included in financial data for the private sector are a variety of business and individual activities subject to governmental control and influence in widely varying degree. As will become evident, the data pertaining to the private sector are quite limited, and insufficient to permit a breakdown between business enterprises and individuals.

The reader will notice that so far in these classifications no reference has been made to financial institutions, whether publicly or privately controlled. Banco de México, Nacional Financiera, and the various other national credit institutions are, of course, a part of the public sector, and likewise deposit and savings banks, financieras, and other such financial organizations are a part of the private sector. However, for purposes of the present analysis it is convenient to consider financial institutions, both public and private, as a separate sector of the economy—the financial sector. The role of financial institutions in financing government, public enterprises, and the nonfinancial private sector is necessarily referred to at various points in the sections which immediately follow. However, a systematic

mination of the sources and uses of funds moving through the
ancial sector is deferred until later in the chapter.

GOVERNMENT FINANCE

The manner in which government sector financial data are presented
in official budget reports makes identification of the actual cash deficit or surplus during any given year or over a period of years extremely difficult. In addition to the problem presented by the existence in
the various budgets of accrual items and expenditure authorizations
which are not closely related to actual receipts and disbursements,
there is the more serious problem arising from the fact that a substantial part of the federal government fiscal operations is conducted
outside the official budget. Furthermore, there exists a complicated
system of transfers and subsidies within the government sector as
well as between the federal government, public enterprises, and the
private sector whose character and financial significance is not
readily determinable from official budget documents. Therefore, for
present purposes it is more convenient, and perhaps more accurate
as well, to attempt to gauge the nature and extent of government
sector financing from data showing net changes in government indebtedness during the period under consideration.

More specifically, our analysis of government finance is based on
data showing government sector indebtedness to banking institutions.
While virtually all of the increase in government indebtedness over
the period was reflected in increased banking system claims, this
index of government borrowing may not be precise for any given year
because of variations in indebtedness to other domestic lenders and
foreigners or because of changes in the aggregate cash balance of the
government sector. But over a period of years the cumulative deficit
of the government sector corresponds closely to the growth of banking system claims. Another drawback with this procedure, however,
is that it does not relate deficits and surpluses in the government
sector to the behavior of governmental receipts and expenditures, and
consequently it will be necessary to introduce a few comments concerning these relationships in the discussion of government sector
deficit financing which follows.

In Table IV-D are shown the aggregate amounts of government
sector indebtedness to banking system institutions, along with the
distribution of claims as between the various groups of institutions,
over the period 1940–1960. As shown, the major share of government

TABLE IV-D

BANKING SYSTEM FINANCING OF GOVERNMENT SECTOR, 1940-1960
(Millions of pesos)

| Year | Government Sector Indebtedness[a] | | | Distribution of Claims | | | | |
| | | | | Monetary System | | Other Credit Institutions | | |
	Total	Securities	Credits	Banco de México	Deposit Banks	National Banks	Financieras	Other
1940	340.0	327.6	12.4	308.4	19.3	8.1	0.1	4.1
1941	480.3	467.9	12.4	454.0	2.2	19.6	0.2	4.3
1942	779.0	766.6	12.4	593.2	9.1	164.8	7.4	4.5
1943	851.8	839.4	12.4	534.5	26.6	282.0	4.7	4.0
1944	1,009.0	1,009.0	-----	617.8	52.5	317.8	4.1	16.8
1945	1,246.7	1,227.8	18.9	692.8	83.6	401.4	8.7	60.2
1946	1,290.9	1,201.1	89.8	751.2	86.7	402.2	2.8	48.0
1947	1,488.2	1,405.2	83.0	964.7	114.4	359.5	1.9	47.7
1948	1,898.9	1,816.7	82.2	1,424.1	107.2	320.2	0.9	46.5
1949	2,150.9	2,146.4	4.5	1,780.7	132.1	193.4	0.3	44.4
1950	2,351.6	2,339.6	12.0	1,725.8	261.3	308.5	1.0	55.0
1951	1,968.1	1,966.7	1.4	1,475.4	200.3	228.0	2.0	62.4
1952	2,242.6	2,240.2	2.4	1,627.6	151.6	403.2	0.2	60.0
1953	2,494.5	2,424.0	70.5	1,794.5	274.9	381.6	0.6	42.9
1954	3,017.3	2,920.7	96.6	2,378.1	261.4	326.8	0.6	50.4
1955	2,991.3	2,917.3	74.0	2,058.7	561.2	256.4	1.8	113.2
1956	3,021.4	2,916.3	104.7	1,535.7	659.1	605.4	5.7	215.5
1957	3,741.7	3,568.0	173.7	1,925.4	788.1	702.8	0.7	324.7
1958	4,412.8	4,345.0	67.8	2,436.9	768.2	590.3	41.5	575.9
1959	4,219.8	4,152.6	67.2	1,601.1	1,069.8	350.8	668.0	530.1
1960	5,509.4	4,992.1	517.3	1,900.5	1,250.4	907.0	802.4	649.1

SOURCE: Annual Reports of Banco de México, S.A.

[a] Includes indebtedness of federal government, state and local governments, and the Federal District.

sector indebtedness was represented by outstanding fixed-interest securities, although short-term credits, principally from Banco de México, were important in some years. Over the period, however, there was relatively little increase in the total amount of banking system credits, nor was there any significant continuing contribution forthcoming from domestic non-bank lenders or from foreign borrowing. In fact, throughout most of the period the foreign indebtedness of the government sector declined as obligations acquired in connection with the nationalization of foreign-owned petroleum properties in the late 1930s, as well as other foreign debts incurred in the early 1940s, were gradually amortized.

In our analysis of government sector deficit financing we may, therefore, focus our attention on the domestic indebtedness of the government sector and in particular on that represented by claims distributed among the various banking system institutions. As shown in Table IV-D, the distribution of these claims changed significantly over the period in response to changes in the overall monetary and financial policy of the government and Banco de México. During the period 1940–1950 Banco de México provided credits equal to about 70 per cent of the total increase in government-sector domestic indebtedness and thereby permitted the straightforward monetization of deficits previously referred to. Since there existed no voluntary market for government securities and no means for forcing the absorption of government securities by private financial institutions or other potential creditors, it appears that Banco de México had little choice but to pursue the course it did during this period—particularly in view of the high priority which was placed on continuation of a relatively high level of public expenditures.

The reader will recall from Chapter III that in 1948 and 1949 banking system reserve requirements were revised in an effort to contain inflationary pressures emanating from excess domestic demand for consumer and investment goods coupled with booming export markets, as well as to influence the allocation of loanable funds as between the various competing uses. Banco de México established high marginal reserve requirements which, as previously explained, were waived provided the deposit banks invested newly acquired funds in accordance with prescribed schedules. This program of selective credit control was to provide the means for significantly altering the pattern of government sector deficit financing in the years to follow, but only after an initial period of experimentation during which the scope and severity of the original scheme was substantially increased.

Beginning in 1950 Banco de México reduced its credits to the government sector while inducing privately owned deposit banks to increase their holdings of government securities. The central bank's claims on government were further reduced in 1951 in association with an overall fiscal surplus and reduction in government sector indebtedness. However, during the three years 1952–1954, when large government sector deficits were again incurred, Banco de México found it necessary to revert to its earlier practice—directly financing upwards of 80 per cent of government sector deficit spending.

In 1955, as previously explained, the reserve scheme was revised so that Banco de México, armed with new powers and also with renewed determination to avoid repetition of the circumstances which led to the previous two devaluations, was able to begin in earnest to shift the pattern of government sector financing. In every year during the six-year period 1955–1960 the government sector required substantial amounts of deficit financing (a total net amount of 2,492.1 million pesos), but during this period Banco de México not only withheld its direct support but actually reduced its claims on the government sector (by 477.6 million pesos).

During this period the private deposit banks and the various nonmonetary financial institutions (especially the private financieras after they became subject to the reserve scheme in 1958) were obliged not only to supply the new deficit financing required by the government sector but also to absorb the securities sloughed off by Banco de México. As we shall see later in the chapter when we take a closer look at the sources and uses of funds moving through the financial sector, to some extent Banco de México provided indirect support to the financing of government sector deficits by expanding its credits to financial institutions and others acquiring government securities. However, it is clear that beginning in 1955 and continuing through 1960 the pattern of government sector deficit financing differed sharply from that which prevailed earlier, with significant consequences for the operation of the money and capital market and the allocation of investable resources.

What in effect occurred was that the burden of financing government sector deficits was shifted from the central bank to other lenders, principally private financial institutions, with the result that these deficits were no longer directly monetized to the degree which formerly had been the practice. Private financial institutions were forced, under threat of penalty, to provide a large volume of relatively low-cost credit to the government sector, and as a consequence a substantial portion of the resources of these institutions which presumably otherwise would have been made available to other borrowers was diverted to the financing of government expenditures. While the government sector was thereby assured of a continuing source of deficit financing with a relatively low inflationary potential, loanable funds became steadily more scarce and costly in the private sector of the economy.

FINANCING OF ENTERPRISES AND INDIVIDUALS

While we would now like to be able to proceed to analyses of the financing of public enterprises and of deficit spending units in the private sector paralleling the above analysis of government sector finance, this unfortunately is not possible because of limitations imposed by the available statistical data. In the official financial statistics, obligations of public enterprises are not usually distinguished from those of private enterprises and individuals. The reason for this deficiency in the statistical record is not entirely clear. To some extent, of course, public and private enterprises are similar, both producing goods and services for sale to the general public and both presumably being subjected to similar standards of financial accountability. Furthermore, as mentioned earlier, the distinction between nominally public and nominally private enterprises in some instances is not clear-cut because of joint financial participation of government and private interests. Likewise, while certain public enterprises are regularly accorded the financial support of the treasury, so also are private expenditures occasionally favored with subsidies and other direct and indirect forms of governmental financial assistance. Yet, in spite of these similarities between the operation of public enterprises and the more strictly commercial activities which characterize private enterprises, it seems reasonable to expect that the financial condition and activities of public enterprises (if not individually, at least as a group) would be regularly disclosed and readily discernible from official statistics. However, as already indicated, this is not the case.

The analysis which follows, therefore, is based on aggregate data showing the amounts and sources of deficit financing by both public and private enterprises as well as by private individuals. Later we shall attempt to build upon this base with such fragmentary (and sometimes not strictly comparable) data as are available in an effort to differentiate between the pattern of financing which has characterized public enterprises and that which appears to have prevailed in the private sector proper.

In Table IV-E is shown the domestic indebtedness of enterprises and individuals during the period 1940–1960 as represented by outstanding securities and other claims held by banking system institutions. In addition to the amounts shown in the table there presumably existed a large and growing volume of indebtedness taking the form of trade credits, consumption loans, and informal agreements whose size and character cannot be ascertained from available statistical data. Also not shown in the table is the amount of financing done by means of issues of fixed- and variable-yield securities to non-bank financial institutions. But even though these items are not included, the data shown in Table IV-E (when compared to those in Table IV-D) reveal that between 1940 and 1960 the recorded domestic indebtedness of enterprises and individuals increased far more rapidly than did that of the government sector.

Also revealed in Table IV-E are the significant changes which occurred in the distribution of claims on enterprises and individuals as between the various financial institutions comprising the banking system. During the period 1940–1950 practically all domestic credits were extended by institutions other than Banco de México. Thus, during the period in which Banco de México underwrote government sector deficits almost singlehandedly, the responsibility for financing deficits elsewhere in the economy was largely assumed by private financial institutions and the various specialized national credit institutions. Much the same pattern is found during the years 1951–1955.

During the period 1956–1960 the pattern shifted somewhat, reflecting the changes which occurred in the pattern of government sector financing previously discussed. Banco de México continued to make only a marginal direct contribution to the financing of deficits of enterprises and individuals in most years. Private deposit banks contributed a much smaller proportion than formerly to the financing of enterprises and individuals while at the same time, it will be recalled, the credits of these institutions to the government sector were being increased under the pressure of the selective credit-control program. The burden of financing the private sector was consequently shifted to other private credit institutions (especially to the financieras) which were less inhibited in the allocation of their funds by the selective credit control program. And, finally, a further large increase in credits to selected enterprises in both the public and private

TABLE IV-E

BANKING SYSTEM FINANCING OF ENTERPRISES AND INDIVIDUALS, 1940–1960

(Millions of pesos)

Year	Indebtedness of Enterprises and Individuals[a]				Distribution of Claims				
		Securities			Monetary System		Other Credit Institutions		
	Total	Debt	Equity	Credit	Banco de México	Deposit Banks	National Banks	Private Institutions	
								Financieras	Other
1940	801.3	22.9	20.9	757.5	83.1	319.7	272.2	4.7	121.6
1941	1,116.9	50.3	23.9	1,042.7	88.1	470.8	359.2	6.9	191.9
1942	1,326.7	39.4	45.8	1,241.5	133.7	548.7	307.8	107.8	228.7
1943	1,809.7	104.5	109.3	1,595.9	200.6	727.1	422.1	184.4	275.5
1944	2,323.0	123.3	157.5	2,042.2	431.5	806.0	426.6	282.7	376.2
1945	2,996.4	189.9	223.7	2,582.8	470.3	934.4	672.9	391.1	527.7
1946	3,830.2	442.2	331.4	3,056.6	824.6	961.6	882.2	542.2	619.6
1947	4,445.1	377.4	373.4	3,694.3	799.5	1,114.3	1,124.8	687.2	719.3
1948	5,312.9	294.2	470.8	4,547.9	794.2	1,361.9	1,616.3	732.5	808.0
1949	6,132.4	596.5	516.0	5,019.9	432.5	1,495.1	2,569.2	746.8	888.8
1950	7,115.7	533.0	570.1	6,012.6	423.7	1,979.7	2,947.9	816.1	948.3
1951	9,035.9	554.6	555.1	7,926.2	650.5	2,371.7	3,727.8	1,111.4	1,174.5
1952	9,960.1	669.8	574.5	8,715.8	769.5	2,527.1	3,936.4	1,348.4	1,378.7
1953	11,551.1	630.5	684.8	10,235.8	1,014.1	2,846.8	4,979.6	1,047.3	1,663.3
1954	14,240.3	811.0	846.6	12,582.7	966.9	3,413.0	6,595.0	1,425.1	1,840.3
1955	15,519.6	843.4	840.7	13,835.5	422.7	4,047.6	7,109.4	1,751.0	2,188.9
1956	17,911.4	730.8	1,124.9	16,055.7	1,043.7	4,551.5	7,252.0	2,453.7	2,610.5
1957	20,261.5	867.7	1,298.1	18,095.7	1,017.0	4,577.5	8,230.0	3,321.9	3,115.1
1958	23,544.1	1,511.8	1,571.9	20,460.4	1,932.4	4,796.8	9,812.5	3,921.1	3,081.3
1959	28,480.3	1,077.4	2,017.2	25,385.7	2,830.0	5,126.4	11,758.4	5,349.2	3,416.3
1960	35,347.0	927.4	2,419.9	31,999.7	3,221.0	5,584.9	15,937.8	7,135.4	3,467.9

SOURCE: Annual reports of Banco de México, S.A.
[a] Includes both public and private enterprises.

sectors was extended by the various specialized national credit institutions which, as we shall later explain, in turn were supported in this activity by Banco de México and foreign loans.

How were these shifts in the sources of credits to enterprises and individuals reflected in the allocation of loanable funds as between public enterprises and the private sector proper? In attempting to answer this question we encounter the statistical problems referred to earlier, but nevertheless it appears that some reliable information concerning this matter can be pieced together.

Public enterprises.—Let us first try to establish the manner in which public enterprises financed their deficits. Estimates of public sector investment and investment financing which are shown in Table IV-F indicate that during the period 1940–1960 public enterprises were able to finance roughly half of their total gross fixed-investment expenditures from internal funds (i.e., from their own gross savings in the form of depreciation allowances and retained earnings). The balance of these expenditures was therefore dependent upon deficit financing. It is worth noting that the deficits were larger relative to the volume of investment expenditures (averaging around 55 per cent) during the decade 1951–1960 than during the 1940s (when they averaged around 40 per cent of the total).

There were three principal sources from which the necessary financing could possibly have been mobilized: the government sector, other domestic sources (i.e., the private sector proper and the financial sector), and the foreign sector. By deducting from the total financing requirements of public enterprises the amounts received in the form of transfers from the government and as foreign loans it is therefore possible to estimate the amount of nongovernmental domestic credits granted to public enterprises. Estimates of the domestic financing of public enterprise investment expenditures based on the procedure just described are shown in Table IV-F. These estimates suggest that an average of roughly 20 per cent of total public enterprise investment expenditures was financed in the domestic money and capital market over the whole period, although the proportion thus financed appears to have varied widely from year to year.

Several additional observations relating to the data shown in Table IV-F seem warranted. First, it is evident that public enterprises relied increasingly upon foreign credits throughout the 1950s. Particularly during the period 1957–1960 foreign credits became an important source of financing, substantially exceeding domestic credits during

TABLE IV-F

FINANCING OF PUBLIC ENTERPRISE INVESTMENT EXPENDITURES, 1940–1960

(Millions of pesos)

Year	Total Investment Expenditures	Sources of Financing			
		Internal Funds[a]	Government Transfers[b]	Foreign Credits[c]	Domestic Credits[d]
1940	147.5	141.5	......	......	6.0
1941	121.4	118.5	......	......	2.9
1942	217.4	130.3	......	45.1	42.0
1943	200.1	163.7	......	—5.3	41.7
1944	236.2	203.4	......	—5.8	38.6
1945	388.3	263.1	......	34.4	90.8
1946	560.6	233.5	......	159.6	167.5
1947	608.5	291.9	......	111.1	205.5
1948	591.3	365.9	......	38.6	186.8
1949	823.0	527.3	34.8	138.7	122.2
1950	1,332.0	724.0	35.9	95.2	476.9
1951	1,466.2	485.9	55.3	117.6	807.4
1952	1,630.2	559.7	64.6	367.6	638.3
1953	1,626.5	877.7	62.5	283.7	402.6
1954	2,232.0	1,051.3	72.6	500.1	608.0
1955	2,487.8	1,259.3	401.9	680.4	146.2
1956	2,566.6	1,378.3	508.3	665.8	14.2
1957	3,043.4	1,437.0	316.7	1,000.3	289.4
1958	3,594.4	881.7	325.5	1,262.7	1,124.5
1959	3,673.1	1,826.9	206.9	713.2	926.1
1960	5,603.9	2,611.1	322.8	2,630.0	40.0

Source: Roberto Santillán López and Aniceto Rosas Figueroa, *Teoría General de las Finanzas Públicas y el Caso de México*, 1962; Carlos Rivera Borbon, *Los Gastos de Transferencia del Gobierno Federal Mexicano*, (México: Universidad Nacional Autónoma de México, 1962) ; Nacional Financiera, S.A.

[a] Santillán López and Rosas Fígueroa, *Teoría General*, p. 218.
[b] Rivera Borbon, *Los Gastos de Transferencia*, p. 84.
[c] Nacional Financiera, S.A., based on data supplied by the Comisión Especial de Financiamientos Exteriores. Figures include credits obtained from the Export-Import Bank, the International Bank for Reconstruction and Development, and from foreign private banks and suppliers.
[d] Computed as a residual.

these years. This development reflects the fact that a growing volume of relatively low-cost foreign loans became available as international lending agencies expanded the scope of their operations and as foreign creditors—including especially foreign private banks and suppliers—became increasingly optimistic about Mexico's debt-servicing ability. Clearly, this growing volume of foreign financing permitted larger public enterprise investment expenditures than otherwise would have been possible, while at the same time reducing the extent to which public enterprises were required to rely on transfers from the federal government and deficit financing in the domestic money and capital market.

A second point illustrated by the data contained in Table IV-F is that transfers from the federal government were lower beginning in 1957 than during the immediately preceding years. This decline in direct government subsidization of public enterprise investment expenditures was, of course, related to increased reliance of public enterprises upon foreign credits. In addition, however, improvement in the ability of public enterprises to finance their investment expenditures from internal funds occurred in 1959 and 1960 as a result of upward adjustments made in prices of certain publicly produced goods and services (e.g., petroleum products and transportation)— which in turn permitted a lower rate of direct governmental subsidization.

Each of these changes in the pattern of public enterprise financing was consistent with the renewed emphasis which, as we have seen, came to be placed on monetary stability during the period following the 1954 devaluation. Thus, both government sector finance and the financing of public enterprises were modified in ways which were intended to permit continued high-level public investment expenditures without giving rise to the monetary instability which had characterized earlier periods. It remains to be seen what were the counterparts of the financial policies employed to these ends in the private sector, and it is to the difficult task of attempting to discern changes in the pattern of private sector finance that we now turn.

Private sector.—The character of private sector financing differs from that of the public sector because fund flows are principally intrasectoral rather than intersectoral. That is, deficit spending units in the private sector are ultimately financed largely by surplus spending units in the same sector. Of course much of this financing is carried out through the intermediation of various financial institutions, and where this occurs the processes involved are reflected in the statistical record—although only dimly, as we shall see. In the case of foreign financing of deficit spending units in the private sector, practically all of which takes the form of direct private investment and is transacted by means of transfers between parent companies based abroad and subsidiaries operating in Mexico, there also is a statistical record which appears in the balance of payments accounts. A problem in this connection, however, is that funds coming into the country in the form of private foreign investment move through domestic financial intermediaries in varying degree and there is no way to distinguish fund flows originating from this source from those transmitting domestic savings from surplus to deficit spending units. Finally, there doubtless is a sizable volume of financing in the private sector for which no record at all is to be found in available financial statistics because the obligations incurred and the claims acquired do not involve financial intermediation or securities issues which are registered with any agency from which the statistical record can be obtained.

Another way in which private sector finance differs from public sector finance is that deficits of individual spending units in the private sector often cannot be related to investment expenditures. We have previously mentioned that in the case of both the government sector and public enterprises as a group, current revenues have regularly been sufficient to cover all current operating expenditures as well as a portion of investment expenditures, so that deficit financing can legitimately be presumed to be attributable to investment expenditures. This presumption is also generally valid for the various component parts of the government sector and for the various public enterprises considered separately. However, in the case of the private sector no such presumption can be defended since, clearly, in addition to instances in which deficit spending is related to investment expenditures, there are numerous other cases in which no such relation exists. For example, a substantial portion of the deficit financing by individual spending units was in support of consumer expenditures and real estate and financial speculation.

Thus, in addition to the fact that the statistical record of financial transactions in the private sector is less complete and less readily decipherable, we see that financial processes in the private sector differ from those found in the public sector. For these reasons analysis of financing in the private sector paralleling that of the public sector is not possible, and our discussion of private sector financing is therefore necessarily limited to a few observations.

It is generally believed by those familiar with the operation of the Mexican financial system that the major share of private investment expenditures is financed directly from gross retained earnings of business enterprises and from the personal savings of individual investors. This appears to be the case both in manufacturing industry and construction and also for agriculture and owner-operated commercial and service industries. It is probably safe to estimate that during the period under consideration between 70 per cent and 90 per cent of investment expenditures in the private sector was financed directly from the savings of investing units.

There are several reasons for expecting internal financing to be relied upon quite heavily. First, most Mexican-owned business enterprises are closely held family or group concerns which are reluctant to turn to outside financing because of the loss of secrecy, diminution of control, and the sharing of profits that would be involved. This also seems to be true of foreign-owned enterprises, although recent "Mexicanization" legislation has been intended to induce greater willingness to admit outside participation and it seems likely that the effect of this legislation will be to induce these enterprises to rely more on the issuance of securities in the domestic market or otherwise to share ownership with Mexican investors. A second reason for believing that private investment expenditures are financed primarily with internal funds is that agriculture, residential construction, and small businesses generally have only limited direct access to the money and capital market—although the availability of credits to finance investment in these areas has presumably been augmented by certain of the specialized national credit institutions as well as by the impact of the selective controls on the allocation of credits extended by private financial institutions. Finally, the cost of credit in the money and capital market is quite high (especially was this the case during the latter part of the 1950s as nominal rates rose and the slowing of inflation narrowed the difference between nominal and real rates of interest), and for this reason also it seems reasonable to believe that private investment expenditures are characteristically financed with internal funds.

If we assume that all external financing of gross private domestic investment expenditures is done by means of issues of fixed-interest securities or with foreign funds, then the foregoing estimate regarding the preponderance of internal funds as the source of financing for private investment expenditures appears to be justified. Thus, from the data in Table IV-G we see that new issues of these sorts of securities by private sector investors amounted to around 5 per cent, and that direct private foreign investment amounted to approximately

TABLE IV-G

FINANCING OF PRIVATE SECTOR INVESTMENT EXPENDITURES, 1940–1960

(Millions of pesos)

Year	Total Private Investment Expenditures	Issues of Fixed-Interest Securities[a]	Direct Foreign Investment Net New Investment	Direct Foreign Investment Reinvested Earnings[b]	Internal Funds[c]
1940	457.0	—	51.3	11.9	—
1941	608.0	56.4	65.6	43.7	442.3
1942	524.0	41.4	77.6	94.6	310.4
1943	659.0	35.5	37.8	41.7	544.0
1944	1,016.0	70.9	102.3	139.2	703.6
1945	1,348.0	125.9	108.6	107.2	1,006.3
1946	2,156.0	170.4	40.7	10.7	1,934.2
1947	2,726.0	68.8	79.1	192.1	2,386.0
1948	2,917.0	44.1	228.7	8.1	2,636.1
1949	3,087.0	186.3	121.9	66.6	2,712.2
1950	3,294.0	202.7	328.7	264.7	2,497.9
1951	3,900.0	92.8	429.0	414.3	2,963.9
1952	4,732.0	201.0	315.7	~ 256.0	3,959.3
1953	4,600.0	302.3	321.8	324.0	3,651.0
1954	5,400.0	274.2	882.3	304.3	3,939.2
1955	7,600.0	247.8	1,061.3	256.2	6,034.7
1956	9,060.0	376.6	1,001.3	537.5	7,144.6
1957	10,124.0	340.4	1,262.5	381.3	8,139.8
1958	10,770.0	1,059.1	785.0	467.5	8,458.4
1959	10,944.0	650.9	820.0	195.0	9,278.1
1960	12,000.0	434.4	−675.0[d]	200.0	10,584.4

Source: Annual reports of Banco de México, S.A., and the Comisión Nacional de Valores.

[a] Annual changes in outstanding private fixed-interest securities as estimated by Comisión Nacional de Valores.
[b] Includes intercompany transfers.
[c] Computed as a residual.
[d] Reflects disinvestment by foreign-owned electric power companies of 1,456.2 millions of pesos ($116.5 million) resulting from the government's purchase on credit of the equity interests of these companies.

an additional 12 per cent, of estimated total gross private investment expenditures over the period under consideration. However, only about 60 per cent of direct private foreign investment was in the form of net new investment, the balance consisting of reinvested earnings of foreign-owned enterprises operating in Mexico. New issues of securities and net new foreign investment together appear to have accounted for somewhat less than 15 per cent of estimated total private investment expenditures, and the balance of more than 85 per cent appears to have been financed from internal funds and other sources.

Some enterprises, of course, occasionally issued variable-yield or equity securities as a means of raising funds for financing investment expenditures, but the extent of this practice in the private sector appears to have been quite limited. In addition, there probably was substantial reliance on what might be termed "semi-external" financing of private enterprises which involved the movement of funds within family or industrial and financial groups, but no statistical evidence is available to establish the extent of this practice. Furthermore it is possible that some portion of private investment expenditures was financed by means of domestic credits not represented by securities issues (or, at least, not securities issues included in the official statistics). While bank credits are nominally of a short-term nature, it is understood that it is not unusual for such credits to be regularly renewed so that, in fact, they are able to be utilized as a source of long-term financing. However, it seems reasonable to believe that the major share of banking system credits to the private sector are employed to finance inventories, trade credits, and other working capital requirements of business enterprises and consumption expenditures and speculative activities of individual borrowers. But in any event, our earlier estimate that between 70 per cent and 90 per cent of gross private domestic investment expenditures was internally financed throughout the period under consideration seems to be a reasonable approximation.

Let us now briefly consider the available evidence regarding the cost and availability of credit in the private sector. As pointed out earlier in this chapter, interest rates were high and tended to rise throughout the period under consideration. However, the high nominal rates were not particularly onerous to borrowers (and favorable to lenders) prior to the years 1956–1960 because almost continuous inflation caused real rates to be relatively low and at times even negative. We also pointed out earlier in the chapter that the government, as selective controls came to be more vigorously applied, was in large measure shielded from the high cost of borrowing because of its ability to force private financial institutions to acquire its relatively low-yielding securities. Public enterprises were less favored in this regard and continued to issue securities yielding interest approximating market rates, but the selective controls also afforded some support to these securities. Furthermore, government grants, access to central bank credits, and eligibility for low-cost foreign loan funds worked to hold down the financing costs of public enterprises. The burden of the high cost of credit therefore fell primarily on the private sector, particularly on investors and consumers who were unable to finance their expenditures from their own funds or funds obtained in lower cost markets abroad.

Financial Sector

It is evident from the foregoing discussion that the various credit and other institutions comprising the financial sector were the principal proximate source of government sector financing. Furthermore, our analysis has shown that while public enterprises and private businesses and individuals had greater access than did government to other lenders, nevertheless financial institutions were the principal source of deficit financing for these borrowers as well. However, we have not yet established the sources of the funds these financial institutions employed in financing the various deficit-spending units. Nor have we considered in any systematic fashion the uses to which financial institutions put the funds at their disposal. Therefore, we now turn to the task of clarifying the nature of fund flows through the financial sector.

It is convenient, first, to consider briefly the banking system as a whole, and then to proceed to separate examinations of the sources and uses of funds in the various components of the system—emphasizing the distinction between monetary institutions (i.e., Banco de México and the privately owned deposit banks) and the various nonmonetary institutions engaged in investment and mortgage banking and fiduciary and other financial activities which involve the issuance of nonmonetary financial claims. Unfortunately, because of the unavailability of the necessary data, a corresponding examination of the sources and uses of funds moving through the non-bank financial intermediaries (e.g., insurance and finance companies, the social security system, and the organized securities markets) is not possible.

BANKING SYSTEM

Table IV-H contains data which show the changes that occurred in the principal asset and liability accounts in the balance sheets of the vari-

TABLE IV-H

CHANGES IN ASSETS AND LIABILITIES OF BANKING SYSTEM INSTITUTIONS, 1940–1960[a]

(Millions of pesos)

	Monetary System			Nonmonetary Credit Institutions		
	Banco de México			National Banks		
	1940–1950	1951–1955	1956–1960	1940–1950	1951–1955	1956–1960
Assets						
Foreign Exchange	2,636.5	2,774.8	128.8	18.1	—3.4	3.5
Claims on Government	1,502.8	332.9	—158.2	297.1	—52.1	505.5
Claims on Enterprises and Individuals	330.6	—1.0	2,798.3	2,666.8	4,161.5	8,828.4
Claims on other Credit Institutions	221.5	177.0	805.9	345.1	214.8	320.1
Other Assets	67.4	105.0	620.4	277.7	1,296.4	312.3
Liabilities						
Money	2,368.1	2,207.3	2,896.9	24.2	86.6	56.8
Quasi-Money	65.9	8.3	115.2	1,803.2	3,372.0	5,846.6
Obligations to Other Credit Institutions	1,764.4	378.7	610.6	722.8	965.3	1,539.7
Other Liabilities	560.4	794.4	572.5	1,054.6	1,193.3	2,526.7

	Deposit Banks			Private Institutions		
	1940–1950	1951–1955	1956–1960	1940–1950	1951–1955	1956–1960
Assets						
Foreign Exchange	—148.8	415.6	—184.3	6.5	24.2	79.6
Claims on Government	252.1	299.9	689.2	51.9	59.0	1,336.5
Claims on Enterprises and Individuals	1,678.1	2,067.9	1,537.3	1,658.2	2,176.0	6,994.9
Claims on Other Credit Institutions	2,086.7	1,044.9	2,436.8	371.9	551.9	1,120.9
Other Assets	136.5	200.3	319.2	175.3	69.2	231.1
Liabilities						
Money	2,712.9	2,235.5	3,415.7	23.3	—1.2	23.2
Quasi-Money	520.2	1,018.9	442.4	1,333.9	2,389.4	7,093.1
Obligations to Other Credit Institutions	221.6	532.3	517.9	679.1	186.4	1,559.1
Other Liabilities	549.9	241.9	422.2	227.5	305.7	1,087.6

Source: Annual reports of Banco de México, S.A.
[a] See notes to Table IV-B.

ous types of institutions comprising the banking system during the three periods 1940–1950, 1951–1955, and 1956–1960. These were the periods which our earlier analysis indicates comprised more or less distinct phases or stages in recent Mexican financial experience. The changes in the liability accounts depict sources of funds and the changes in the asset accounts depict uses of funds.

During the period 1940–1950 the peso value of the resources of the banking system as a whole increased by nearly nine times, and during each of the two subsequent five-year periods, 1951–1955 and 1956–1960, there was, roughly speaking, a further doubling—so that by the end of 1960 the undeflated value of banking assets (including intra-system claims) was in excess of thirty times the value of these assets at the end of 1939. Of course these figures reflect the inflation which occurred in the intervening years as well as the growth in intrasystem claims. But even after allowance for these distorting factors, it is clear that the banking system grew at a substantially more rapid rate over the period than did the economy as a whole.

The relatively rapid growth of the banking system reflects the fact that banking processes—essentially the processes of financial intermediation—became increasingly important in the industrial and commercial life of the country as well as to governmental operations. That the main stimulus to the growth of the banking system emanated from the industrial, commercial, and consumer demand for banking services is evidenced by the fact that the claims of the system on enterprises and individuals increased at a substantially more rapid rate than did other banking system assets. And that the stimulus from this source became increasingly important is clear from the fact that during the years 1956–1960 almost 70 per cent of the increase in banking system assets was registered as claims against enterprises and individuals, as compared to 53 per cent and 43 per cent respectively, during the periods 1951–1955 and 1940–1950.

The comparisons cited in the previous paragraph might appear to contradict our earlier finding that in the latter part of the 1950s credit became progressively more scarce and costly in the private sector as loan funds were diverted from the financing of private sector to the financing of government deficits. This proposition is re-examined below within the framework of our sources-and-uses of funds analysis and we shall find ample confirmation that the credit resources of private banking institutions were, during these years, diverted in increasing amounts to the support of government sector deficits.

While the comparisons cited above do not contradict this finding they do relate closely to it. What they indicate is that the extreme tightness that developed in the market for loan funds in the latter part of the 1950s was a product of both mounting demand on the part of enterprises and individuals for banking system credits and a sizable diversion of funds of private lending institutions to the government sector.

Monetary institutions.—We have previously referred to certain characteristics of the balance sheets of Banco de México and the private deposit banks, and to changes over time in the principal asset and liability accounts. As a part of the analysis of the behavior of the money supply we presented in Table IV-B a combined balance sheet for monetary system institutions which reveals the changes in the assets and nonmonetary liabilities accounting for changes in the money supply. And, in support of our analysis of the financing of deficits in the public and private sectors of the economy, we showed in Table IV-D and Table IV-E changes in the amounts of credits extended to government and to enterprises and individuals by Banco de México and the deposit banks. But while we have examined certain aspects of their operations and experience, we have not yet considered separately and in detail the sources and uses of funds flowing through these monetary institutions.

Table IV-H contains a summary of the changes that occurred in the principal asset and liability accounts of Banco de México and the deposit banks during the three periods 1940–1950, 1951–1955, and 1956–1960. Considering first the data for Banco de México, it is evident that a significant change occurred in the use of the resources of this institution. During the period 1940–1950, and also the period 1951–1955, Banco de México was primarily engaged in financing government deficits and in attempting to maintain an adequate stock of foreign-exchange reserves. Relatively little continuing support was granted to enterprises and individuals or to other credit institutions during these years. During the period 1956–1960, however, Banco de México failed to make any net direct contribution to the financing of government sector deficits, while its claims on enterprises and individuals (principally public enterprises) and on credit institutions (principally national institutions) were substantially increased.

We have previously described how Banco de México employed selective credit controls as the means for relieving itself of the necessity for directly financing government sector deficits. However, it is clear from the data contained in Table IV-H that Banco de México did not wholly withdraw its support from public sector deficit financing, but rather that it merely changed from its earlier practice of purchasing government securities to that of directly financing public enterprises and, to a lesser extent, of supporting increased lending by the various specialized national credit institutions. By this means Banco de México not only augmented the financial resources of selected public agencies but it also introduced into the banking system funds which were adequate to support expansion of the money supply at a rate approximating that which had previously occurred on the basis of increases in credits to government and in the foreign-exchange holdings of the monetary system.

The changes which are apparent from the accounts of the deposit banks differ from, but are quite consistent with, those which occurred in the activities of Banco de México. During the period 1956–1960 credits to the government sector increased more rapidly than formerly while growth in claims on enterprises and individuals was relatively less important as a component of the total growth in deposit bank assets. Here we see unmistakable evidence of the diversion of private credit resources to the financing of government deficits in the years following 1955.

An examination of the asset accounts of the deposit banks also reveals a sizable increase in claims on other credit institutions. This movement of funds from the deposit banks to other institutions occurred throughout the entire period 1940–1960 but was especially marked during the years 1956–1960. More than 50 per cent of the total growth in deposit bank assets during this latter period consisted of increased claims on other credit institutions, while the comparable figure for the period 1940–1955 was less than 40 per cent. To some extent, of course, these intrasystem claims reflect increases in deposit-bank reserves maintained with Banco de México. However, the figures also reflect a movement of funds from the deposit banks to affiliated credit institutions (especially to the private financieras, often by way of various fiduciary institutions) which, throughout much of the period, were freer from the restrictions imposed on the deposit banks. We see reflected in this development not only increasing integration of the money and capital market but also a tendency for the process of financial intermediation to become more complex as the funds of ultimate lenders were transmitted less directly through the financial system to ultimate borrowers.

The principal source of deposit-bank funds throughout the period under consideration was, of course, checking deposits. As previously noted, the growth of these deposits was relatively constant and accounted for a major share of the increase in the money supply. Other sources of funds are reflected in the growth of quasi-monetary liabilities (especially foreign-currency deposits), claims on other banking institutions, and capital and other miscellaneous liability accounts.

It is clear from Table IV-H that growth of deposit-bank assets was quite limited relative to growth of the assets of the banking system as a whole, especially following 1955. The increase in deposit-bank assets amounted to but 22 per cent of the total increase in banking system assets (including intrasystem claims) during the 1940–1960 period, and during the years 1956–1960 the comparable percentage was less than 17 per cent. Thus, deposit banking became a progressively less important part of the overall banking system. The record of growth of the resources of Banco de México was much the same, so that not only deposit banking but also the monetary system as a whole became progressively less important relative to nonmonetary credit institutions.

Nonmonetary institutions.—As previously explained, there are two main types of nonmonetary credit institutions: the national banks and the privately owned institutions. We shall focus our attention on the items in the combined balance sheets of the national and private institutions, but where it seems appropriate, separate consideration will be given to the operations of the dominant institutions in each group, namely Nacional Financiera and the private financieras .

We see from the data shown in Table IV-H that during the period under consideration, increases in the resources of the nonmonetary national credit institutions accounted for about one-third of the increase in assets of the banking system as a whole. Nearly 80 per cent of the increase in assets of these institutions was in the form of claims on enterprises and individuals, representing nearly 45 per cent of the total volume of credits channeled by the banking system as a whole to this group of borrowers. The share of the funds moving through these institutions to enterprises and individuals increased somewhat during the period 1956–1960 as compared to 1940–1955 (85 per cent as compared to 74 per cent). Likewise, the contribution made by these institutions to the financing of government sector deficits became relatively more significant following 1955 (they absorbed somewhat more than 25 per cent of the total increase in banking system claims on government during the period 1956–1960 as compared to only 9 per cent during the earlier period).

The major sources of the funds at the disposal of the national non-monetary credit institutions during the period 1940–1960 were bond issues and foreign loans. Additions to capital and loans from other financial institutions also constituted significant sources of funds.

As previously indicated, Nacional Financiera is the dominant non-monetary national credit institution, and therefore the sources and uses of the funds of this institution are of special interest. Unfortunately, however, there is no way to determine precisely the extent to which Nacional Financiera accounted for the various sources and uses of funds shown for all nonmonetary financial institutions in Table IV-H. Nacional Financiera does not make comparable data available in its own periodic public documents and Banco de México does not disclose data it compiles on the operations of individual institutions other than itself. However, figures in the annual reports of Nacional Financiera suggest that in recent years its resources amounted to between 30 per cent and 40 per cent of the total combined resources of all nonmonetary national credit institutions excluding those of Banco de México. In addition to its own funds, Nacional Financiera administers various public trust funds and also guarantees a sizable volume of debt obligations for a variety of borrowers, these latter operations constituting a quite significant aspect of Nacional Financiera operations. Recent studies indicate that Nacional Financiera relied increasingly on foreign loans and issues of fixed-interest securities as a source of funds during the period under consideration while progressively curtailing credits from other banks and various deposit liabilities. The main uses of Nacional Financiera funds are in support of infrastructure-type and other investment expenditures in industry and manufacturing in both the public and private sectors—although a relatively small and declining proportion of Nacional Financiera funds also has been made available to various trade and service industries, other financial institutions, and governmental units.

Turning now to the private, nonmonetary credit institutions, we see from the data in Table IV-H that their assets increased more rapidly following 1955 than formerly. Thus, during the period 1956–1960 these institutions accounted for about one-third of the total increase in banking system assets while during the period 1940–1955 they accounted for only about a sixth of the total increase. Funds at the disposal of private nonmonetary credit institutions were employed largely to finance enterprises and individuals. Thus, nearly 75 per cent of the increase in assets of these institutions was represented by increases in claims on enterprises and individuals over the period 1940–1960, the percentage being somewhat lower during the period 1956–1960 than formerly. Prior to 1955 these institutions contributed very little support to government sector deficits. However, during the period 1956–1960 they accounted for somewhat more than 50 per cent of the increase in total banking system claims on the government sector, an amount equal to nearly 15 per cent of the increase in their assets during this period.

In spite of the increased flow of funds from the private, nonmonetary institutions to the government sector during the period 1956–1960 (and particularly during 1958–1960), these institutions continued to be a major source of funds for financing deficits of enterprises and individuals, accounting for roughly 35 per cent of total banking system credits to these borrowers. This was a larger share of the total financing of enterprises and individuals than was supplied by these institutions during the period 1940–1955, when the comparable figure was 26 per cent.

One final comment on the pattern of fund usage by private, nonmonetary credit institutions as a whole. As shown by the data contained in Table IV-H, these institutions employed a significant proportion of their funds to acquire claims on other credit institutions (although, significantly, the proportion of new funds used for this purpose was lower in the period following 1955 than formerly). Some portion of these claims no doubt represented reserve deposits, but the major part represented holdings of securities issued by other financial institutions (principally the various nonmonetary national credit agencies) and credits to the deposit banks. It appears, then, that in addition to their support of public sector deficits by means of direct credits to government and public enterprises, these institutions afforded some indirect support to public sector deficits through the intermediation of the national, nonmonetary credit institutions.

An examination of the changes which occurred in the liabilities of the private, nonmonetary credit institutions reveals that the principal source of the funds at the disposal of these institutions through-

out the period was deposits received from enterprises and individuals
—which are shown as increased quasi-monetary liabilities in Table
IV-H. Also quite significant as sources of funds were issues of claims
to other financial institutions—especially fiduciaries—and additions
to capital.

The most important type of private, nonmonetary credit institution
in recent years has been financial societies—the so-called financieras.
The resources of these institutions increased from 8.3 million pesos
in 1940 to 916.5 million pesos in 1950; by the end of 1955 the corresponding figure stood at 1,994.6 million and by the end of 1960 at
9,057.8 million. The proportion of the total resources of all private,
nonmonetary credit institutions accounted for by the financieras increased from 4.5 per cent in 1940 to 37.9 per cent in 1950, 37.6 per
cent in 1955, and 60.1 per cent in 1960. Over 70 per cent of the
growth in total resources of all private financial institutions during
the period 1956–1960 was accounted for by the financieras.

The principal sources of funds at the disposal of the financieras
were deposits denominated in national and foreign currencies (the
latter increasing in relative importance over the years immediately
following the 1954 devaluation). The major share of financiera deposits took the form of liabilities to enterprises and individuals, but
other financial institutions were also quite important as a source of
funds. The principal uses of financiera funds were various sorts of
loans and credits to enterprises and individuals and other financial
institutions, although following the extension of the selective-credit–
control program to the financieras in 1958, a substantial increase in
credits to government is evident. Indeed, during the years 1958–
1960 the proportion of financiera resources taking the form of claims
on government increased from practically nil to nearly 9 per cent.
During this period, of the total increase in claims on government
held by the private, nonmonetary credit institutions, roughly 60 per
cent was accounted for by the financieras, reflecting the impact of
selective credit controls. The flow of financiera funds to enterprises
and individuals and other financial institutions continued to increase
during the 1958–1960 period but had it not been for the requirements of the control program, and given the same rate of increase in
loanable funds, it seems clear that the flow of financiera credits to
these nongovernment borrowers would have been greater than was
the case.

Other financial intermediaries.—As indicated earlier, data limitations prevent analyses of the various non-bank financial intermediaries such as insurance and finance companies, the social security trust funds, and the organized securities markets of the sort offered above for the various monetary and nonmonetary credit institutions comprising the banking system. What fragmentary information is available on "extra-bank" financing indicates that the non-bank financial institutions were relatively unimportant throughout the whole period under consideration, but beyond this general appraisal little can be said in the present context.

The overall picture which emerges from our examination of the financial sector and its operation during the years 1940–1960 can be summarized as follows. The importance of the monetary system in the process of financial intermediation declined as both Banco de México and the private deposit banks provided a progressively smaller share of the deficit financing of government, public enterprises, and the private sector proper. The relative importance of nonmonetary credit institutions correspondingly increased, the growth in volume of funds moving through these institutions being especially marked in the years 1956–1960. Numerous significant changes occurred in the sources and uses of banking system funds. The most significant seem to have been, on the sources side, a growing reliance on issues of quasi-monetary claims and an increasing volume of intrasystem fund flows. The most significant changes on the uses side appear to have been an increased volume of credit extended to the government sector by all credit institutions other than Banco de México, and assumption by various nonmonetary credit institutions (especially Nacional Financiera and the private financieras) of greater responsibility for financing enterprises and individuals.

Conclusion

It is hoped that after this description of Mexican monetary and financial experience during the 1940–1960 period the reader is better able to understand what this experience consisted of both in terms of specific developments and general trends. If the "what" and "how" of recent Mexican monetary and financial experience have been presented clearly and accurately, then the purpose of this chapter has been successfully fulfilled.

It remains to explain why Mexican monetary and financial experience during this period was what it was. In particular, we need to examine the reasons for the changes which occurred in policies and practices as well as in instruments and institutions. Clearly our consideration of these matters must be cast in more speculative and theoretical terms than we have heretofore employed. It is to this task that we turn in the two chapters which follow.

PART III . . . THE 1940–1960 PERIOD—ANALYSIS

CHAPTER V

INTERNAL STABILITY AND EXTERNAL EQUILIBRIUM

Introduction

CHANGES IN MONETARY VARIABLES brought about by
the monetary authorities in an effort to exercise control over the behavior of the domestic price level and the international balance of
payments must influence the aggregate volume of expenditures in
order to be effective. However, the extent to which monetary measures are capable of influencing expenditures is dependent upon the
degree to which the measures taken result in modification of the
amount and rapidity of monetary circulation and also upon the responsiveness of spending decisions to the cost and availability of loan
funds. Thus the effectiveness of monetary policy in maintaining (or
re-establishing) financial and economic stability hinges, first, on the
ability of the authorities to control the money supply and thereby influence conditions in the loanable-funds market and, second, on an
appropriate responsiveness of spending decisions.

The quantity of money and the velocity of its circulation is governed by a number of factors, some of which are more amenable to
the control of the authorities than others. In particular, the extent to
which various nonmonetary financial assets serve as substitutes for

strictly monetary claims may constitute an important limitation on the ability of Banco de México to influence the cost and availability of credit by means of quantitative controls restricted to the commercial banking system. Likewise, disturbances emanating from outside the economy, and acting through the balance of international payments, may also operate to limit the effectiveness of traditional instruments of monetary policy. The task of promoting domestic monetary stability and external financial equilibrium tends to be complicated, and the effectiveness of monetary policy in achieving these ends is subject to numerous limitations.

In this chapter we propose to examine some of the principal limitations imposed on the Mexican monetary authorities in their efforts to achieve and maintain domestic stability and external equilibrium. At the outset we admit to a degree of skepticism regarding the effectiveness of monetary policy in the circumstances in which most lesser developed countries find themselves. Particularly in a country like Mexico—which must of necessity maintain free currency convertibility, which because of the character of her international trade is especially vulnerable to disequilibrating influences from abroad, and which as a consequence of the past record of inflation and devaluation is subject to large-scale capital movements in response to changes in appraisals of exchange risk—do there exist serious limitations on the ability of the authorities to pursue stabilization policies by means of the traditional instruments of monetary control. However, Banco de México has been able to overcome some of the difficulties encountered in its efforts to achieve domestic stability and external equilibrium by extending its regulatory influence to nonmonetary financial institutions and to the market for quasi-monetary instruments, by supplementing traditional quantitative controls with qualitative (or selective) controls, and by means of various other expediencies.

Our procedure in this chapter is to analyze the behavior of monetary and quasi-monetary liabilities of banking system institutions, and the underlying supply-and-demand conditions in the money and capital market, with the purpose of gauging the degree of control exercised by Banco de México over these variables. This procedure, of course, requires that we isolate those parameters governing the behavior of the various banking system liabilities which are under the direct control of the monetary authorities, distinguishing these from other parameters which are not so amenable to control. Our findings are employed as a basis for evaluating the effectiveness of Mexican monetary and financial policy and also for commenting on the merits of the so-called monetarist-structuralist controversy which has commanded so much attention in recent years.

Behavior of Money and Quasi-Money

For purposes of our analysis the money supply is considered to consist of the total amount of coin, currency, and checking deposits denominated in national currency held by other than banking system institutions and units of government. That is, the money supply is defined to include all monetary claims against banking system institutions held by enterprises and individuals. Monetary claims are, of course, the most perfectly liquid of all the many types of outstanding obligations of financial institutions and other borrowers. In addition, monetary claims are differentiated from other instruments employed for mobilizing resources in the financial markets by the fact that they do not yield interest to holders.

Money is desired principally for its convenience in effecting purchases and for paying debts, although it also is employed as a means of storing wealth or value. Of course all sorts of financial instruments are capable of fulfilling the latter function, but none except monetary claims (and also to a limited extent checking deposits denominated in foreign currencies) are utilized directly for making payments. In other words, the distinguishing characteristic of money as defined here is its usefulness both as the basic means of effecting transactions and as one among many other means of storing wealth.

All sorts of nonmonetary financial claims are constantly being exchanged for money in anticipation of expenditures for goods, services, productive factors, or for other financial instruments, including foreign exchange. Thus, all outstanding nonmonetary claims in varying degree constitute potential sources of financing for expenditures —a fact which explains why, for some sorts of analysis, it may be preferable to focus upon the whole range of financial claims, both monetary and nonmonetary, which can be readily converted into goods, services, or other things without undue delay or serious loss of value. Clearly, those financial claims which can be converted into money without difficulty do constitute close substitutes for money— and for this reason it is appropriate to refer to such liquid claims as "quasi-money."

Figure 5– A

RELATION OF MONEY SUPPLY AND QUASI-MONEY TO GROSS NATIONAL PRODUCT

(Billions of pesos – 1940 to 1960)

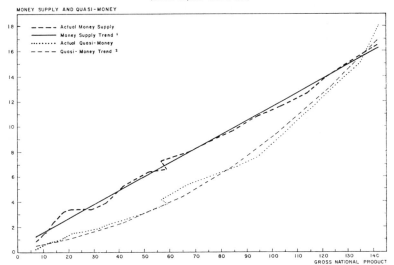

Source: Annual reports of Banco de México, S.A.

[1] The secular trend in the growth of the monetary liabilities of the banking system during the period 1940–1960 may be expressed as: M = 119 GNP — 0.477

[2] The secular trend in the growth of the quasi-monetary liabilities of the banking system during the period 1940–1960 may be expressed as: Log. Q = 2.879 — 0.01296 GNP

STATISTICAL COMPARISONS

Because of the potential interchangability of money and quasi-money, it is not possible to study the behavior of money without at the same time being concerned to some extent with the behavior of quasi-money. However, the behavior of the one will be closely related to the behavior of the other only if they are being regularly substituted for one another on a large scale. Actually, as shown in Figure 5-A, our observations of the behavior of the money supply and quasi-money reveal no significant correlation between the growth of these two variables during the period 1940–1960. We find that while the monetary liabilities of the banking system increased in more or less direct proportion to gross national product, quasi-monetary liabilities increased regularly over time as a percentage of gross national product. As a consequence the monetary liabilities of the system declined as a proportion of the total obligations of banking system institutions, while quasi-monetary liabilities increased in relative importance. It does not appear that the growth of quasi-monetary liabilities resulted to any significant extent from a substitution of holdings of these claims for money balances; nor does it appear that the behavior of the money supply, and its virtually constant relationship to gross national product, was in any significant way governed by the behavior of quasi-monetary liabilities of banking system institutions. Furthermore, short-run deviations from the respective secular growth paths of monetary and quasi-monetary liabilities do not appear to have been significantly correlated with one another.

Some qualification is necessary, however, since the overwhelming factor governing the growth of both money and quasi-money appears to be growth of national product. The fact that both the money supply and the volume of outstanding quasi-monetary claims are positively correlated with gross national product naturally tends to produce a positive correlation between the two monetary variables, thereby off-setting the negative correlation which would result from a substantial degree of substitutability between money and quasi-money. Furthermore, the extent to which quasi-money serves as a substitute for money may be reflected in the failure of the money supply to increase relative to gross national product (i.e., in the absence of a decline in the income velocity of circulation with the growth of national product). But since we cannot know whether or not there would have been a tendency for this to occur in the absence of large-scale growth of quasi-monetary claims, speculation along these lines seems unlikely to be fruitful.

The main point for present purposes is that money and quasi-money appear to have behaved more or less independently and that for this reason it seems appropriate to analyze the behavior of each separately. Therefore, our procedure in the remainder of this chapter is to examine first the factors governing the supply of and the demand for money, and to reserve until later consideration of the behavior of quasi-monetary claims against banking system institutions. By means of this procedure we hope to demonstrate the influence, or lack thereof, of monetary policy measures on the behavior of the money supply, other principal types of financial claims, and the overall operation of the financial system.

SUPPLY OF AND DEMAND FOR MONEY

The quantity of money in circulation (or the money supply) is governed on the one hand by the central bank working in conjunction with commercial banks and on the other hand by decisions on the part of wealth owners regarding what part of their wealth to hold in money form. The control exercised by the central bank over the monetary circulation is for the most part dependent upon influences exercised on the behavior of commercial banks—but, as will be demonstrated, this control is partial at best.

As already indicated, it is evident from an examination of the statistical record that the Mexican money supply maintained a more or less constant relationship to gross national product during the period 1940–1960, fluctuating within the 12–14 per cent range except for the war years, when the percentages were somewhat higher. This implies that the annual velocity of circulation ranged between 7 and 8 and that increments in the money supply ranging from 12 to 14 pesos were required to support each 100-peso increase in gross national product. These relationships might seem to suggest that it is a simple matter to induce an increase (or decrease) in the aggregate volume of expenditures by manipulation of the money supply—i.e., by means of variations in the reserve base of the monetary system sufficient to produce credit expansion (or contraction) and thereby create (or destroy) the desired amount of monetary claims. In fact, however, the evidence reveals that changes in expenditures for current output have not been closely correlated with changes in the reserves of the monetary institutions. Nor has the money supply behaved in close accordance with changes in these reserves, especially that component of the money supply consisting of checking deposits. While the money supply bears a linear relationship to gross national product, expansionary monetary policies do not appear to have caused growth in expenditures but, rather, the causal relationship appears to run in the opposite direction.

The fact that money balances were maintained in more or less constant proportion to gross national product suggests that these balances were desired principally for transactions purposes. It appears that money balances were not very responsive to changes in market rates of interest; indeed, those few instances in which a significant increase in liquidity preference is evident were clearly associated with special circumstances, such as the large influx of short-term capital in connection with the Korean crisis of 1950 and the absolute decline in gross national product which occurred in 1953. In short, to the extent that money balances were occasionally substituted for other financial claims or for goods (or vice versa), it appears that the principal motivating factor was uncertainty regarding exchange-rate stability or the level of output and employment in the domestic economy rather than expectations regarding changes in the level and structure of interest rates.

Control of the Money Supply

Monetary analysis is often premised on the assumption that the money supply is fixed at will by action of the central bank. However, this may not be a realistic assumption, especially for a lesser developed country such as Mexico in which exogenous events in the foreign sector govern to a considerable degree not only the behavior of the money supply but also the level of domestic interest rates and of national income and employment. Mexico, like most countries heavily involved in the production of primary products for export is subject to substantial fluctuations in foreign exchange receipts, and these fluctuations in turn are reflected in the country's balance of international payments, monetary reserves, and monetary circulation. We find that developments in the foreign sector, as reflected in the balance of international payments, at times exercise a fundamentally important influence on the operation of the monetary system and that as a consequence the power of Banco de México to control the behavior of the money supply and the level of interest rates in some circumstances is closely circumscribed.

A crucial factor governing the country's balance of payments experience is, of course, the degree of confidence on the part of wealth holders in the stability of the peso. The reader will recall that Mexico has experienced three substantial devaluations since the depression of the 1930s and that the external value of the peso has fallen from 3.60 to the dollar in 1937 to the present 12.50. As a consequence of this experience any evident weakness in the country's external payments position produces expectations of further devaluation—which in turn tend to further worsen the payments position and to reduce the effectiveness of any monetary measures Banco de México may take in an attempt to alleviate the situation.

For example, when adverse developments occur in export markets the Mexican economy is at the same time often confronted with the dual problem of domestic recession and an adverse balance of international payments. If Banco de México acts to increase the money supply in an effort to check the decline in domestic economic activity, the payments imbalance becomes even more acute as a consequence of the stimulus afforded imports. The further losses in foreign exchange reserves, in turn, tend to curtail the credit base and thereby work to offset the effect of Banco de México efforts to increase the money supply. If Banco de México is able to effect an increase in the money supply under these circumstances (i.e., if the increase in money supply resulting from Banco de México actions is greater than the decrease resulting from foreign exchange losses), the heightened exchange risk brought about by depletion of reserves, coupled with domestic credit expansion, provokes capital flight as sophisticated wealth holders become alerted to the possibility of further devaluation. Speculation against the peso is facilitated not only by the easier credit conditions in the domestic market but also by the policy of supporting the market values of a wide range of quasi-monetary claims at par. The result is that Banco de México ends up financing speculation against the peso by introducing additional liquidity into the system in its efforts to ease conditions in the domestic market and at the same time prevent disruptive declines in prices in the market for financial claims—with no significant stimulus being afforded domestic economic activity.

CONTROLLED AND UNCONTROLLED CAUSES OF
VARIATIONS IN THE MONEY SUPPLY

The limitations on the power of Banco de México to control the money supply are strikingly revealed by an examination of the behavior of certain items in the balance sheets of the monetary system institutions over time. Some of these items (namely, the rediscounts and other credits extended by Banco de México, the legally required security holdings of the deposit and savings banks, and the cash balances and paid-in capital accounts of these latter institutions) are capable of being controlled either directly or indirectly by the monetary authorities, and by means of induced variations in these items attempts are made to exercise control over the quantity of money in circulation. However the remaining nonmonetary items in the combined balance sheets of Banco de México and the deposit and savings banks (namely the foreign exchange reserves, treasury deposits, and other asset and liability accounts of Banco de México, and the credits, foreign exchange holdings, nonmonetary liabilities, and other asset and liability accounts of the deposit and savings banks) are not subject to direct control by the monetary authorities but rather are dependent upon developments in the money and capital market and the operations of borrowers and lenders in the market as well as upon the country's balance of payments experience.

As shown in Figure 5-B, changes in the variables governing the be-

Figure 5 – B

RELATION BETWEEN CONTROLLED AND UNCONTROLLED CAUSES OF VARIATION IN MONEY SUPPLY [1]
(Millions of pesos)

Source: Annual reports of Banco de México, S.A.

[1] The correlation between quarterly changes of net controlled and uncontrolled causes of variation in the money supply, assuming no lags, is — 0.611.

[2] Includes changes in the foreign exchange reserves, treasury deposits, and other asset and liability accounts of Banco de México, and credits, foreign exchange holdings, nonmonetary liabilities, and other asset and liability accounts of the deposit and savings banks. The changes shown are the net result of yearly changes of these items.

[3] Includes changes in Banco de México rediscounts and other credits, and in legally required security holdings, cash balances, and paid-in capital accounts of deposit and savings banks. The changes shown are the net result of changes in each of these items.

havior of the money supply which are subject to the control of the monetary authorities tend to be associated with contrary, although usually somewhat less intense, reactions in those remaining variables governing the behavior of the money supply which are beyond the control of the monetary authorities. Thus we see illustrated graphically the fact that the ability of Banco de México to control the money supply is limited by the demand of the public for money balances— which in turn is evidently governed principally by the level of gross national product. In other words, when the monetary authorities attempt to maintain the money supply at a level which is at variance with that desired by the community, equilibrium in the supply of and demand for money balances tends to be re-established by adjustments on the demand side.

There are numerous ways, in addition to variations in spending for goods, in which the public might choose to adjust to actions taken by the monetary authorities. For example, wealth holders with undesired money balances may choose either to convert these funds into other types of financial assets or they may reduce their liquidity by extinguishing existing liabilities. Similarly, when money balances in excess of those willingly supplied by the monetary authorities are desired, there may occur a liquidation of nonmonetary financed assets or an increase of borrowing.

FOREIGN EXCHANGE LIQUIDITY TRAP

Whatever form the process of adjustment takes, there ultimately results an impact on Mexico's balance of international payments—whether reflected in the current account (as a consequence of adjustments in expenditures for imports associated with variations in income and liquidity) or in the capital account (as a consequence of changes in demand for financial claims denominated in foreign currencies principally motivated by changes in appraisals of exchange risk but also coupled with differentials in interest yields obtainable on domestic and foreign financial claims). For example, the reaction to changes in those variables which the monetary authorities are able to influence by means of general quantitative controls in an effort to induce monetary expansion is that an excess supply of money is, to some extent and either directly or indirectly, converted into claims on foreign exchange. The tendency for expansionary monetary policies to manifest themselves in an adverse balance of international payments limits in very substantial degree the ability of the authorities to pursue such policies as a means of stimulating the level of domestic economic activity.

A similar situation exists in the case of restrictive monetary policies. Such policies, of course, involve an attempt to curtail growth of the money supply and to heighten the cost and limit the availability of bank credit. However, if there is excess demand for money, an inflow of foreign exchange will tend to develop (whether directly by means of conversion of liquid foreign currency assets into pesos, or indirectly as a result of the tendency for restrictive policies to produce a balance of payments surplus). In any case, the behavior of the balance of payments tends to limit the effect of restrictive monetary policies on the cost and availability of credit and thereby on investment and consumption expenditures. In the short run the existing amount of liquid foreign exchange assets held by residents sets an upper limit on the operation of the compensatory mechanism, but over a longer period adjustments producing a surplus on current account in the balance of international payments (and perhaps also in the long-term capital account) could provide large and continuing offsets to restrictive monetary policies.

Thus in the case of both restrictive and expansionary monetary policies compensatory forces operate to limit the power of the monetary authorities to control the money supply and to establish desired conditions in the domestic money and capital market. The behavior of the money supply is thus governed principally by the transactions demand for money which in turn is largely determined by the growth of gross national product. Expansionary pressures exerted by the monetary authorities in the internal market in an effort to counter a domestic recession are rather quickly manifested in balance of payments difficulties, while restrictive pressures introduced in an effort to counter inflationary tendencies in the domestic market are likewise offset by compensating adjustments of a similar sort.

Numerous examples drawn from recent Mexican experience could be cited to illustrate the processes at work, but perhaps two will be sufficient. Following the devaluation in mid-1954 and throughout 1956, Banco de México followed restrictive policies in an effort to re-establish confidence in the peso at the new exchange parity. Nevertheless, in spite of the restrictive policies the money supply continued to increase in more or less constant proportion to gross national product at progressively higher price levels. The main impetus to the monetary expansion which occurred was an increase of almost two and one-half times in the foreign exchange reserves of Banco de México—which, in addition to revaluation of existing reserves, was principally the result of repatriation of Mexican short-term capital (especially from the United States), but also to some extent was due to improvement in Mexico's balance of payments on current account. A second example is found in the country's experience during the years 1956–1959, during which the authorities attempted to ease credit conditions in an effort to stimulate the rate of growth of domestic production. Again, however, the money supply continued to maintain a virtually constant relation to gross national product as balance of payment deficits, short-term capital outflows, and other offsetting factors limited the effectiveness of the expansionary actions of Banco de México. These two examples suggest that in some circumstances the central bank may be confronted with a sort of foreign exchange liquidity trap which effectively frustrates the efforts of the authorities to exercise control over the money supply and the aggregate level of expenditures by means of traditional quantitive instruments of monetary management.

In an economy such as that of Mexico strong demand for exports, and a consequent favorable balance of international payments, tends to be associated with periods of high-level activity and inflationary pressures in the domestic economy, while domestic recession tends to be associated with slackened demand for exports and balance of payment difficulties. It is because of the high degree of responsiveness of the domestic economy to external influences that a conflict between stability and external equilibrium is especially likely to arise. Particularly when there is a slackening in the demand for exports, a slowing in the rate of growth of domestic output, and a decline in official holdings of foreign exchange reserves does there develop a conflict between the objectives of domestic stability and external equilibrium because of vulnerability of the peso to adverse speculation.

GRAPHICAL REPRESENTATION

Our argument is premised on the observed fact that short-term capital movements, motivated either by changes in appraisals of the risk of exchange rate instability or by interest rate differentials as between Mexican and foreign financial markets, are capable of exercising a strong influence on monetary reserves and the money supply and thereby on the aggregate volume of domestic expenditures and level of overall economic activity. This situation, coupled with the policy of maintaining free currency convertibility and the heavy dependence of Mexico on export earnings, imposes limitations on the ability of the monetary authorities to control the money supply and conditions in the domestic money and capital market.

These propositions are depicted graphically in Figure 5-C. In the graph the prevailing rate of interest in the domestic money market is measured along the I axis, the amount of money in circulation is measured along the M axis, the degree of exchange risk (stated in terms of a discount factor) is measured along the R axis, and the amount of foreign exchange assets, other than official reserves, held by Mexicans is measured along the F axis. The L_N curve depicts the demand for national money as a function of the domestic interest rate, the R curve depicts exchange risk as a function of the size of the money supply, the F curve depicts the amount of foreign exchange which residents wish to hold as protection against foreign exchange risk (given the level of the interest rate in the domestic market) and the L_F curve depicts the demand for foreign exchange as a function of the interest rate in the domestic market (given the degree of exchange risk).

The relationships depicted in Figure 5-C between conditions in

Figure 5 – C

RELATION BETWEEN CONDITIONS IN DOMESTIC AND FOREIGN FINANCIAL MARKETS

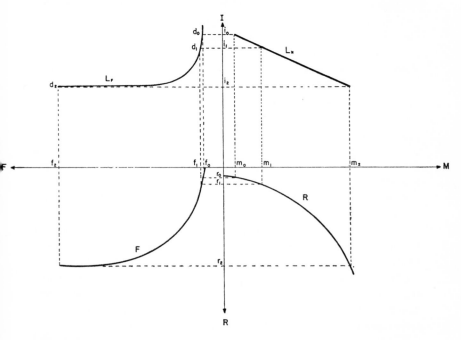

the domestic money and capital market and those in the foreign exchange market are as follows. The demand for money (L_N) and the supply of money (m_1) determine the interest rate (i_1). The degree of exchange risk associated with m_1 is r_1 and, given the level of the interest rate in the domestic market, wealth holders will seek to hedge against this risk by holding foreign exchange in the amount of f_1. Thus the demand for foreign exchange (L_F) is shown to be a function of the domestic money supply and of the associated level of domestic interest rate and degree of exchange risk. At some minimal level of money supply (e.g., m_0) and relatively high level of the domestic interest rate (e.g., i_0), exchange risk virtually disappears and the demand for foreign exchange becomes fixed at some low level (e.g. f_0) as determined by the minimum requirements of foreign trade. However, as the money supply is increased and domestic interest rates tend to fall, exchange risk increases and speculative considerations induce an increase in the amount of foreign exchange demanded as wealth holders attempt to maintain an optimal balance between assets denominated in domestic and foreign currencies. Exchange speculation is motivated by appraisals that yields obtainable on foreign exchange holdings, plus possible devaluation profits, outweigh the higher yields obtainable on peso assets minus possible devaluation losses.

Explicit recognition of the role of exchange risk in our model makes it possible to explain the substantial prevailing disparities in interest rates obtainable in Mexico and in foreign financial centers such as New York. Furthermore the model illustrates the relationship between foreign exchange speculation and domestic monetary policy, and shows how expansion of the money supply is capable of producing a balance of payments deficit and a drain on the country's foreign exchange reserves.

Wealth holders are willing to hold peso assets, including money, as long as the domestic interest rate and the convenience of holding wealth in this form is judged to cover their exchange risk and the opportunity cost of not holding foreign assets. Of course, wealth holders will differ in their appraisals in this regard, but clearly domestic monetary expansion will induce progressively more switching from domestic to foreign assets. Successive increases in the money supply and decreases in the interest rate will lead to progressively larger flows of funds into foreign assets as wealth holders seek to hedge against the increasing risk of devaluation and take advantage of diminishing interest rate differentials. At some combination of money supply and interest rate (m_2, i_2, in the diagram) there develops a consensus that the exchange risk can no longer be covered by yields in the domestic market, and at this juncture the demand for foreign exchange becomes infinitely elastic and the demand for money, and other financial assets denominated in pesos, becomes completely inelastic with respect to the rate of interest.

Of course expansion in the level of domestic economic activity (which generally would occur in response to increased demand for exports and corresponding increases in foreign exchange reserves) causes both the L_N and L_F curves to shift outward from the origin and thus would normally be associated with corresponding shifts in the R and F functions. If not wholly negated by increases in the money supply, the result would be an increase in domestic interest rates and, in turn, a greater willingness on the part of wealth holders to hold peso assets. Because of the higher level of domestic economic activity and the associated improvement in domestic investment opportunities and opportunities for profitable lending in the domestic market, resources previously sent abroad tend to be repatriated and foreign investors and lenders are induced to further augment the supply of foreign exchange. The money supply tends to be enlarged along with the growth of foreign exchange reserves, but because there is no need to afford further stimulus to the domestic economy the monetary authorities are in a position to impose restrictive measures and thereby to exercise an influence over conditions in the money and capital market. In short, when the domestic economy is experiencing rapid growth and the demand for money balances is consequently increasing, the monetary authorities are in a reasonably good position to follow policies conducive to maintenance of domestic and external stability. However, when the rate of economic growth is low, or negative, and the narrow limits within which expansion policy can be pursued prior to the limitation imposed by the foreign exchange liquidity trap have already been exploited, there exists no further possibility for monetary stimulus to the economy—and indeed any efforts to provide such stimulus can only have destructive consequences.

All of the foregoing indicates that the behavior of the money supply is dependent upon a number of variables, many of which are beyond the control of the monetary authorities, and that therefore it is usually inappropriate beyond rather narrow limits to consider the money supply as an exogenous variable subject to control by the monetary authorities. The monetary authorities are, in effect, constrained from pursuing other than passive policies by developments in the domestic economy, the foreign sector, and by preferences (and suspicions) of wealth holders. It is because of these limitations on the ability of the monetary authorities to control the money supply and conditions in the money and capital markets by means of traditional quantitative controls that the policy prescriptions of traditional monetary theory often have had little relevance to the circumstances in which the country has found itself.

Control of Quasi-Money

In Chapter II we examined the various sorts of financial instruments employed in the money and capital market and concluded that, because of policies pursued by Banco de México, Nacional Financiera, and ultimately, the federal government in supporting the market values of a wide range of securities, almost all of the nonmonetary indebtedness of financial intermediaries possesses the character of quasi-money. Likewise, in Chapter III we observed that during the 1950s controls exercised by Banco de México were extended to certain nonmonetary financial institutions and that as a consequence the position of these institutions vis-à-vis the central bank and the commercial banks was substantially altered. It remains to consider how these developments were related to one another and also to the problem of maintaining stability and external equilibrium.

GROWTH OF QUASI-MONETARY CLAIMS

We have previously indicated that while in theory the growth of quasi-money might be at the expense of growth in money holdings, the statistical record fails to reveal any significant correlation between variations in these two aggregates. While the money supply maintained a virtually constant relation to GNP, outstanding quasi-monetary claims regularly increased relative to GNP—with the result that quasi-monetary claims increased relative to, but probably not at the expense of, growth in the money supply.

The increase in the outstanding volume of quasi-monetary claims was, of course, closely related to growth in the indebtedness of financial institutions and other borrowers capable of supplying such claims. All sorts of financial intermediaries contributed to the supply of quasi-money. Among the private institutions, those which accounted for the largest share were the deposit and savings banks, and, especially during the 1950s, the private financieras. Among the national institutions the principal issuers of quasi-monetary claims were the specialized credit agencies, with Nacional Financiera presumably being the major source.

These statements are supported by the data shown in Table V-A. As shown, 53.3 per cent of the total increase in quasi-monetary obligations of banking system institutions which occurred between 1940 and 1960 was accounted for by obligations of private institutions—and of this amount over 80 per cent was attributable to deposit and savings banks and financieras. Nonmonetary national institutions accounted for about 45 per cent of the growth of quasi-monetary claims over the period.

As long as the nonmonetary institutions issuing large amounts of

TABLE V-A

ORIGIN OF QUASI-MONETARY CLAIMS, 1940–1960[a]

(Millions of pesos)

| Year | Total | Private Institutions | | | National Institutions | |
		Deposit and Saving	Financieras	Other	Banco de México	Other
1940	397.9	152.8	4.5	101.9	33.5	105.2
1941	539.2	194.3	3.1	154.5	20.4	166.9
1942	693.0	215.9	54.4	192.5	31.3	198.9
1943	981.5	329.8	91.0	233.1	11.4	316.2
1944	1,353.7	447.5	159.7	309.8	55.5	381.2
1945	1,887.7	609.2	213.4	440.3	54.6	570.2
1946	2,084.6	627.2	183.9	523.8	54.6	695.1
1947	2,425.6	630.2	198.4	539.5	170.5	887.0
1948	3,011.9	804.3	241.5	577.3	220.2	1,168.6
1949	3,589.7	944.4	245.6	645.2	250.2	1,504.3
1950	4,131.6	1,084.9	229.3	786.6	69.8	1,961.0
1951	5,432.8	1,315.5	425.1	964.1	87.5	2,640.6
1952	6,000.6	1,614.3	488.8	1,085.5	87.5	2,724.5
1953	7,020.1	1,779.5	513.4	1,313.5	105.8	3,307.9
1954	9,766.1	2,550.7	802.0	1,295.8	103.3	5,014.3
1955	10,920.2	2,917.1	1,044.7	1,547.3	78.1	5,333.0
1956	12,229.8	3,244.3	1,529.1	1,938.1	116.7	5,401.6
1957	13,879.6	3,946.4	2,228.2	2,169.3	135.6	5,400.1
1958	16,340.0	4,595.7	2,931.9	2,124.3	142.4	6,545.7
1959	18,755.9	4,448.3	4,261.6	2,292.3	145.6	7,608.1
1960	24,402.7	4,707.0	5,826.2	2,496.6	193.3	11,179.6

Source: Annual reports of Banco de México, S.A.

[a] Quasi-monetary claims include all domestic and foreign currency obligations of banking system institutions to enterprises and individuals except monetary liabilities and capital account items.

quasi-monetary instruments remained largely exempt from the sorts of controls imposed on the commercial banks, there was an increasing limitation on the ability of Banco de México to influence conditions in the money and capital market by means of the traditional instruments of monetary policy applied to the commercial banks. In particular, it seems clear that the spectacular growth of financieras following the 1954 devaluation created a serious problem for the monetary authorities because the operations of these institutions assumed a progressively more important influence in the money and capital market and thereby on the behavior of interest rates, the aggregate level of expenditures, the price level, and the balance of international payments. The additional liquidity introduced into the financial system by the financieras clearly compounded the difficulty of maintaining domestic stability and external equilibrium.

The problem presented by the large-scale growth of quasi-money can be summarized as follows. In the first place, to the extent that quasi-monetary instruments were capable of serving as substitutes for money, their issuance would tend to reduce demand for money balances held for speculative purposes—or, in other words, to increase the velocity of monetary circulation. By freeing money balances for transactions purposes, in effect financieras and other institutions issuing quasi-monetary claims would be able to augment the effective money supply. As will be recalled, however, the statistical evidence shows that the growth in quasi-money was not associated with a secular increase in the income velocity of money circulation, suggesting that the problem was that of a potential rather than an actual substitution of quasi-money for money balances and, ultimately, other things. The important problem presented by the growth of quasi-money was, therefore, the increased danger of large-scale liquidation—liquidation motivated by desire on the part of wealth holders either to convert their financial claims into goods (thereby producing inflationary pressures in the domestic market) or to convert these domestic claims into claims denominated in foreign currencies (thereby supporting adverse speculation against the peso). Given the concern on the part of the monetary authorities to avoid further inflation and devaluation, and given the established policies of supporting the market values of virtually all financial claims and of maintaining free convertibility of the peso into foreign currencies at fixed rates of exchange, the only available means of defending against the potential disrupting influence of further growth of quasi-money was extension of controls to issuing institutions.

EXTENSION OF CONTROLS

As we have previously seen, the measures adopted consisted principally of extension of the system of selective controls, originally applied only to commercial banks, to include the financieras and also the savings and mortgage-lending institutions. The effect of this action was to reduce to some extent the advantage which these institutions had come to hold over the commercial banks in competing for deposits and other sorts of funds in the market, and also to divert some of the resources of these nonmonetary institutions to those applications deemed to be most consistent with the requirements of selected deficit spending units for noninflationary sources of credit— most notably the government and certain public sector enterprises.

In addition to extension of selective controls to encompass intermediary institutions accounting for the major share of quasi-money, an absolute limit on the annual rate of growth of financiera deposits and various other short-term, highly liquid obligations was introduced in 1960. The limit was set at 12 per cent per year with the intention of keeping the growth of these financiera obligations at rates below the secular trend, which in some prior years had reached rates of 30 per cent, while at the same time encouraging issues of long-term bonds. More fundamentally the purpose of this measure was to obviate the potential danger of large-scale liquidations by financiera depositors and the unsettling consequences which such a development would necessarily have entailed. The effect of this measure was to curtail the rate of financiera growth, but not to the 12 per cent rate since large amounts of deposit liabilities were converted into long-term bonds and additional new issues of these bonds were stimulated.

The imposition of a maximum limit on the growth rate of specified financiera obligations represented a radical departure from existing control techniques employed by Banco de México—a type of regulatory activity for which there existed no satisfactory basis on which to establish suitable criteria. Clearly, the intent of the authorities was to gain some further control over the volume of liquidity put into the system by the financieras and thereby to reduce the potential danger that Banco de México might be called on to support the liquidation of financiera obligations to finance speculation against the peso or to support an upward spiral of the domestic price level. However, in choosing between alternative rates of growth to impose, Banco de México was faced with the necessity of weighing various conflicting requirements against one another: namely, that of promoting a properly balanced development of financial institutions; that of assuring financially sound practices on the part of individual institutions; and that of appropriately facilitating the mobilization and allocation of resources necessary for financing overall economic development. It seems clear that the growth rate limitation imposed upon the financieras was arbitrarily chosen, and was not premised on sophisticated calculations of the various consequences and their relative importances.

The same 12 per cent annual growth rate limit applied to deposit obligations of the financieras was also applied to *cédulas hipotecarias* issued by mortgage-lending institutions located in Mexico City. Previously, Banco de México had been forced on several occasions to support these instruments in the market, especially in 1954, with the result that a sizable proportion of outstanding issues was acquired at heavy expense and under impropitious circumstances. The purpose of regulating the growth of *cédulas hipotecarias* was principally that of permitting Banco de México to dispose of the sizable share of outstanding issues it had accumulated and also to obviate the necessity of repeated support to maintain orderly market conditions. Clearly, however, a related consideration was that of preventing a situation in the future in which Banco de México might again be forced into supporting liquidations of these instruments made with the purpose of speculating against the peso. While the limitation imposed on the growth of *cédulas hipotecarias* was quite arbitrary, it did have the effect, on the one hand, of moderating subsequent temporary increases in issues of these instruments and, on the other hand, of inducing mortgage banks to be more judicious in their scrutiny of the economic merits of the various types of real estate collateral upon which these issues were based.

AN EVALUATION

Had Banco de México not extended its controls to savings banks, financieras, and mortgage-lending institutions, the effectiveness of the controls exercised over monetary institutions would have been even further reduced. Or, looked at another way, in the absence of controls imposed on the creation of quasi-money, the stringency of controls applied to the monetary institutions would have had to be greater in order to achieve the same degree of stabilizing influence. While the appropriateness of the selective controls, supplemented by limitations on the growth rates of selected liabilities, as applied to institutions responsible for large amounts of quasi-money is subject to question on other grounds, clearly these controls served to alleviate to some extent existing restraints on the effectiveness of traditional monetary controls—which, as we have already argued, were largely the product of the vulnerability of the Mexican financial system to external influences.

Even in spite of the extension of Banco de México controls to financieras and other large-scale issuers of quasi-money, these nonmonetary institutions continued to grow throughout the latter half of the 1950s at a substantially higher rate than did monetary system institutions. This is explained by the fact that the nonmonetary institutions, most notably the financieras, retained an advantage in the competition for funds because they continued to be able to utilize resources at their disposal for financing activities producing higher returns. Furthermore, while the extension of controls clearly had the effect of diminishing issues of short-term financiera obligations and *cédulas hipotecarias*, it failed to arrest the growth of quasi-money as a whole. Consequently, as issues of other types of quasi-monetary instruments were accelerated, the liquidity of the system continued to increase, and along with this there was the continued danger to the commodity and foreign exchange markets posed by the possibility of large-scale liquidations of quasi-monetary claims.

Assurance of the liquidity of quasi-monetary claims was dependent upon continued underwriting by Banco de México. While there is no evidence to suggest that serious consideration was given to the possibility of withholding official support from the markets for these instruments, it did become clear during the latter half of the 1950s that continuation of this policy (which was intended to assure orderly conditions in the financial markets and thereby to promote the development of these markets) had significant undesirable consequences. In effect the problem confronting the authorities was that of choosing between the risks inherent in abandoning the long-standing practice of supporting the market values of nonmonetary financial instruments and the risks inherent in permitting continuation of rapid growth in the outstanding volume of quasi-money. As we shall see, since 1960 the practice of supporting market values at par has been curtailed, thereby reducing to some extent the liquidity of quasi-monetary claims.

Monetarist-Structuralist Controversy

Our analysis of the problem of maintaining, or re-establishing, internal financial stability and external payments equilibrium in the Mexican circumstances leads to conclusions concerning the efficacy of monetary policy which are at odds with the prescriptions offered by both the so-called monetarists and structuralists. Consequently it may be useful to state explicitly in what respects we differ with these competing orthodoxies—useful because it forces us to relate our conclusions to the issues raised in the controversy which has developed between representatives of these two viewpoints, and perhaps also because we may be able to throw some new light, based on study of Mexico's experience, on issues which have been too long obscured by doctrinal differences.

THE PROTAGONISTS

The monetarist and structuralist positions are best represented by two agencies of the United Nations, namely the International Monetary Fund (IMF) and the Economic Commission for Latin America (ECLA). The controversy which has developed between these two agencies is centered on the question of the relationship between monetary stability and economic development. However, much more is involved than differences in analysis and judgment of a strictly economic or technical sort pertaining to this question, and the controversy is in fact rooted in fundamental differences of an ideological sort. The monetarists attach great importance to the free functioning of markets and the price mechanism as the appropriate means for achieving an efficient allocation of productive resources and thereby the highest possible sustainable rate of economic growth. The structuralists, on the other hand, are less impressed with the efficacy of free-market forces and evidence a preference for conscious interference with the operation of the price mechanism based on plans designed to overcome what are believed to be the inherent limitations of market forces within the Latin American context. Clearly, basic political and doctrinal issues are involved in the monetarist-structuralist controversy, but for our purposes it is better to leave these aside and to focus instead on unresolved differences of a technical, analytical sort pertaining to financial aspects of the process of economic development.

ANALYSIS AND POLICY PRESCRIPTIONS

A basic tenet of the monetarist argument is that inflation distorts market processes and the allocation of productive factors in such a manner as to reduce efficiency and overall economic development, and consequently monetarists place a high premium on price stability. Furthermore, they urge developing countries to adopt strong anti-inflationary policies in the belief that maintenance of stable exchange rates and free currency convertibility are essential to expansion of international trade and investment, upon which it is assumed economic improvement in the underdeveloped countries is dependent. According to the monetarist view, inflation and currency instability is a phenomenon which results from unwarranted expansion of money and credit, which in turn produces an excess of demand relative to the available supply of goods and services and thereby stimulates an upward spiral of prices. According to this view, the basic difficulty is attributable to insufficient restraint and inept application of the traditional quantitative instruments of monetary control on the part of monetary authorities in the various Latin American countries.

The structuralist explanation of inflation contrasts sharply with the monetarist thesis. Stated in simplest terms, it is the structuralist argument that increases on the side of demand and on the side of supply do not coincide because of factor immobility and other structural rigidities which characterize Latin American economies, and that chronic inflation is the product of resulting imbalances or bottlenecks which develop in the productive and distributive processes. In the circumstances envisaged by the structuralists, restraint in the expansion of money and credit is neither a necessary nor desirable means of dealing with the difficulty, and indeed they argue that such a policy may cause serious harm by preventing further growth in the productive capacity of certain sectors of the economy vital to the overall development process. For the structuralists inflation is a symptom and not a cause of the difficulties confronted by Latin American countries in attempting to achieve improvement in their economic circumstances, and consequently, according to the structuralist view, it would be a serious mistake to emphasize the goal of domestic monetary stability and external financial equilibrium at the expense of efforts to correct the more fundamental structural impediments to economic growth and development.

As is to be expected, the policy prescriptions offered by proponents of the monetarist and structuralist viewpoints vary as widely as do their respective diagnoses of the problem. The monetarists are inclined to advocate orthodox monetary and fiscal policies designed to produce price stability and free currency convertibility at fixed rates of exchange, believing that by these means efficient allocation of resources would be facilitated and the maximum sustainable rate of economic growth would be achieved. The structuralists, on the other hand, favor the use of more comprehensive and direct techniques of economic planning to overcome rigidities in specific commodity and factor markets which are supposed to limit capital formation of an appropriate sort and otherwise to inhibit the process of economic growth and development. Stated in even more simple terms, structuralists focus upon conditions in the commodity and factor markets and are willing to tolerate the consequences of financial instability necessary to achieve the improvements they seek to effect, while the monetarists focus upon conditions in the money and capital markets and are confident that beneficial adjustments in the commodity and factor markets will work themselves out if a stable financial environment is assured.

Both the monetarist and structuralist arguments are premised on the assumption (not often explicitly stated) that the monetary authorities are faced with the necessity of choosing between restrictive policies designed to prevent inflation and expansionist policies designed to remove structural imbalances. However, neither party to the controversy bothers to consider whether or not in practice such a choice really exists, i.e., whether or not the authorities really are able to control the rate of monetary and credit expansion and thereby the level of interest rates and aggregate expenditures. Our analysis of Mexican experience suggest that failure to consider this question represents a vital missing link in both arguments. As a result of this omission each side is led to embrace a polar position. Stated in terms of the concepts and relationships developed in connection with our discussion of Figure 5-C, the monetarists appear to believe that it is impossible to escape falling into the foreign exchange liquidity trap when expansionist monetary policies are followed, while the structuralists appear to believe that expansionist monetary policies can be followed without any danger of falling into the foreign exchange liquidity trap. Of course circumstances can be imagined in which either the monetarist or the structuralist position may be the correct one, but surely neither view of the matter possesses universal validity. The factors governing the supply of and demand for money need to be investigated for each country and under differing circumstances before an informed judgment can be made regarding the powers of a monetary authority and the consequences of one particular course of action or another—and this sort of analysis neither party to the controversy has evidenced any willingness to undertake.

MEXICAN SYNTHESIS

For reasons we have previously attempted to explain, Mexican monetary policy is premised on a combination of conventional quantitative controls of an indirect sort and of various selective and other types of direct controls aimed at achieving domestic stability and external stability without unduly restricting public investment expenditures and other programs designed to overcome structural imbalances inhibiting economic growth and development. The fundamental objective of this system of controls is to provide a sufficient check on consumption and low-priority investment expenditures to permit achievement of financial stability while at the same time providing adequate financing for investment projects deemed to be essential to removal of structural impediments to further growth of the economy. In short, the system of controls devised by the Mexican authorities are intended to prevent the excess demand feared by the monetarists while at the same time permitting large-scale investment expenditures of the sort advocated by the structuralists. This is not to say that the Mexicans have hit upon an ideal balance, or that there are not serious deficiencies in the Mexican system, but rather the intent of these observations is to illustrate how the Mexican experiences and circumstances have combined to bring about an imperfect but workable synthesis (or compromise) of the different policies advocated by dogmatists of both the monetarist and structuralist persuasion.

FINAL COMMENT

It is indeed unfortunate that the IMF and the ECLA—both branches of the same corpus—in attempting to carry out their responsibilities to provide expert counsel to Latin American countries should find it necessary to offer such dissimiliar and often flatly contradictory advice concerning the relationship between financial stability and economic development. In the same way that the ECLA has been insufficiently sensitive to the disastrous consequences which can follow from inadequate concern for financial stability, the IMF has been too unwilling to admit the legitimacy of employing selective credit controls and other planning techniques to cope with the fundamentally important problem of structural imbalance. The fact that both of these agencies are partially supported by Latin American countries and that the resources put at their disposal have been dissipated in internecine warfare and in coercing various countries to follow policies not of their own choosing, and often against their own best interests, instead of for more constructive purposes makes the situation all the more distressing. Surely the Latin American countries, and all member countries for that matter, are entitled to expect that in the future every effort will be made to develop guides to action which are both theoretically respectable and practically applicable to the dual problems of monetary instability and structural imbalances confronted by all Latin American countries.

Conclusion

In this chapter we have attempted to explain the nature of the problem Mexico has encountered in its efforts to maintain domestic monetary stability and external financial equilibrium as well as the rationale of the various policies and techniques of control employed in an effort to achieve the stabilization goal without unduly restraining the growth and development of the overall economy. We have shown that because of this interdependence of conditions in the markets for goods and for money and other financial claims, as well as because of the interrelationships between conditions in domestic and foreign markets (both financial markets and goods markets), destabilizing influences originating in any one sector of the economy are readily transferred to other sectors and the economic system as a whole. We have focused our attention on the limitations of conventional or orthodox monetary policies in the Mexican circumstances, finding that the power of the monetary authorities to effectively carry out the stabilization function by means of these policies is limited at best. We find, however, that by means of various selective and other direct controls the Mexican authorities have been able to overcome some of the difficulties which seem to be inherent in the simultaneous pursuit of the goals of financial stabilization and of rapid economic growth. Finally, we have concluded that the record of Mexican experience and achievement in attempting to cope with the dual problems of monetary stability and economic development has relevance to the so-called monetarist-structuralist controversy which has received so much attention in recent years.

Our purpose has been to offer a satisfactory theoretical explanation of the stabilization problem and of the various policies designed to promote stability without unduly limiting growth. However, we have not as yet offered any systematic explanation of the institutional development, changes in the structure of financial claims, and of the nature of processes at work in the money and capital market. We shall attempt in the following chapter to remedy this remaining deficiency in our explanation of Mexican financial development during the period 1940–1960.

CHAPTER VI

FINANCIAL PROCESSES AND ECONOMIC GROWTH

Introduction

IN FOREGOING CHAPTERS we have described the Mexican monetary and financial system, the policies and institutions governing its operation, and its development over time. We have reviewed the record of Mexican financial experience during the period 1940–1960, with emphasis on relationships between the degree of financial stability achieved and the pattern of fund flows. In particular, in the immediately preceding chapter we offered an explanation of relationships between the monetary and financial policies of the government and the record of domestic stability and external equilibrium. It remains to analyze the operation of the financial system as a whole and the relation of financial processes to output growth, and this is the task to which we turn in the present chapter.

More specifically, in this chapter we attempt to formulate a satisfactory explanation of three of the most outstanding characteristics of recent Mexican financial development: the pattern of growth in domestic indebtedness, the changing nature of financial intermediation, and the behavior of liquidity and yields in the money and capital market. We endeavor to demonstrate interrelationships between these phenomena and also between financial processes generally and the behavior of such variables as prices and interest rates, savings and capital formation, and overall economic growth.

Our analysis of the record of Mexican financial development requires reformulation of the statistical data already discussed in earlier chapters. For readers not already familiar with the somewhat unconventional concepts and measures employed, some attention to definitions and methodology will be necessary. Our procedure necessarily involves a certain amount of repetition, but it nevertheless seems to be justified, not only because it permits the record of recent Mexican financial development to be concisely summarized but also because it reveals patterns in this development not otherwise readily apparent.

Growth of Domestic Indebtedness

Domestic indebtedness consists of two sorts, obligations of ultimate borrowers, which we designate as direct debt, and obligations of financial intermediaries to ultimate lenders, which we designate as indirect debt. Ultimate borrowers are the nonfinancial deficit-spending units in the economy, and direct debt therefore consists of the total outstanding volume of financial obligations of government, public enterprises, and private enterprises and individuals— whether to ultimate lenders or financial institutions. Similarly, ultimate lenders are the nonfinancial surplus-spending units in the economy, and indirect debt therefore consists of the total outstanding obligations of financial intermediary institutions to government, public enterprises, and private enterprises and individuals. We shall first review the pattern of growth in direct debt before turning to consideration of the behavior of indirect debt.

DIRECT DEBT

Estimates of the growth of direct debt during the period under consideration are shown in Table VI-A. The data include all outstanding fixed-interest obligations of government and of enterprises and individuals as recorded by the Comisión Nacional de Valores, and all other claims on government and enterprises and individuals held by banking system institutions as recorded by Banco de México. An indeterminable amount of direct indebtedness taking the form of credits from other than banking system institutions, of equity securities held outside the banking system, and of interpersonal loans is not included in the figures; however, these latter types of indebtedness are pre-

TABLE VI-A

STRUCTURE OF DOMESTIC INDEBTEDNESS, 1940–1960

(Millions of pesos)

Year	Direct Debt[a] Origin Total	Origin Government	Origin Enterprises and Individuals	Type Fixed-Interest Securities	Type Other Banking System Credits	Indirect Debt[b] Origin Total	Origin Monetary System	Origin Non-monetary Institutions	Type Money	Type Quasi-Money	Type Other
1940	1,290.6	466.2	824.4	520.7	769.9	1,728.0	1,282.3	445.7	1,060.4	397.9	269.7
1941	1,789.4	623.9	1,165.5	734.3	1,055.1	2,130.8	1,525.6	605.2	1,269.5	539.2	322.1
1942	2,228.2	821.2	1,407.0	974.4	1,253.9	2,808.9	2,018.1	790.8	1,749.9	693.0	366.0
1943	2,758.6	956.4	1,802.2	1,150.3	1,608.3	4,063.5	2,989.3	1,074.2	2,672.9	981.5	409.1
1944	3,089.9	762.5	2,315.0	1,047.7	2,042.2	5,137.1	3,727.1	1,410.0	3,279.9	1,353.7	503.5
1945	3,963.9	974.9	2,989.0	1,362.2	2,601.7	5,982.2	4,041.7	1,940.5	3,539.5	1,887.7	555.0
1946	5,040.5	1,320.5	3,720.0	1,894.1	3,146.4	6,180.6	3,998.2	2,182.4	3,460.8	2,084.6	635.2
1947	5,816.4	1,390.9	4,425.5	2,039.1	3,777.3	6,601.0	4,065.9	2,535.1	3,438.7	2,425.6	736.7
1948	6,945.4	1,628.8	5,316.6	2,315.3	4,630.1	7,812.1	4,721.3	3,090.8	3,916.9	3,011.5	883.7
1949	8,146.7	2,180.2	5,966.5	3,122.3	5,024.4	9,354.5	5,296.1	4,058.4	4,352.9	3,589.7	1,411.9
1950	9,286.4	2,127.8	7,158.6	3,261.8	6,024.6	11,456.4	6,868.5	4,587.9	5,988.5	4,131.6	1,336.3
1951	11,155.4	1,915.4	9,240.0	3,227.8	7,927.6	13,619.2	7,815.8	5,803.4	6,800.9	5,432.8	1,385.5
1952	12,556.3	2,283.5	10,272.8	3,838.1	8,718.2	14,595.2	8,371.7	6,223.5	7,073.0	6,000.6	1,516.4
1953	14,425.1	2,302.0	12,123.1	4,118.8	10,306.3	16,312.1	8,925.0	7,387.1	7,652.9	7,020.1	1,639.1
1954	18,013.2	2,973.0	15,040.2	5,333.9	12,679.3	20,539.4	10,664.3	9,875.1	8,723.5	9,766.1	2,049.8
1955	19,933.7	3,057.6	16,876.1	6,024.2	13,909.5	24,114.0	12,760.7	11,353.3	10,516.8	10,920.2	2,677.0
1956	22,755.3	3,382.7	19,372.6	6,594.9	16,160.4	27,306.5	14,153.2	13,153.3	11,692.2	12,229.8	3,384.5
1957	25,917.1	3,905.5	22,011.6	7,647.7	18,269.4	29,862.2	15,471.2	14,391.0	12,493.4	13,879.6	3,489.2
1958	30,600.2	4,628.8	25,971.4	10,072.0	20,528.2	32,971.6	16,310.4	16,661.2	13,386.9	16,340.0	3,244.7
1959	36,503.5	4,965.9	31,537.6	11,050.6	25,452.9	38,015.9	18,108.7	19,907.2	15,434.3	18,755.9	3,825.7
1960	45,397.0	7,498.2	37,898.8	12,880.0	32,517.0	45,227.3	19,516.3	25,711.0	16,909.3	24,402.8	3,915.2

Source: Annual reports of Banco de México, S.A., and the Comisión Nacional de Valores.

a Includes outstanding fixed-interest securities issued by government and enterprises and individuals as reported by Comisión Nacional de Valores and banking system credits other than those represented by fixed-interest securities as reported by Banco de México.
b Includes all obligations of banking system institutions to government and to enterprises and individuals.

sumed to constitute a relatively small percentage of the total amount outstanding.

As shown in the table, recorded direct indebtedness increased from about 1.3 billion pesos in 1940 to about 45.4 billion pesos in 1960—an increase from 17.7 per cent to 33.8 per cent of gross national product, for these two years respectively. The growth in recorded direct indebtedness relative to gross national product was substantially greater between 1955 and 1960 than during the earlier period. Another characteristic, evident from the figures, of the growth pattern of direct indebtedness is a tendency for the share of the total accounted for by enterprises and individuals to increase relative to the share accounted for by government. In 1940 enterprises and individuals accounted for about 65 per cent of the total while by 1960 this proportion had risen to nearly 85 per cent. Finally, short- and intermediate-term banking system credits accounted for most of direct debt throughout the period, and the share of the total accounted for by outstanding fixed-interest securities evidenced a tendency to decline, falling from 40 per cent in 1940 to less than 30 per cent in 1960. What is the explanation of these developments?

The basic explanation of the growth of direct debt relative to national product is found in the institutional fact that deficit spending was a regular occurrence in the government and enterprise sectors of the economy while surpluses were regularly achieved by nonbusiness spending units in the private sector whose current income was in excess of that required for financing consumption and household investment expenditures. These surpluses were made available to deficit spending units either with or without the intermediation of financial institutions. In either case, direct indebtedness of the chronic deficit sectors cumulatively increased. If there had been no regularity in this pattern, and instead government and enterprises were alternatingly deficit and then surplus sectors, and the same situation had prevailed for nonbusiness spending units in the private sector, direct debt would have tended to be self-canceling and would not have grown in the cumulative fashion which we find. Clearly, then, one explanation of the growth pattern of direct debt is the characteristic distribution of income and spending which prevailed during the period under consideration.

The tendency for enterprises and individuals to account for an increasing share of direct debt indicates on the one hand an increasing willingness of lenders to hold debt instruments of the sort enterprises and individuals were capable of issuing and on the other hand an increasing reliance upon deficit financing on the part of these spending units. It is apparent that the growth of industrial and commercial activity and the increased amounts of credit made available to finance construction and expansion of productive capacity, as well as inventories and purchases of consumer durable goods, were closely interrelated phenomena.

It should be noted that the decline which occurred in the proportion of direct debt accounted for by government does not imply a corresponding decline in the contribution of the public sector as a whole to the growth of direct indebtedness. While the available statistics do not permit the portion of the increase in direct debt accounted for by public enterprises to be readily distinguished from that accounted for by private enterprises and individuals, it nevertheless is clear that the contribution of public enterprises increased continuously throughout the period and that consequently the share of total direct debt accounted for by the public sector as a whole declined to a lesser extent than did the share accounted for by government alone. Indeed, when the evidence produced in Chapter IV (see especially Table IV-F) is considered in conjunction with the figures shown in Table VI-A, it appears that during the 1955–1960 period the indebtedness of the public sector as a whole may have increased relative to that of the private sector, reflecting the diversion of credit resources from private to public sector which was examined in detail in the earlier chapter. During the same period the composition of domestically held public debt changed as securities issues and other borrowing by public enterprises increased relative to borrowing by government. These developments are attributable on the one hand to the increased amounts of deficit financing required to support public investment expenditures and on the other hand to policy changes which required public enterprises to depend to a greater extent upon their own financial arrangements.

The final characteristic of the pattern of direct indebtedness deserving of comment is the heavy dependence of enterprises and individuals on short- and intermediate-term banking system credits. It seems reasonable to suppose that the principal explanation of this situation is to be found, throughout most of the period, in limited availability of long-term financing. So long as lenders anticipated inflation and periodic devaluation, they would be understandably reluctant to enter into long-term contracts except at such high interest rates as to be prohibitive to borrowers. Long-term credits tended to be restricted to government and to public enterprises accorded preferential access to the limited amount of available funds, and other borrowers were forced to depend almost wholly on shorter-term credit arrangements. However, during the period of rising interest rates and relatively stable prices, the proportion of total direct debt accounted for by banking system credits increased only slightly, reflecting increased activity in the long-term end of the credit market.

INDIRECT DEBT

The movement of funds from ultimate lenders to ultimate borrowers depended heavily upon acquisitions of direct-debt claims by financial intermediary institutions. These institutions, in turn, depended upon issues of their own obligations to ultimate lenders as their principal source of loanable funds. In addition, financial institutions incurred a growing volume of obligations to one another, and consequently the total amount of their indebtedness (indirect debt plus intrasystem claims) increased by more than did indebtedness to ultimate lenders alone. We shall later consider the growth pattern of intrasystem obligations within the context of our examination of the development of techniques of financial intermediation, but first it is convenient to discuss the behavior of indirect debt.

Shown in Table VI-A is a breakdown of the indirect indebtedness of all banking system institutions. Comparable data for insurance companies, social security trust funds, and the various other so-called auxiliary institutions are not available—and therefore the figures understate to some extent the total volume of outstanding indirect debt. However, the data for indirect debt are more comprehensive than those for direct debt. This can be seen from the fact that total obligations of financial institutions to ultimate lenders exceeded the total recorded indebtedness of ultimate borrowers for most of the period. By definition, direct debt must be at least equal to indirect debt and, unless all debt obligations of ultimate borrowers are held by financial intermediaries, direct debt must exceed indirect debt. Were comprehensive data available they would necessarily show that direct debt exceeded the indirect debt throughout the period. They probably also would reveal that during the earlier part of the period indirect debt was nearly as large as direct debt (indicating that practically all direct debt was held by financial intermediaries), and that in the latter part of the period indirect debt increased a little less rapidly than direct debt (indicating that a somewhat larger proportion of direct debt came to be held by ultimate lenders). While it is difficult to estimate, it seems reasonable to suppose that by 1960 the total indebtedness of ultimate borrowers exceeded total indirect indebtedness by no less than 30 per cent and perhaps by substantially more.

In any case it is clear that financial intermediaries were the locus of the loanable funds market throughout the period under consideration, that ultimate borrowers and lenders dealt directly with one another to only a limited extent, and that deficit-spending units were financed largely by means of funds obtained from banking system institutions. A principal explanation of the overwhelming importance of indirect financing is that the kinds of financial claims lenders preferred to hold differed from the kinds of financial obligations borrowers preferred to assume so that financial intermediaries, because of their ability to convert financial instruments from one form to another, were able to effect the necessary linkage between surplus- and deficit-spending units. Thus, for example, ultimate lenders had a strong preference for monetary and quasi-monetary claims which only the banking system institutions were capable of issuing, and were not much interested in holding bonds, mortgages, and other debt instruments which could be issued by government, public enterprises, and ultimate borrowers in the private sector.

However, to the extent that outstanding indirect debt did decline as a percentage of direct debt in the latter part of the period, ultimate lenders evidenced an increased willingness to hold claims on ultimate borrowers. This development was associated with innovations in direct debt instruments, with shifts in the preferences of borrowers and lenders resulting from changes in market conditions and prevailing expectations, and with an increase in the volume of direct transactions between borrowers and lenders. However, it also reflects a change which occurred in the character of financial intermediation. As ultimate lenders became more receptive to direct securities, financial intermediaries began to market previously acquired holdings instead of relying exclusively on additional issues of their own obligations as the means of mobilizing funds for purchasing additional direct securities for their own accounts. By so doing the intermediaries continued to serve as the principal channel through which funds moved from ultimate lenders to ultimate borrowers, but without leaving quite so large a residue relative to earlier years in the form of indirect debt. Furthermore, by occasionally acting as dealers in direct debt the intermediaries served to bolster the development of the money and capital market—making available to both borrowers and lenders the benefits of their superior ability to appraise the quality of direct debt instruments (and in some cases lending their guarantee to such instruments), as well as their superior distributional facilities.

The most outstanding change which occurred over the period in the structure of indirect indebtedness is reflected in the declining share originating in the monetary system. As shown in Table VI-A, in 1940 the monetary system accounted for 74.2 per cent of recorded indirect debt obligations while in 1960 the comparable figure was 43.6 per cent. This development, of course, was associated with a decline in the importance of money relative to nonmonetary indirect debt. In 1940 money accounted for 61.3 per cent of recorded indirect indebtedness, the balance being accounted for by other sorts of banking system obligations to ultimate lenders; by 1960 these proportions were nearly reversed with nonmonetary claims accounting for 62.6 per cent and money for 37.4 per cent of the total.

There are several separate but related explanations of the relative decline of the monetary system and of money in the process of financial intermediation. The first relates to the policy followed by the government and the central bank of supporting the market values of a wide range of nonmonetary financial claims, according them a high degree of liquidity, and thereby making them close money substitutes. This policy worked to gradually overcome reluctance on the part of ultimate lenders to hold claims other than money (in much the same fashion as a greater willingness to hold deposit claims instead of coin and currency, and coin and currency instead of full-bodied metallic money, had developed during earlier periods). A second explanatory factor is found in the relatively high yields obtainable on many types of nonmonetary claims and the consequent high opportunity cost of holding one's assets in money form. A third factor was that certain nonmonetary claims (principally deposits denominated in foreign currencies) afforded protection from the risk of currency devaluation as well as an attractive yield, and were consequently preferred to money and other sorts of claims by certain classes of lenders.

This interpretation of the decline in the relative importance of money is incomplete, however, without some further explanation of the reasons for supporting the prices of nonmonetary claims in the market and for permitting the sizable growth of foreign currency deposits which occurred. The reason for the policy of underwriting

the liquidity of a wide range of indirect financial assets was, on the
one hand, to develop confidence on the part of lenders and thereby
to promote the development of the money and capital market and,
on the other hand, to forestall market disorders which might prove
disruptive to the operation of the monetary and financial system and
the overall economy. Once adopted, the support policy proved difficult to abandon and was continued with only minor modifications
throughout the whole period. It perhaps should be added in this
connection that this policy had detrimental as well as beneficial
effects—especially in the latter part of the period, when greater free-
dom to employ traditional monetary policy measures based on adjustments in the yields of outstanding financial instruments became
desirable. In the case of foreign currency deposits, their growth was
permitted so that wealth holders could hedge against the risk of devaluation within the country instead of transferring funds to foreign
financial markets, with a consequent drain on foreign exchange
reserves.

Development of Financial Intermediation

We have seen that the movement of funds between
ultimate lenders and ultimate borrowers depended heavily upon the
linkage provided by financial intermediaries throughout the entire
period under consideration. The character of this linkage changed
with the growth which occurred in the volume of funds moving
through the financial system as new techniques of intermediation
were developed in response to changes in the policies of the government and the central bank and to changes in preferences of borrowers
and lenders and in the loanable funds market.

Before turning to an examination of the processes of financial intermediation, it may be worthwhile to briefly summarize relevant
points developed in Chapter IV. We found that the monetary system
declined in relative importance in the intermediary process as both
Banco de México and the private deposit banks provided a progressively smaller share of the deficit financing of government, public
enterprises, and the private sector proper. The relative importance of
nonmonetary institutions correspondingly increased, the growth in
the volume of funds moving through these institutions being
especially marked in the years 1956–1960. Numerous changes were
noted in the sources and uses of funds moving through the financial
system. On the sources side the most significant were a growing re-

liance on issues of quasi-monetary claims and an increasing volume of intrasystem fund flows. On the uses side, the most significant were an increased volume of credit to the government sector on the part of all credit institutions other than Banco de México, and assumption by the various nonmonetary credit institutions (especially Nacional Financiera and the private financieras) of increasing responsibility for financing deficits of enterprises and individuals.

GROWTH OF INTERMEDIARY INSTITUTIONS

The volume of funds channeled to ultimate borrowers by intermediary institutions is largely reflected in the direct-debt holdings of these institutions. However, because these institutions occasionally act as dealers in direct-debt instruments, buying such instruments and subsequently selling them, evidence of their intermediary function is not fully revealed by an examination of their balance sheets. Similarly, the volume of funds mobilized from ultimate borrowers is reflected in the outstanding volume of the indirect-debt obligations of intermediary institutions as shown in their balance sheets—again except for instances in which funds are raised by selling previously acquired direct-debt instruments. Obviously, for all financial intermediary institutions taken together, the growth of direct-debt claims must approximate fairly closely the growth of indirect-debt obligations. However, for individual institutions and groups of institutions the growth in primary-debt claims and indirect-debt obligations is often unequal because a substantial volume of funds is either received from or directed to other intermediary institutions, resulting in sizable intrasystem net debtor or net creditor positions.

These remarks are intended to assist the reader in interpreting the data shown in Table VI-B. The table shows the amounts of direct-debt claims, of indirect-debt obligations, and of net intrasystem indebtedness for the banking system as a whole, as well as for the major component parts of the system. The peso value of the indirect-debt obligations of the banking system as a whole increased by more than six times during the 1940–1950 period, and during each of the two subsequent five-year periods (1951–1955 and 1956–1960) there was, roughly speaking, a further doubling of banking system obligations held by ultimate lenders. By the end of 1960 the undeflated value of outstanding indirect-debt obligations of the banking system was in excess of twenty-five times the value of these obligations at the end of 1940. A similar but somewhat more rapid growth occurred

TABLE VI-B

CLAIMS AND OBLIGATIONS OF FINANCIAL INTERMEDIARIES, 1940–1960

(Millions of pesos)

	All Banking System Institutions			Monetary System — Banco de México			Monetary System — Deposit Banks			Nonmonetary Institutions — National			Nonmonetary Institutions — Private		
Year	Direct-Debt Claims[a]	Indirect Debt Obligations[b]	Net Intra-system Claims[c]	Direct-Debt Claims[a]	Indirect Debt Obligations[b]	Net Intra-system Claims[c]	Direct-Debt Claims[a]	Indirect Debt Obligations[b]	Net Intra-system Claims[c]	Direct-Debt Claims[a]	Indirect Debt Obligations[b]	Net Intra-system Claims[c]	Direct-Debt Claims[a]	Indirect Debt Obligations[b]	Net Intra-system Claims[c]
1940	1,141.3	1,728.0	8.6	391.5	741.3	−235.3	339.0	541.0	202.1	280.3	289.7	19.5	130.5	156.0	22.3
1941	1,597.2	2,130.8	−13.7	542.1	865.6	−227.7	473.0	659.7	173.0	378.8	388.9	30.5	203.3	216.3	10.5
1942	2,105.7	2,808.9	−26.0	726.9	1,118.4	−345.1	557.8	899.7	331.0	472.6	415.5	−43.7	348.4	375.3	31.8
1943	2,661.5	4,063.5	−97.0	735.1	1,565.6	−686.9	753.7	1,423.7	670.9	704.1	537.1	−155.9	468.6	537.1	74.9
1944	3,332.0	5,137.1	−28.0	1,049.3	1,911.1	−883.5	858.5	1,821.0	906.4	744.4	630.4	−162.6	679.8	774.6	111.7
1945	4,243.1	5,982.2	−8.8	1,163.1	1,803.3	−1,038.5	1,018.0	2,238.4	1,154.7	1,074.3	850.5	−234.0	987.9	1,090.0	108.8
1946	5,121.1	6,180.6	−65.9	1,575.8	1,874.5	−771.3	1,048.3	2,123.7	1,014.8	1,284.4	1,010.8	−264.0	1,212.6	1,171.6	−45.4
1947	5,933.3	6,601.0	−36.9	1,764.2	2,008.6	−447.9	1,228.7	2,057.3	811.3	1,484.3	1,235.1	−232.2	1,456.1	1,300.0	−168.1
1948	7,211.8	7,812.1	−48.6	2,218.3	2,411.7	−404.5	1,469.1	2,309.6	799.2	1,936.5	1,616.0	−309.7	1,587.9	1,475.2	−133.6
1949	8,283.3	9,354.5	−70.4	2,213.2	2,752.4	−499.5	1,627.2	2,543.7	851.0	2,762.6	2,445.5	−323.9	1,680.3	1,612.9	−98.0
1950	9,467.3	11,456.4	−366.0	2,149.5	3,128.2	−1,651.4	2,241.0	3,740.3	1,946.9	3,256.4	2,750.4	−364.1	1,820.4	1,837.5	−297.4
1951	11,004.0	13,619.2	32.1	2,125.9	3,699.7	−868.0	2,572.0	4,116.1	1,506.5	3,955.8	3,437.6	−613.2	2,350.3	2,365.8	6.8
1952	12,202.7	14,595.2	−141.5	2,397.1	3,923.7	−767.0	2,678.7	4,448.0	1,680.2	4,339.6	3,523.4	−971.5	2,787.3	2,700.1	−83.2
1953	14,045.6	16,312.1	−400.8	2,808.6	3,106.4	−778.5	3,121.7	4,818.6	1,650.3	5,361.2	4,272.9	−1,631.9	2,754.1	3,114.2	359.3
1954	17,257.6	20,539.4	245.1	3,345.0	4,896.6	−953.4	3,674.4	5,767.7	1,973.4	6,921.8	6,327.3	−1,040.2	3,316.4	3,547.8	265.3
1955	18,510.9	24,114.0	−14.3	2,481.4	5,537.5	−1,853.1	4,608.8	7,223.2	2,459.5	7,365.8	6,930.4	−1,114.6	4,055.4	4,422.9	493.4
1956	20,932.8	27,306.5	205.2	2,579.4	6,383.7	−1,864.7	5,210.6	7,769.5	2,492.5	7,857.4	7,509.0	−965.4	5,285.4	5,644.3	542.8
1957	24,003.2	29,862.2	−60.3	2,942.4	6,853.8	−1,739.1	5,365.6	8,617.4	3,191.3	8,932.8	7,424.5	−1,743.2	6,762.4	6,966.5	230.7
1958	27,956.9	32,971.6	−46.6	4,369.3	7,228.6	−1,856.6	5,565.0	9,081.8	3,179.9	10,402.8	8,690.8	−1,820.4	7,619.8	7,970.4	450.5
1959	32,700.1	38,015.9	111.3	4,331.1	7,876.5	−1,820.1	6,196.2	10,232.2	3,850.9	12,109.2	10,052.0	−1,926.0	9,963.6	9,855.2	6.5
1960	40,856.4	45,227.3	420.4	5,121.5	8,571.9	−1,657.8	6,835.3	10,944.4	4,378.4	16,699.7	13,712.5	−2,334.2	12,386.8	12,053.3	55.2

Source: Annual reports of Banco de México, S.A.

a Includes claims on government and enterprises and individuals.
b Includes obligations to government and enterprises and individuals.
c Difference between claims on other banking system institutions and obligations to other banking system institutions. Minus sign indicates net obligations.

in the direct-debt holdings of banking system institutions, the unde-flated value of these claims increasing by more than thirty-five times between 1940 and 1960. Gross national product in current prices increased by only about eighteen times over the same period.

This growth of the indirect debt obligations and the direct debt claims of banking institutions relative to the value of current output reflects the fact that financial intermediation tended to become in-creasingly important in the industrial and commercial life of the country as well as in the fiscal operations of government. The main stimulus to the growth of financial intermediation emanated from the industrial, commercial, and consumer demand for credit and banking services, as evidenced by the fact that obligations to enter-prises and individuals accounted for the major share of the indirect indebtedness of banking system institutions, amounting to around 90 per cent of the total over the whole period.

This statement might appear to contradict our previous findings that in the latter part of the 1950s credit became progressively more scarce and costly in the private sector as loan funds were diverted from the financing of government sector deficits. Unquestionably the loanable funds market became progressively tighter, and cer-tainly there occurred a substantial diversion of the credit resources of private lending institutions. Indeed this last phenomenon is illus-trated by the data in Table VI-B, which show that the private deposit banks were substantial net intrasystem lenders while Banco de Méx-ico and the other national lending institutions were substantial net borrowers. The fact that private credit institutions acquired a grow-ing share of the outstanding debt obligations of the government sec-tor reflects this development even more clearly. Thus, while the major share of the indirect indebtedness of banking system institutions was consistently accounted for by enterprises and individuals, the tight-ness which developed in the loanable-funds market during the latter part of the 1950s was a product of both mounting demand for credit on the part of enterprises and individuals and a sizable diversion of the resources of private lending institutions to the government sector.

INTRASYSTEM INDEBTEDNESS

The transfer of funds from private to national credit institutions was not always effected directly. While the deposit banks were the main source of the intrasystem movement of funds, these funds often passed through the accounts of one or more intervening institutions in the process of moving from their origin within the system (i.e., from the institution incurring the original indebtedness to ultimate lenders) to their destination (i.e., the institution acquiring the relevant direct-debt claims from ultimate borrowers).

A practice which became common in the latter half of the 1950s was for funds to be channeled from deposit banks to private financieras, often by way of fiduciary institutions, and from there either to ultimate borrowers or national credit institutions. This process is illustrated by figures on intrasystem indebtedness of selected private banking system institutions shown in Table VI-C. As shown, the growth in intrasystem claims of the deposit banks regularly outpaced that of the intrasystem obligations of these institutions, with the result that a very sizable net creditor position developed over the period—and especially following imposition of the selective credit-controls beginning in 1949. Throughout the first half of the 1950s all but a relatively small portion of the intrasystem credits of the deposit banks apparently was channeled directly to national banking institutions. However, beginning in 1956 and throughout the remainder of the 1950s a growing volume of intrasystem credits was channeled through the private financieras—the majority of these credits originating with the deposit banks. This flow continued without interruption following application of the requirements of the selective credit-control program to the financieras in 1958, but thereafter the intrasystem claims of the financieras constituted a substantially larger percentage of the intrasystem obligations of these institutions reflecting a larger flow of funds from the financieras to the national credit institutions in accordance with the newly imposed regulations. Other specific instances could be cited of intrasystem movements of funds both among private institutions and among national institutions as well as between the two, but none would be so clear cut or as quantitatively important as that involving the financieras. Furthermore, the impact of the policies of the government and the central bank on the intrasystem movement of funds is more clearly evident in the case of the financieras than in any other instance we might choose to consider. It is important to recognize, however, that the development of the financieras and their overall role in the increasingly complex process of financial intermediation is not explainable wholly in terms of public policies, but requires in addition some attention to the effects of changes in the preferences of borrowers and lenders as well as to the influence of market forces.

TABLE VI-C

INTRASYSTEM CLAIMS AND OBLIGATIONS OF SELECTED PRIVATE BANKING SYSTEM INSTITUTIONS, 1940–1960[a]

(Millions of pesos)

Year	Deposit Banks			Financieras			Savings Institutions			Mortgage Banks		
	Claims	Obligations	Net	Claims	Obligations	Net	Claims	Obligations	Net	Claims	Obligations	Net
1940	271.4	69.3	202.1	2.7	—	2.7	13.1	.1	13.0	.5	7.3	−6.8
1941	280.0	107.0	173.0	1.9	2.8	−0.9	13.1	—	13.1	.6	16.7	−16.1
1942	495.3	164.3	331.0	17.7	27.6	−9.9	28.1	.6	27.5	10.5	17.7	−7.2
1943	872.7	201.8	670.9	42.0	58.2	−16.2	81.0	1.5	79.5	7.9	19.1	−11.2
1944	1,135.4	229.0	906.4	47.5	62.4	−14.9	104.4	.1	104.3	9.2	23.1	−13.9
1945	1,419.3	264.6	1,154.7	50.9	89.7	−38.8	139.1	.1	139.0	7.9	22.2	−14.3
1946	1,333.4	318.6	1,014.8	53.7	235.9	−182.2	126.9	.2	126.7	8.0	41.4	−33.4
1947	1,166.1	354.8	811.3	45.2	307.6	−262.4	100.2	.5	99.7	8.0	73.1	−65.1
1948	1,231.5	432.3	799.2	41.3	271.9	−230.6	125.1	6.2	118.9	9.3	96.3	−87.0
1949	1,320.6	469.6	851.0	40.8	286.0	−245.2	173.4	24.9	148.5	12.4	79.3	−66.9
1950	2,230.7	283.8	1,946.9	46.6	346.6	−300.0	240.5	10.8	229.7	16.1	63.3	−47.2
1951	2,095.8	589.3	1,506.5	65.1	450.9	−385.8	330.6	2.1	228.5	14.4	54.8	−40.4
1952	2,247.9	567.7	1,608.2	80.9	575.8	−494.9	363.7	33.4	330.3	21.4	66.6	−45.2
1953	2,317.2	666.9	1,650.3	72.7	238.4	−165.7	448.0	34.8	413.2	33.9	60.6	−26.7
1954	2,723.5	750.1	1,973.4	83.8	305.1	−221.3	477.0	34.7	442.3	27.9	126.1	−98.2
1955	3,275.6	816.1	2,459.5	136.2	325.9	−189.7	596.0	37.6	558.4	55.6	86.1	−30.5
1956	3,440.7	948.2	2,492.5	140.4	481.2	−340.8	743.0	7.2	735.8	62.9	82.5	−19.6
1957	4,178.8	987.5	3,191.3	272.8	701.6	−428.8	698.7	0.4	698.3	73.6	126.9	−53.3
1958	4,474.7	1,294.8	3,179.9	442.3	1,027.7	−585.4	881.2	1.7	879.5	62.7	122.6	−59.9
1959	5,162.1	1,311.2	3,850.9	627.2	1,447.4	−820.2	610.7	0.2	610.5	92.1	105.4	−13.3
1960	5,712.4	1,334.0	4,378.4	831.8	1,860.2	−1,028.4	894.3	0.1	894.2	88.8	169.8	−81.0

Source: Annual reports of Banco de México, S.A.

[a] Figures include claims on and obligations to both national and private banking system institutions.

Savings, Capital Formation, and Output Growth

We have so far examined Mexican monetary and financial experience from several points of view, but always based the analysis on available financial statistics. We have referred to the real factors which underlie the financial experience and processes with which we are principally concerned, but the behavior of these underlying real factors has not been discussed in any detail. In this section, therefore, we review the record of savings, capital formation, and output growth during the period under consideration, and attempt to reconcile this record with our interpretation of Mexico's recent monetary and financial experience.

The Mexican record of savings, capital formation, and output growth during the period 1940–1960 is summarized in Table VI-D. At the outset it is necessary to indicate the limitations of the data. In the first place, the output and investment figures are more in the nature of estimates than of measurements and are therefore subject to substantial error. This is especially true of the figures shown for gross investment expenditures, the private sector component of which is widely believed to be understated; but the figures shown for gross national product are also not very reliable—as evidenced by the substantial upward revision in 1963 of official estimates for the period beginning with 1950. In this latter connection, for present purposes we shall employ the earlier estimates—those relevant to policy decisions during the period under consideration. A second data limitation is that the figures shown for net foreign investment represent estimates based on the difference between the value of imports and the value of exports (i.e., the balance of international payments on current account), and as such they reflect not only short- and long-term capital movements (i.e., the balance on capital account) but also variations in Banco de México's holdings of foreign exchange reserves and net errors and omissions. Consequently the estimates thus obtained, quite apart from the reliability of the underlying data, are not very accurate indexes of the amounts of foreign savings available for financing investment expenditures in Mexico. Third, the estimates of gross savings of government, public enterprises, and private enterprises and individuals are based on figures taken from both the national income accounts and official financial statistics, even though the data from these two sources are not strictly comparable on conceptual grounds. In short, the data with which we must work are not very satisfactory, and therefore it is to be expected that analysis based on such data will produce results that are less than fully satisfying. Nevertheless the results obtained appear to be reasonably consistent with the foregoing interpretation of Mexican monetary and financial experience, and also the estimates of savings, capital formation, and output growth appear to reveal certain important dimensions of this experience which are not otherwise evident.

SOURCES OF SAVINGS

As indicated by the data contained in Table VI-D, gross domestic savings tended to increase as a percentage of gross national product, although with sizable year-to-year variations. During the three subperiods 1940–1950, 1951–1955, and 1956–1960 the percentages were, respectively, 12.7, 13.4, and 13.9. At the same time, however, gross domestic savings tended to decrease as a percentage of gross national investment as an increasing proportion of this investment came to be financed with foreign savings. During the above three subperiods the percentages of investment financed with domestic savings were, respectively, 98.7, 94.3, and 91.6, with the balance being accounted for by net foreign investment. We previously noted this tendency toward increasing reliance on foreign financing, and indicated that credits obtained by public enterprises from foreign government and international lending agencies accounted for the bulk of new foreign financing.

The ultimate sources of domestic savings were, of course, the government sector, public enterprises, and the private sector. Table VI-D contains estimates of the volume of savings accounted for by each of these sources. As indicated, the proportion of total domestic savings accounted for by government was substantially lower during the period 1956–1960 (18.9 per cent) than during the previous five-year period (24.4 per cent), and somewhat lower than during the period 1940–1950 (20.2 per cent). Public enterprise savings, as a percentage of total domestic savings, were practically constant in each of the three subperiods (around 10 per cent) so that variations in the relative importance of public sector savings were almost wholly accounted for by government. Accordingly, private sector savings, which accounted for somewhat more than two-thirds of total domestic savings over the entire period, evidenced a tendency to increase as a share of the total during the last five years of the period.

As the data in Table VI-D show, savings in the private sector regularly exceeded private sector investment expenditures, with the

TABLE VI-D

ESTIMATES OF SAVINGS, INVESTMENT, AND OUTPUT, 1940–1960

(Millions of pesos)

Year	Gross Domestic Savings				Net Foreign Investment[d]	Gross National Investment				Gross National Product[e]	
	Total	Government[a]	Public Enterprises[b]	Private Sector[c]		Total	Government	Public Enterprises	Private Sector	Current Prices	1950 Prices
1940	939.5	145.0	141.5	653.0	−146.3	793.2	188.7	147.5	457.0	7,300	20,700
1941	868.3	116.8	118.5	633.0	123.4	991.7	262.3	121.4	608.0	8,800	23,300
1942	1,123.7	110.7	130.3	882.7	−107.2	1,016.5	275.1	217.4	524.0	10,700	26,400
1943	1,782.7	287.0	163.7	1,332.0	−497.6	1,285.1	426.0	200.1	659.0	13,700	27,400
1944	1,863.7	474.1	203.4	1,186.2	−124.2	1,739.5	487.3	236.2	1,016.0	17,700	29,700
1945	2,307.4	451.8	263.1	1,592.5	−6.8	2,300.6	564.3	388.3	1,348.0	20,500	32,000
1946	2,442.1	479.1	233.5	1,729.5	844.4	3,286.5	569.9	560.6	2,156.0	26,100	34,100
1947	3,346.6	711.7	291.9	2,343.0	810.5	4,157.1	822.6	608.5	2,726.0	29,000	34,500
1948	4,203.3	998.7	365.7	2,838.7	345.0	4,548.3	1,040.0	591.3	2,917.0	31,700	36,100
1949	5,446.6	1,101.5	527.3	3,817.8	−395.4	5,051.2	1,141.2	823.0	3,087.0	35,200	37,600
1950	6,414.6	1,342.6	724.0	4,348.0	−455.0	5,959.6	1,333.6	1,332.0	3,294.0	41,500	41,500
1951	5,159.2	2,025.4	485.9	2,647.9	1,722.2	6,881.4	1,515.2	1,466.2	3,900.0	51,800	44,500
1952	7,256.4	2,044.4	559.7	4,652.3	892.7	8,149.1	1,786.9	1,630.2	4,732.0	58,300	45,000
1953	7,063.9	1,860.3	877.7	4,325.9	789.7	7,853.6	1,627.2	1,626.5	4,600.0	56,300	44,400
1954	9,489.7	2,343.2	1,051.3	6,095.2	275.6	9,765.3	2,133.3	2,232.0	5,400.0	66,478	47,800
1955	13,381.0	2,050.0	1,259.3	10,071.7	−1,121.3	12,259.7	2,171.9	2,487.8	7,600.0	84,000	52,500
1956	13,547.5	2,822.2	1,378.3	9,347.0	445.0	13,992.6	2,365.9	2,566.6	9,060.1	94,000	56,000
1957	14,145.3	3,018.1	1,437.0	9,690.2	1,925.0	16,070.3	2,902.9	3,043.4	10,124.0	103,000	58,000
1958	15,016.2	3,081.9	881.7	11,052.6	2,270.0	17,286.2	2,921.8	3,594.4	10,770.0	114,000	60,600
1959	17,420.2	2,817.7	1,826.9	12,775.6	396.3	17,816.5	3,179.6	3,673.1	10,944.0	122,000	63,400
1960	18,597.0	3,169.1	2,611.1	12,816.8	2,175.0	20,772.0	3,168.1	5,603.9	12,000.0	134,400	67,000

Source: Annual reports of Banco de México, S.A.; and Roberto Santillán López and Aniceto Rosas Figueroa, *Teoría General de las Finanzas Públicas y el Caso de México*, 1962.

a Represents public investment financed internally with the fiscal resources of the federal and local governments, as shown by Santillán López and Rosas Figueroa, p. 218.
b Represents public investment financed internally with the resources of public enterprises, as shown by Santillán López and Rosas Figueroa, p. 218.
c Computed as a residual. Figures arrived at by subtracting net foreign investment, government savings, and public enterprise savings from total gross national investment.
d Balance on current account as shown in the balance of international payments. Negative figures indicate a current account surplus.
e The 1963 revisions of gross national product estimates for the period 1950–1960 are as follows:

	1950	1951	1952	1953	1954	1955	1956	1957	1958	1959	1960
Current Prices	40,577	52,311	58,643	58,437	71,540	87,349	99,323	114,225	127,152	136,200	154,137
1950 Prices	40,577	43,621	45,366	45,618	50,391	54,767	58,214	62,708	66,177	68,119	73,482

result that a surplus of transferable savings was available for financing the deficit in the public sector occasioned by an excess of investment expenditures over current savings. We have previously examined the financial processes involved in the intersectoral transfer of savings. Indeed, as we have seen, the country's monetary and financial experience throughout the period under consideration was characterized to a significant degree by the processes employed in effecting the transfer of savings from the private sector to the support of public sector deficits.

Additional light is shed on these processes by comparisons of the records of savings and investment by the individual sectors. We see that total government sector savings over the period 1940–1960 were somewhat in excess of total government sector investment expenditures. The record in this regard has varied considerably from year to year and from subperiod to subperiod. During the period 1940–1950, government sector savings amounted to 87.5 per cent of government sector investment expenditures while during the periods 1951–1955 and 1956–1960, savings exceeded investment (the percentages were, respectively, 111.8 and 102.5). The fact that government accounted for savings in excess of its investment expenditures did not obviate the necessity of deficit financing because a sizable portion of government sector savings were transferred to public enterprises and other deficit-spending units in the public and private sectors and employed to finance the retirement of previously incurred foreign indebtedness. Indeed, as shown by comparison of the data shown in Table IV-D with that shown in Table VI-D, the cumulative deficit of the government sector equalled approximately 23 per cent of the volume of government investment expenditures over the period 1940–1960. Similar comparisons of the savings and investment expenditures accounted for by public enterprises reveal that this sector saved less than half of the amount required to finance its investment expenditures over the entire period 1940–1960 (for the three subperiods the percentages were 60.5, 44.8, and 44.0 respectively).

When we consider the public sector as a whole the picture emerges even more clearly. The combined savings of government and public enterprises amounted to 76.0 per cent and 77.9 per cent, respectively, of total public sector investment during the periods 1940–1950 and 1951–1955. During the period 1956–1960, however, the comparable percentage declined to 69.8 per cent, a development which indicates why foreign financing became relatively more important and why the domestic money and capital market was called upon to provide a proportionately larger volume of public sector financing than formerly.

We have previously indicated that only a relatively small percentage of private investment was financed from savings transferred through the intermediation of the institutional framework of the money and capital market from surplus to deficit spending units, probably between 10 per cent and 20 per cent of total domestic savings. The amount of private sector savings transferred by means of these institutions to the public sector appears to have comprised an even smaller share of total domestic savings, perhaps between 5 per cent and 10 per cent. Thus, transferrable savings which probably amounted to no more than 30 per cent of total domestic savings, and perhaps to as little as 15 per cent of such savings, appear to have constituted the real basis for the processes of financial intermediation examined in earlier sections of this chapter.

CAPITAL FORMATION AND OUTPUT GROWTH

As indicated in Table VI-D, the proportion of gross national product represented by domestic investment expenditures evidenced a tendency to increase, rising from 12.9 per cent during the subperiod 1940–1950 and 14.2 per cent during the subperiod 1951–1955 to 15.2 per cent during the last five years of the period. The proportionate contributions of the public and private sectors of roughly 40 per cent and 60 per cent, respectively, to the total volume of investment expenditures were remarkably constant over the period. Within the public sector, however, there was a tendency for public enterprise investment expenditures to increase relative to those of government (public enterprises accounted for 56.0 per cent of total public sector investment expenditures during the years 1956–1960 as compared to 50.6 per cent and 42.4 per cent, respectively, during the earlier subperiods 1951–1955 and 1940–1950).

The final aspect of the behavior of the real factors underlying Mexican monetary and financial experience which is deserving of comment was the tendency for the rate of growth of real gross national product to decline in the latter part of the 1950s. When the data contained in Table VI-D are adjusted to allow for the effect of price level changes they indicate that the average annual rate of growth in real gross national product declined during 1956–1960 as compared to 1951–1955. Over these same two periods the percentage of gross national product being invested tended to increase; that is, a higher investment-output ratio appears to have prevailed during the latter period. Apparently, what occurred was a decline in the real productivity of new or marginal capital formation. The revised estimates of gross national product indicate that the rate of growth in real output averaged somewhat higher in both the 1951–1955 and the 1956–1960 periods, although the average rate indicated for the latter period remains below that for the former (See Table VI-D, note e). No corresponding revision has as yet been made of official estimates of investment expenditures. It should be added at this point that the available statistical evidence for the period since 1960 indicates that a substantially higher rate of output growth has been achieved in the past several years.

Perhaps a tendency for the growth rate to decline in spite of a rising rate of real investment expenditures was inevitable during the stage of Mexican economic development under review. Certainly the productivity of investment during the period 1940–1950 was extraordinarily high, reflecting both intensive utilization of capacity and extensive deferral of maintenance and replacement. The decline in the productivity of investment in the following years clearly reflects the growing importance of replacement investment made necessary by the depreciation of capital goods accumulated over previous years. It probably also indicates that high-yield, short-pay-out projects were no longer so numerous as in earlier years—in part because many of these had already been exploited and in part for other reasons, e.g., declining world market prices for export products, etc. Also important in explaining this development is the fact that large-scale investments were being made in such things as transportation and communication facilities which, while basic to economic development, were necessarily limited in the yield they were capable of producing over the short run. Finally, it seems probable that industries in the initial stages of development during the 1950s were more capital intensive than was the case for their counterparts during the 1940s.

But in addition to these factors it may be that the tendency for investment productivity to decline was also related to difficulty experienced in achieving an efficient allocation of investable resources.

Indeed, judging from the government's actions in establishing various inter-agency coordinating and planning groups during the latter half of the 1950s, it appears that more efficient resource allocation was recognized as a serious problem. Clearly this was a problem that bore closely upon the operation of the monetary and financial system, since one of the fundamental responsibilities of this system, as is true of the financial system of all market economies, is to facilitate the movement of investable resources to their most productive applications. It may well be that the prior record of inflation and successive devaluations, coupled with the particular monetary and financial policies being followed in an effort to avoid repetition of this experience and with the oligopolistic structure of private financial and industrial activities, combined in the latter part of the 1950s to reduce the effectiveness of the financial system in this respect. It seems probable that an important related factor contributing to misallocation of investable resources was the limited movement of financial resources between borrowers and lenders in the private sector.

Another implication of the distressing behavior of the relationship between capital formation and output growth that became apparent during the latter half of the 1950s was that an increasing volume of domestic savings would be necessary in order to re-establish the growth rate of prior years. This situation also reflected on the operation of the financial system since, in addition to that of promoting efficient allocation of investable resources, a second fundamental responsibility of any such system is to generate a flow of savings and investment sufficient to support an adequate rate of output growth. Again it may well be that the system was inhibited in performing this function well during the latter part of the 1950s by the combined effect of past experience and current policies on expectations of potential savers and investors.

These observations are not intended to suggest, of course, that the apparent slowing of the rate of output growth during the latter part of the 1950s is attributable to failure of the financial system to perform properly. Such an interpretation would clearly be invalid since a large variety of factors—real as well as financial, economic as well as political, and domestic as well as foreign—combined to contribute to this development. What the observations are intended to indicate, however, is that the behavior of these real factors was related to developments in the financial sphere, and that the tendency for the rate of growth of the Mexican economy to diminish, which was apparent by 1960, reflected difficulties in the monetary and financial sphere as well as difficulties of other sorts.

Operation of Loanable-Funds Market

The foregoing discussion of the growth of debt and the development of financial intermediation is incomplete without further elaboration of the role played by the money and capital, or loanable funds, market. It is therefore necessary to examine more carefully than heretofore the operation of the loanable funds market as well as the factors governing market behavior.

MARKET EQUILIBRIUM AND THE PROCESS OF ADJUSTMENT

Issues of direct debt by ultimate borrowers must necessarily be equal in aggregate amount to acquisitions of debt claims by ultimate lenders, either directly or indirectly through financial intermediaries. Before debt instruments are issued, prospective ultimate borrowers must decide that spending in excess of current income is warranted or necessary. Likewise, before direct debt instruments are acquired, ultimate lenders (or intermediary institutions acting for them) must decide that it is desirable or necessary that not all of current income be spent on goods but rather that some portion should be reserved for purchasing claims, either with or without intermediation of financial institutions, on deficit spending units. Clearly the factors underlying these decisions on both sides of the loanable funds market are numerous and varied, and clearly also propensities to borrow and to lend are subject to change, and do change, in response to changing circumstances. Furthermore, borrowing and lending decisions, particularly when the public sector is involved, are not always premised on calculations of prospective financial gain nor are borrowers and lenders, particularly the latter, always permitted to make their decisons free from compulsions of one sort or another. Nevertheless the necessary ex post balance between the amount of new indebtedness incurred by ultimate borrowers and the amount of loanable funds employed in the acquisition of new direct debt instruments is brought about essentially by the working of market forces, as modified by government intervention and controls, which, by producing terms of lending sufficiently attractive to lenders and terms of borrowing sufficiently onerous to borrowers, produce equality between the supply of and the demand for loanable funds.

Equilibrium exists in the loanable funds market when the demand for loanable funds, i.e., the scheduled or planned net issues of debt instruments by ultimate borrowers, is equal to the supply of loanable funds, i.e., the scheduled or planned acquisitions of direct claims by ultimate lenders and financial intermediaries acting on their behalf. Given an initial equilibrium position, the loanable funds market will remain in equilibrium if new issues of direct debt instruments by ultimate borrowers are equal to the incremental demand for direct debt claims by ultimate lenders. If there is excess demand in the loanable funds market, i.e., if scheduled or planned issues exceed scheduled or planned acquisitions, interest rates will rise and other terms of lending will tighten (and vice versa in the case of excess supply) so that, *ex post*, issues will equal acquisitions, the demand for loanable funds will equal the supply, and borrowing will equal lending.

Of course the operation of the loanable funds market, as well as the factors underlying the operation of this market, is closely related to demand and supply conditions in the goods market. If there is excess demand in the goods market, i.e., if scheduled or planned purchases of goods exceed scheduled or planned production, prices will rise and, assuming the availability of the necessary productive resources, output will increase. Any such adjustments in the goods market, in turn, will cause repercussions in the loanable funds market. We shall examine in more detail a bit farther on the relations between the operation of the two markets as they adjust to a disequilibrium situation, but the point to be emphasized here is that changes in the level of interest rates and prices, as well as changes in the volume of deficit financing and in physical output, are all closely interrelated phenomena.

RELATION TO INTEREST RATE AND PRICE-LEVEL BEHAVIOR

We have shown earlier in this chapter that the flow of loan funds from ultimate lenders to ultimate borrowers increased at a rate exceeding the growth of gross national product, especially during the years 1956–1960. Nominal rates of interest were relatively high and rose modestly throughout the 1950s, the rise being somewhat more pronounced following 1955. The price level also increased, but the average annual rate of increase was substantially lower after 1955 than before. When nominal interest rates are adjusted for price level changes it is found that the real cost of borrowing was much higher during the 1956–1960 period than formerly. How can these developments be explained?

It seems clear that the larger volume of transactions between ultimate borrowers and ultimate lenders, and the higher real cost of loan funds in the 1956–1960 period as compared to earlier years, was associated with shifts in borrowing and lending propensities. Of course borrowing and lending decisions are influenced by a number of factors. Presumably one factor which contributed significantly to the relatively faster growth of direct indebtedness following 1955 was shifts in the pattern of income and expenditure which were related on the one hand to changes in expectations regarding further inflation and devaluation and on the other hand to the decline in the rate of output growth which occurred during the latter part of this period —developments which together tended to produce relatively larger budget imbalances than formerly.

While available statistical data do not permit examination of the pattern of income distribution, spending, and financial transactions by sectors, we have produced estimates which indicate that public sector deficits were relatively larger during the years 1956–1960 (averaging 1.9 per cent of gross national product) than during the period 1940–1955 (when the comparable figure was 1.2 per cent). The relevant data are shown in Table VI-D. Similarly, we found that domestic issues of debt instruments by government amounted to 28.9 per cent of government sector investment expenditures during the years 1956–1960 as compared to 18.4 per cent during the years 1940– 1955. These findings indicate that the slowing of the rate of output growth in association with a decline in the rate of inflation produced, or at least was accompanied by, changes in the pattern of income and expenditure such that public sector deficits, and corresponding surpluses in the private sector, required an enlarged flow of loan funds from the one to the other.

The increasing volume of borrowing and the rising real cost of loanable funds during the 1956–1960 period was associated with a sizable increase in the ratio of liquid financial claims (money and quasi-money) to gross national product and in the proportion of total liquid financial claims denominated in foreign currencies. Thus the ratio of liquid claims to gross national product increased from 25.5 per cent in 1955 to 30.7 per cent in 1960 after fluctuating in the 20–26 per cent range throughout the period 1940–1950. The proportion of liquid claims stated in foreign currencies increased from

34.2 per cent to 42 per cent between 1955 and 1960, the comparable figure for 1950 being 28.3 per cent. These ratios are evidence that lenders became increasingly fearful of further inflation and devaluation and consequently were highly reluctant to enter into long-term peso contracts—in spite of the progressively higher interest inducement to do so. These same expectations, of course, worked to reduce the reluctance of business and individual spending units in the private sector to operate on borrowed funds. The manifestation of these expectations in borrowing and lending propensities in the private sector, coupled with the increasing demands of the public sector for non-inflationary credits, naturally worked to produce a high degree of tightness in the market for loanable funds.

As previously indicated, developments in the loanable funds market which affect the level of interest rates and propensities to borrow and lend also influence the operation of the goods market. Thus, for example, the heightened demand for loanable funds relative to the supply which became manifest following 1955, in addition to causing an increase in the real cost of borrowing, worked to reduce upward pressures on prices and also, presumably, to diminish the rate of output growth. During the 1956–1960 period the wholesale price index increased at an average annual rate of less than 4 per cent and the average annual rate of output growth, according to contemporary estimates, was about 4.6 per cent, while the comparable figures for the 1951–1955 period were 9.4 per cent and 5.7 per cent respectively. Of course many factors in addition to influences stemming from the loanable funds market were important in causing the slowing of inflation and output growth in the latter period. Furthermore, developments in the loanable funds market were themselves subject to influence from the behavior of prices and output in the goods market. The point we wish to make here, however, is simply that associated with the appearance of excess demand in the loanable funds market was substantial diminution of excess demand in the goods market.

GRAPHICAL REPRESENTATION

In the previous section we suggested an interpretation of certain aspects of recent Mexican financial experience which focused upon relationships between the behavior of interest rates, the volume of deficit financing in the loanable funds market, and the level of prices and output in the goods market. The argument was premised on a general equilibrium theory of the operation of the economy, and it is therefore appropriate that the essential character of this theory be made explicit in somewhat more formal terms.

There are assumed to be two markets, the market for current output (i.e., the goods market) and the market for financial claims (i.e., the loanable funds market). If equilibrium prevails in one of these markets it also must prevail in the other; or, alternatively, if disequilibrium exists in either market, adjustments will tend to work themselves out in both markets.

Consider the relationships depicted in Figure 6-A. The *GG* curve

Figure 6 – A

EQUILIBRIUM CONDITIONS IN THE GOODS AND LOANABLE FUNDS MARKETS

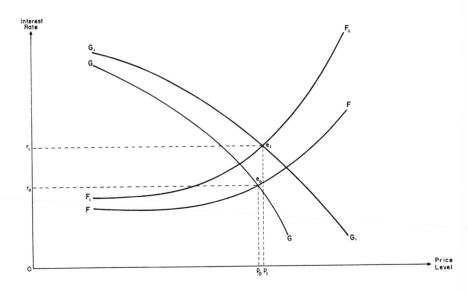

shows alternative combinations of price level and interest rate consistent with equilibrium in the goods market, assuming a given level of real output and a given amount of financial claims in circulation. Likewise, the *FF* curve shows alternative combinations of price level and interest rate consistent with equilibrium in the loanable funds market, assuming a given level of real output and a given amount of outstanding financial claims. Equilibrium in both the goods and the loanable funds market would prevail when the price level-interest rate combination is that represented by point e_0, the point of intersection of the GG and FF curves.

The effect of an autonomous increase in the demand for goods would be to shift the GG curve upward, so that some combination of higher prices and higher interest rates would be required to re-establish equilibrium in the goods market. Likewise, the effect of an autonomous increase in the demand for loanable funds would be to shift the FF curve upward so that some combination of higher interest rates and lower prices would be required to re-establish equilibrium in this market. In the case of simultaneous upward shifts of both the GG and FF curves the effect would be to raise interest rates, but the influence on the price level would depend upon the shapes of the curves and the magnitude of their shifting. These relationships are illustrated by the G_1G_1 and the F_1F_1 curves in Figure 6-A.

Numerous other sorts of changes in both the goods and loanable funds markets could be assumed and their effects analyzed within the framework of the simple general equilibrium model depicted in Figure 6-A. Thus, for example, we could consider the effect of an increase in the output of goods or of an increase in the supply of loanable funds on the GG and FF curves and the equilibrium level of prices and interest rates in the goods and loanable funds markets. However, since we are principally concerned with the path of adjustment followed by the Mexican economy in recent years in response to increases in demand for goods and loanable funds, perhaps sufficient illustrations of the adjustment mechanism have been offered.

Within this framework let us reconsider the record of price level and interest rate changes. It will be recalled that this record suggests that the Mexican economy adjusted primarily by way of price increases during the period 1950–1955, while during the period 1956–1960 adjustment was reflected primarily in interest rate increases, i.e., increasing real cost of loanable funds. This is clearly illustrated by Figure 6-B, which incorporates price level and real interest rate combinations for the years 1949–1961 into functions depicting conditions in the loanable funds market. Between 1949 and 1955 the price level increased rapidly while the real rate of interest remained more or less constant at a relatively low level. In contrast, between 1955 and 1961 the real rate of interest rose sharply while the price level rose only moderately.

The new situation which developed following the 1954 devaluation

Figure 6 – B
RELATION BETWEEN INTEREST RATE AND PRICE LEVEL

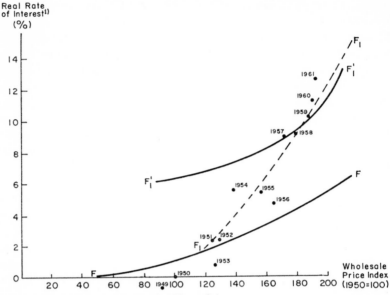

Source: Annual reports of Banco de México, S.A.

1 The "real rate of interest" for each year is computed as the difference between a five-year moving average of annual rates of increase in the wholesale price index (centered on the third year) and the estimated average nominal rate of interest for each year (as shown in Table IV-A).

and its aftermath can be interpreted within the framework of the model as either an upward shift in the FF curve (as shown by curve $F'_1F'_1$), or as a movement along an unchanged FF curve from the relatively horizontal to the relatively vertical portion (as depicted by curve F_1F_1). In any case it is evident that in the latter part of the 1950s the basic conditions of supply and demand in the loanable funds market, as modified by the various controls and other actions of the monetary authorities, were such as to force recurrent upward shifts in the GG curve to be manifested to a much greater extent in higher interest rates and to a much lesser extent in higher prices than was formerly the case.

RELATION TO RATE OF OUTPUT GROWTH

We have already shown that in the latter half of the 1950s, during the period in which restrictive monetary policies were bringing about sharply higher interest rates and substantially slower increases in the price level, there was evident a tendency for the rate of overall economic growth to be somewhat lower than in previous years. This latter aspect of recent Mexican experience was to some extent the result of adjustments in financial processes and resource utilization which were a necessary accompaniment of the stabilization program.

These processes of adjustment can be illustrated in terms of a general equilibrium model which incorporates forces operating in both the financial and goods market in the manner previously described. However, this model is devised in such a way as to emphasize the relationship between developments in the financial and goods markets and the level of current output rather than to focus upon the behavior of the price level. The relevant relationships are depicted in Figure 6-C.

The *GG* curve in the upper diagram shows alternative combinations of output level and interest rate consistent with equilibrium in the goods market (i.e., consistent with equality between the supply of savings and the demand for investable resources). Under conditions in which investment demand is responsive to changes in interest rate, the curve depicting equilibrium conditions in the goods market would be downward sloping to the right, as shown in the upper diagram. The *FF* curve shows alternative combinations of output level and interest rate consistent with equilibrium in the loanable funds market (i.e., consistent with equality between the supply of money and the demand for money balances). Under conditions in which the demand for money balances is a function of both interest rate and income level and in which the money supply is determined autonomously by the monetary authority the *FF* curve would be upward sloping to the right, again as depicted in the upper diagram. The point of intersection of the *GG* and *FF* curves indicates the unique combination of income level and interest rate at which both the goods market and the money market can be in equilibrium simultaneously.

However, there are reasons for believing that the general functional relationships depicted in the upper diagram are not those relevant to the circumstances of Mexico during the latter half of the 1950s. For example, it seems reasonable to believe that in the Mexican environment investment expenditures were governed principally by changes in income level rather than by changes in interest rate. The principal reason is that expenditures in the private sector were largely

Figure 6 – C

RELATION BETWEEN INTEREST RATE AND OUTPUT

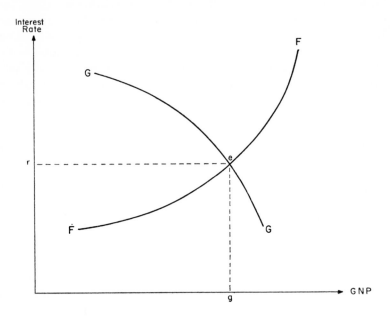

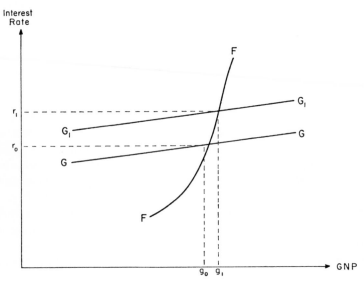

financed with the savings of the investing unit rather than with borrowed funds and that expenditures in the public sector were governed by the requirements for sustaining an adequate rate of economic growth rather than by profitability considerations. Other factors such as the relative scarcity of capital and the high import content of many investment projects also served to make investment expenditures relatively unresponsive to interest rate changes. In the case of savings, since consumption expenditures tended to be governed principally by income (because per capita income was relatively low, because of the power of the demonstration effect, etc.), so also did the supply of savings. In short, for various reasons the GG curve representative of circumstances in the Mexican economy during the latter half of the 1950s is more or less horizontal, as shown in the lower diagram in Figure 6-C.

There are also reasons for supposing that the function depicting conditions in the money market had special characteristics. Since the demand for money was governed principally by transactions requirements and was little affected by speculative considerations (speculative activities being concentrated in the market for nonmonetary financial instruments, including foreign exchange, and in the goods market), money balances were principally determined by income level rather than by interest rate considerations. On the supply side, because of the inability of the monetary authority to achieve its objectives by means of quantitative controls, the money supply was governed principally by transactions requirements, including those stemming from the needs of the public sector for deficit financing. Consequently the FF function representative of circumstances prevailing in the Mexican money market during the latter half of the 1950s can be presumed to be nearly vertical—at least in the range in which intersection with the GG function occurs.

The main implication of the GG and FF functions depicted in the lower diagram shown in Figure 6-C is that the level of output was particularly responsive to changes in supply and demand conditions in the money market (i.e., to shifts in the FF function) while the level of interest rates was not easily controllable by monetary measures of a quantitative sort. For example, given the policy of restricting the means of payment to the minimum amount necessary for effecting transactions, upward shifts in the GG curve were manifested to a greater extent in higher interest rates and to a lesser extent in increases in the level of output than would otherwise have been the case.

Within this analytical framework it is easy to comprehend the logic of the stabilization program carried out during the latter half of the 1950s. Widespread expectation of further inflation following the 1954 devaluation had the effect of shifting the GG curve upward (as shown by the curve G_1G_1). For the same reason there was a general unwillingness to hold money balances in excess of the minimum requirements for transactions purposes. The monetary authorities steadfastly refused to permit expansion of the money supply beyond the level consistent with achievement of domestic stability and external equilibrium, while at the same time attempting to facilitate growth in output by various nonquantitative means. The result was a sharply higher level of interest rates and a lower rate of output growth than would have occurred under less restrictive monetary policies. The purpose of the monetary restriction, of course, was to dispel the prevailing inflationary psychology and thereby to re-establish an environment in which expansionary forces (whether emanating from the goods market or the money market) could be expected to manifest themselves in increases in the level of output but without increases in the domestic price level and balance of payments disequilibrium. As we shall see in the next chapter, the performance of the Mexican economy since 1960 demonstrates the success of the stabilization program in achieving this objective.

Conclusion

The lengthy description and analysis of Mexican monetary and financial experience during the 1940–1960 period, as contained in Chapters II through VI, has been intended to give the reader an understanding of what occurred during these years, how the monetary and financial system operated under the various circumstances in which the country found itself, and also why the forces at work in the different situations manifested themselves as they did. It remains to review and interpret events since 1960, to indicate some of the contemporary monetary and financial problems confronting Mexico, and to suggest possible alternative courses of future policy. It is to these tasks that we turn in the final chapter which follows.

PART IV . . . DEVELOPMENTS SINCE 1960

CHAPTER VII

RECENT EXPERIENCE AND FUTURE DEVELOPMENT

Introduction

WE BELIEVE the record of Mexican financial experience as described and analyzed in this book is deserving of study for several reasons. First, Mexico is today confronted with numerous financial problems of significance for the country's program of economic development, and understanding of these problems and of the alternative courses of action open to monetary and fiscal authorities is dependent upon awareness of reasons for past experience and current trends. Second, analysis of the experience of Mexico reveals relationships between financial and real aspects of economic development which contribute to better understanding at the theoretical level of the requirements for intelligent financial planning for development—whether for Mexico or other countries. Third, a systematic recording and interpretation of Mexican experience provides a basis for comparative studies of financial aspects of economic development, whether of similarly situated countries (e.g., Mexico, Argentina, and Brazil) or of countries in differing economic and financial circumstances (e.g., Mexico, Ecuador, and Haiti).

International comparative studies promise not only to contribute to understanding of the financial side of the development process but also, and perhaps more importantly, to facilitate a fruitful interchange of information regarding financial policies, institutions, instruments, and techniques of control of great practical usefulness to those in positions of decision-making responsibility. Indeed, such comparative studies are an essential step in international technical assistance in the financial sphere—assistance which in many respects the lesser developed countries are better suited to offer one another than are the relatively advanced countries whose experiences, institutional structures, and interests and viewpoints are quite different from those of countries in greatest need of advice and guidance.

In the foregoing sections of this book we have described the Mexican financial system and the processes and policies underlying its operation, and have examined relationships between Mexican financial development and the stability and growth of the overall economy. In this final chapter we review experience since 1960, emphasizing those contemporary trends and problem areas which seem likely to be of greatest significance for the future, and propose policy guides which are believed to be consistent with further progress toward the development of a more effective financial system.

Review of Experience since 1960

Several fundamental changes in the Mexican financial system which have substantially altered the nature of the money and capital market occurred in the first several years of the 1960s. First, and foremost, confidence in the country's ability to maintain domestic monetary stability and external financial equilibrium was firmly established—so that the prime policy consideration no longer had to be that of countering undesirable speculation based on adverse expectations with regard to the future of the currency. The early 1960s also witnessed resumption of a higher rate of economic growth, giving rise to confidence on the part of private investors and vindicating stabilization policies which during the latter part of the 1950s were widely criticized for unduly restricting the pace of economic activity. Finally, in the absence of serious inflationary and balance of payments difficulties, it became possible for the monetary authorities to introduce greater ease into the financial markets, thereby inducing a decline in interest rates.

INSTITUTIONAL DEVELOPMENT

The institutional structure developed over the years has remained virtually unchanged during the 1960s except for the establishment of several public trust funds designed to augment the flow of credit to selected lines of activity which, for one reason or another, were judged to be unduly restricted by insufficient credit on appropriate terms. In general these funds are employed as a basis for affording guarantees to private credit institutions against default on the part of certain classes of borrowers and also as a source of financing for discounting of paper acquired by these institutions in extending credits to the specified types of borrowers. In other words, the special funds supplement the resources of the established private credit institutions both by reducing lenders' risk (through the guarantee arrangement) and by increasing the liquidity of lenders' claims (through the discount privilege).

Actually the special trust funds are not a new development; rather, their expanded role since 1960 represents extension into new fields of an innovation introduced in the mid-1950s with the establishment of a fund to assist in meeting the financing requirements of small- and medium-sized enterprises (Fondo de Garantía y Fomento a la Industria Mediana y Pequeña, established in 1954 under the jurisdiction of Nacional Financiera) and a fund to increase the flow of credits from private credit institutions into agricultural ventures (Fondo de Garantía y Fomento para la Agricultura, Ganadería y Avicultura, established in 1954 under the jurisdiction of Banco de México). Three similar funds were subsequently created under Nacional Financiera's jurisdiction, namely: Fondo de Garantía y Fomento del Turismo (1957); Fondo del Programa Nacional Fronterizo (1961); and Fondo para la Exploración, Explotación y Beneficio de Minerales no Metálicas (1962). And three additional such funds were established in 1963 under Banco de México's jurisdiction, two for the purpose of facilitating the financing of residential construction (Fondo de Operación y Descuento Bancario de la Vivienda and Fondo de Garantía y Apoyo a los Créditos para la Vivienda), and one for the purpose of providing additional credits to exporters of manufactured products (Fondo para el Fomento de las Exportaciones de Productos Manufacturados). The only fund not administered either by Banco de México or Nacional Financiera is the Fondo de Garantía y Fomento de la Artesanía, established in 1961 under

the administrative jurisdiction of Banco Nacional de Fomento Cooperativo.

Each of these special trust funds is capitalized somewhat differ-
ently. For example, the fund for small- and medium-sized enterprises
operates on an initial contribution from the federal government, a
loan from the Inter-American Development Bank, and accumulated
earnings. The Fondo de Operación y Descuento Bancario de la Vivienda is funded principally with credits from the United States
Agency for International Development and the Inter-American Development Bank, made available under the Alliance for Progress program. The fund designed to foster the flow of private credits to agricultural enterprises, after operating for a number of years on capital
provided by the federal government, is now also supported by United
States credits transmitted through the Agency for International Development. A final example is the special export promotion fund
which draws its resources mainly from a 10-per-cent ad valorem tax
levied on nonessential imports.

Each of the trust funds is necessarily administered on the basis of
quite different criteria. In the case of the fund for small- and medium-
sized enterprises, eligibility under the guarantee and discount provisions is restricted to borrowing firms with a total capitalization of
no more than 10 million pesos. In the case of the funds designed to
assist financing of residential construction, eligibility is determined
by type of collateral and only mortgages backed by so called low-cost
housing qualify. A third example is found in the special fund for augmenting export credits, which is restricted in its guarantee operations
to coverage of political risks.

The common characteristic of the discount and guarantee functions of all these publicly administered trust funds is that they are
integrated with the lending activities of the private credit institutions
in such a way as to leave with the lending institutions not only responsibility for establishing the credit worthiness of individual applicants and the merits of the activities for which credit is sought, but
also for sharing to some extent in the risk associated with each loan.
Thus while the trust funds serve to reduce the risk and increase the
liquidity of certain types of debt instruments (thereby tending to
lower the cost and increase the availability of credit on a selective
basis), the private lending institutions continue to have ample incen-
tive to grant credit on an economic basis and in accordance with the
overall priorities established by the authorities.

The organizational structure of the Mexican financial system as of the end of 1964 is depicted in Table VII-A, including relationships between the federal government, the Ministry of Finance, Banco de México and the other policy-making and regulatory agencies, and the various national and private credit institutions. The position of the newly established trust funds within the overall system is also indicated. As revealed by comparison with Table II-A and Table II-B, with the exception of the growth in number of branches of certain private institutions and the expanded role of the publicly administered trust funds, there have been no significant changes in the national and private components of the banking system since 1960. However, the resources of the banking system have grown substantially and it is this growth rather than further elaboration of the institutional structure which has been the principal characteristic of Mexican financial development in these last few years.

POLICY MEASURES

While the basic goals of monetary and financial policy have continued essentially unchanged, circumstances since 1962 have permitted the authorities to place greater emphasis on full employment and rapid growth and to be somewhat less fully absorbed in the task of domestic and external stabilization than was possible during the latter part of the 1950s and during 1960, 1961, and the first half of 1962. Furthermore, while the basic instruments of monetary and financial policy have continued to consist principally of the quantitative and selective credit controls exercised by Banco de México, during the past several years somewhat greater reliance has been placed on fiscal policies and somewhat larger scope has been permitted for the working of market forces in the financial sphere.

Banco de México has continued to occasionally revise the reserve requirements imposed on the deposit and savings banks, the financieras, and the mortgage credit institutions in accordance with changing circumstances and objectives. The security reserve and directed credit devices in particular have continued to be employed on the one hand to force the private credit institutions to finance requisite amounts of public sector deficits and on the other hand to induce the desired allocation of available credits among competing applications in the private sector. In this latter connection, increasing priority has been given to low-cost housing construction and to the financing of industrial exports, thereby reinforcing the effectiveness of the special

TABLE VII-A

ORGANIZATION OF MEXICAN FINANCIAL SYSTEM, 1964

FEDERAL GOVERNMENT
Secretaría de Hacienda y Crédito Público

Banco de México, S.A.
Director General appointed by Board of
Directors after nomination by the President
Board of Directors consists of 9 members
5 directors appointed by federal government
4 directors designated by private credit
institutions

Comisión Nacional Bancaria
Chairman appointed by federal government
Executive Committee consists of 6 members
Chairman and 5 members appointed by
Secretaría de Hacienda
Full Commission consists of 9 members
6 members of Executive Committee
1 member designated by deposit banks
2 members designated by other banking
system institutions

Comisión Nacional de Valores
Chairman appointed by Secretaría de Hacienda
Commission consists of 10 members
Chairman and 1 representative of each
of the following:
Secretaría de Hacienda y Crédito Público
Secretaría de Industria y Comercio
Banco de México, S.A.
Nacional Financiera, S.A.
Banco Nacional Hipotecario Urbano y
Obras Públicas
Comisión Nacional Bancaria
Asociación de Banqueros de México
Asociación Mexicana de Instituciones
de Seguros
Bolsa de Valores

Comisión Nacional de Seguros
Chairman appointed by federal government
Executive Committee consists of 5 members
Chairman and 4 members appointed by
Secretaría de Hacienda

National Credit Institutions
Banco Nacional de Crédito Agrícola y Ganadero
Banco Nacional Hipotecario Urbano y de Obras
Públicas
Nacional Financiera, S.A.
Banco Nacional de Crédito Ejidal
Banco Nacional de Comercio Exterior
Banco Nacional de Fomento Cooperativo
Banco Nacional del Pequeño Comercio del D.F.
Banco Nacional del Ejército y la Armada, S.A.
Banco Nacional Cinematográfico, S.A.
Banco Nacional de Transportes, S.A.
Financiera Nacional Azucarera, S.A.

Public Trust Funds
Fondo de Garantía y Fomento a la Industria
Mediana y Pequeña
Fondo de Garantía y Fomento para la Agricultura
Ganadería y Avicultura
Fondo de Garantía y Fomento del Turismo
Fondo de Garantía y Fomento de la Artesanía
Fondo del Programa Nacional Fronterizo
Fondo para la Explotación y Beneficio de Minerales
no Metálicas
Fondo de Operación y Descuento Bancario de la
Vivienda
Fondo de Garantía y Apoyo a los Créditos para la
Vivienda
Fondo para el Fomento de las Exportaciones de
Productos Manufacturados

Other National Institutions[a]
Nacional Monte de Piedad
Almacenes Nacionales de Depósito
Union Nacional de Productores de Azúcar
Instituto Mexicano del Seguro Social
Patronato de Ahorro Nacional
Instituto de Seguridad y Servicios Sociales de
los Trabajadores del Estado

ll Commission consists of 7 members
5 members of Executive Committee
2 members appointed by Secretaría de
Hacienda after designation by insurance
companies

Private Credit Institutions
Deposit Banks (103—with 1,118 branches and agencies)
Savings Banks (117—mostly departments of deposit
banks, with 1,128 branches and agencies)
Financieras (97—with 31 branches and agencies)
Mortgage Banks (26—with 13 branches and agencies)
Capitalization Banks (13—with 22 branches and
agencies)
Fiduciary Institutions (122—mostly departments of
deposit banks, with 791 branches and agencies)
Savings and Loan Banks for Family Housing (3)

Other Private Institutions[b]
Insurance Companies (66—with 47 branches and
agencies)
Finance Companies (14)
Mutual Funds (4)
Securities Exchanges (3)
Credit Unions (61—with 6 branches)
General Deposit Warehouses (26—with 15 branches)
Clearing House Associations (11)

Source: Banco de México, S.A.
[a] Excludes special pension funds established for employees of government agencies and
public enterprises.
[b] Excludes private industrial pension funds.

trust funds operating in these areas. The reserve requirements in effect as the end of 1964 are shown in Table VII-B, along with changes in these requirements during the previous four years.

In addition to selective credit control exercised by means of variations in reserve requirements, the authorities have occasionally intervened more directly, especially in the case of the financieras. The limitation imposed on the rate of growth of short-term financiera obligations, originally introduced in 1960, has continued in effect and has been strengthened by a prohibition introduced in 1964 against financiera acceptance of loans and deposits for terms of less than 180 days. The purpose of these and related measures was to curtail increases in the degree of liquidity in the domestic market (by forcing the financieras to employ longer term instruments as the means of mobilizing their resources), to strengthen the financial condition of the financieras (by bringing about a better matching of the term structure of claims and obligations), and in general to improve

TABLE VII-B

RESERVE REQUIREMENTS, 1960–1964

(Percentages)

Institutions and Instruments	End of 1960 Cash	End of 1960 Directed Investments	End of 1964 Cash	End of 1964 Directed Investments	Credits	Securities
Deposit and Savings Banks						
Demand and time deposits						
In domestic currency						
Demand: Federal District	15	60	15	60	{12.5 Medium term; 2.5 Secured industrial; 5.0 Production}	{25.0 Federal government; 10.0 Other official; 5.0 Industrial}
Interior	15	55	15	55	{12.5 Medium term; 2.5 Secured industrial; 25.0 Production}	{10.0 Federal government; 5.0 Industrial}
Over 90 days	15	85	10	90	{15.0 Medium term; 25.0 Production; 25.0 Distribution of consumer goods}	{20.0 Federal government; 5.0 Industrial}
In foreign currencies						
Deposits as of 8/1/55	20	5	20	5		5.0 Federal government
Additions to 8/1/55 deposits	25	75	25	75	10.0 Manufactured exports	65.0 Federal government
Savings deposits						
In domestic and foreign currencies						
Deposits as of 8/31/55	10		10			
Additions to 8/31/55 deposits	10	90	10	90[a]	15.0 Medium term	{37.5 Federal government; 37.5 Industrial}
In domestic currency						
Additions to 6/1/63 deposits			5	70[b]	{5.0 Medium term; 50.0 Low-cost housing}	{2.0 Federal government; 13.0 Industrial}

Financieras[c]
Other than demand and time deposits and bonds

In domestic currency					
Obligations as of 5/4/60	1	19	19		{ 3.0 Federal government { 16.0 Other official
Additions to 5/4/60 obligations	1	99	99[d]	80.0 Other approved	{ 3.0 Federal government { 16.0 Other official
In foreign currencies					
Obligations as of 3/6/59	1	24	24	5.0 Manufactured exports	19.0 Other official
Additions to 3/6/59 obligations	25	75	75[d]		75.0 Federal government
Mortgage Credit Banks					
Bonds and *Cédulas Hipotecarias*	3				3.0 Federal government

Source: Annual reports of Banco de México, S.A.
[a] Reduced to 25 per cent when investments in government and industrial securities reach 20 per cent of savings deposits as of August 31, 1955.
[b] Reduced to 50 per cent when credits in support of low-cost housing amount to 30 per cent of savings deposits as of June 1, 1963.
[c] For demand and time liabilities similar to those of the deposit banks, reserve requirements imposed on the financieras are the same as those for the deposit banks. Outstanding issues of financiera bonds are not subject to reserve requirements.
[d] For financieras with total domestic currency obligations ranging between 20 and 50 million pesos, increases in these obligations exceeding 1 per cent per month are subject to a 100 per cent cash reserve requirement.

the overall structure of domestic indebtedness (by inducing a gradual separation of the money market and the capital market).

Associated with these measures were actions which reflected desire on the part of the authorities to move toward a lower, more rational structure of interest rates. Especially significant in connection with interest rates was the initiation of a policy of gradual withdrawal of official support from the market for fixed-yield securities, thereby permitting market forces greater scope in determining security values and relative interest rates. Curtailment of price supporting actions in the long-term securities market has also worked to promote separation of the money and capital markets. The goal of a lower overall structure of interest rates has been pursued by means of a policy of general monetary ease supplemented by fiscal actions and foreign borrowing. These latter actions have been motivated, in part at least, by the desire to stimulate an increased volume of private investment expenditures by increasing the availability of credits for this purpose.

Government revenues have been increased as a result of reformulation of the federal income tax in 1963 and also because of improvements in tax administration. Growth in the volume of goods and services produced, coupled with selective upward rate revisions, have permitted a similar increase in the revenues of public enterprises. Public sector expenditures have also grown, however, as a result of increasing investment expenditures and also because of mounting administrative costs and larger expenditures under various subsidy and public welfare programs. As a consequence, the public sector has continued to require substantial amounts of deficit financing. Deficits have been financed largely in the domestic money and capital market with the assistance of the selective credit control scheme. But the tendency already apparent in the latter part of the 1950s to rely increasingly on foreign borrowing for this purpose has also continued, thereby easing to some extent the pressure of public sector financing requirements in the domestic market.

Along with the increasing reliance on foreign borrowing there has become evident a growing concern on the part of the Mexican authorities over the size and structure of foreign indebtedness, both because of the burden of debt service and because of recognition of the need to maintain and further improve the country's credit standing in the international capital market. Perhaps the most significant development so far during the 1960s in this connection has been the successful marketing on three occasions of Mexican government bonds in the New York market, an action which not only served to lengthen the average maturity of Mexican foreign indebtedness but which also served to pave the way for further reliance on this practice in the future. In addition, a program has recently been initiated to develop more effective, centralized administrative control over the volume and terms of foreign borrowing by individual public sector entities.

STATISTICAL RECORD

Mexican financial experience and the overall performance of the Mexican economy during the period 1960–1964 is summarized in Table VII-C.

Domestic finance.—The money supply increased at an average annual rate of 15.9 per cent between the end of 1960 and the end of 1964, exceeding the rate of growth of aggregate expenditures for current output. The tendency toward a lower velocity of monetary circulation became especially pronounced in 1963 and 1964, reflecting a greater willingness to hold money balances. Checking deposits continued to increase relative to coin and currency as a proportion of the money supply, extending the trend which has been evident for many years.

Quasi-monetary obligations of banking system institutions continued to increase relative to both the money supply and gross national product throughout the period, the divergence of rates of increase becoming especially pronounced following 1962. The overall liquidity of the financial system (as measured by the ratio of money plus quasi-money to gross national product) increased from 26.8 at the end of 1960 to 34.4 at the end of 1964. According to this index, the liquidity of the system increased 28.4 per cent during 1963 and 1964. The substantial increase in foreign exchange holdings realized during these years was an important source of this increase in liquidity. Significantly, however, the proportion of total liquid financial claims consisting of deposits denominated in foreign currencies declined progressively following 1961.

The total volume of banking system claims on the government and enterprises and individuals nearly doubled between the end of 1960 and the end of 1964, by far the biggest increase occurring during the latter year. Over the whole period, credits to government accounted for 20.1 per cent of the increase in banking system claims, but the large increase during 1964 resulted in somewhat greater degree from expansion of credits to government. The main source of government financing was the private institutions—reflecting Banco de México reserve requirements—while all parts of the banking system, other than Banco de México, substantially increased their claims on enterprises and individuals. The flow of banking system credits channeled through the nonmonetary institutions, both national and private, became somewhat larger relative to the volume of credits extended by the monetary institutions, reflecting continuation of the decline which has been underway for many years in the relative importance of the monetary institutions. Finally, as evidenced by the increase of intrasystem claims, the movement of funds between banking system institutions increased substantially, suggesting that the processes of financial intermediation continued to grow in complexity.

The securities market became increasingly active during the period, especially in 1963 and 1964. During these latter two years the outstanding amount of fixed-interest securities increased by 61.7 per cent, principally as a result of sizable new issues of indirect securities by public and private financial institutions. Between the end of 1960 and the end of 1964 the proportion of outstanding fixed-interest securities representing obligations of private sector entities (financial and industrial) increased from 23.7 per cent to 28.7 per cent. As already noted, an especially significant development during 1963 and 1964 was evidence of somewhat greater flexibility in the market prices of these securities, reflecting curtailment of supporting activities on the part of issuing agencies. While the stock market continued to be relatively unimportant as a source of new capital funds, during 1964 both the volume of trading and market prices increased greatly, reflecting not only the high level of industrial activity but also greater interest on the part of both domestic and foreign capital in participating in Mexican economic development through this medium.

Government revenues increased by more than 50 per cent between 1960 and 1964. Expenditures likewise increased, this in association with a growing volume of investment expenditures and also because of mounting administrative costs and larger expenditures under various subsidy and public welfare programs. The government sector continued to require substantial amounts of deficit financing from both the domestic market and abroad. The domestic component of government sector deficit financing was provided by private financial institutions, but the pressure of government sector requirements in the domestic market, as well as the pressure of the deficit financing requirements of public enterprises, was eased by continuation of the practice of relying on foreign borrowing for these purposes. Public sector borrowing abroad was especially large in 1964.

A high degree of price stability was maintained throughout 1960–1963—the wholesale price index increased only 3.4 per cent during those years—extending the favorable record achieved during the latter part of the 1950s. Between 1963 and 1964, however, in association with the higher degree of liquidity in the financial system and increased pressure on capacity in some producing sectors, the index of wholesale prices increased by 4.2 per cent.

Interest rates continued to rise in 1960 and 1961 as a result of tightness in the money and capital market produced by a combination of limited overall credit expansion and the policy of diverting a substantial portion of the resources of the private credit institutions to support of public sector deficits. Consequently the high interest rate structure was especially restrictive of expenditures in the private sector. Beginning in the latter part of 1962 and continuing through 1964 the authorities pursued a less restrictive policy, effected by a combination of expansion in the reserve base of the monetary system and of somewhat reduced pressure on the private credit institutions to finance public sector deficits. The average level of interest rates, according to our composite index, appears to have declined by about two percentage points (from 14.4 per cent to 12.4 per cent) during 1963 and 1964, the stimulating effect of which tended to be augmented during 1964 by the moderate rise in the general level of prices already referred to.

International finance.—During 1960 and 1961 Mexico experienced a further depletion of official holdings of foreign exchange in association with a continued balance of payments deficit on current account and what appears to have been a very substantial outflow of short-term capital, especially during 1961. Deficits on current account continued to be incurred in 1962, 1963, and 1964 (the amount becoming very large in the latter year), but the effect of this factor on the overall balance of international payments was more than compensated for by inflows of long-term capital and by cessation of speculative short-term outflows, so that a substantial net increase in official holdings of foreign exchange was achieved over these years.

The inflow of foreign capital, both that resulting from public sector borrowing abroad and from direct private foreign investment, has been quite large in recent years, far surpassing the rate of inflow realized during the 1950s. Especially during 1964 did Mexico rely heavily upon foreign financing; the balance on capital account during that year was nearly double that for any preceding year during the 1960s and greatly in excess of amounts ever previously recorded. The major factor explaining the 1964 figure is the large net increase in public sector foreign indebtedness which occurred during the year.

Along with the growth in foreign borrowing, larger remissions of interest and profits abroad have been necessary. Interest payments in connection with official foreign indebtedness and remission of profits and other outflows in connection with direct private foreign investments have mounted during the 1960s, not only in absolute terms but also relative to foreign exchange earnings on current account. In 1960 a total of $171 million was required for these purposes while in 1964 the comparable figure was $297 million; these amounts represented 11.2 per cent and 16.2 per cent, respectively, of the total dollar value of Mexican exports of goods and services (including tourist receipts) in these two years.

Production, investment, and domestic savings.—Turning now to a brief consideration of the behavior of the real variables of the economy, we see that after continuation into 1960 and 1961 of the relatively low growth trend established in the latter half of the 1950s, the level of output began increasing at a higher rate in 1962. During the three-year period 1962–1964 the gross national product in real terms increased at an average annual rate of 7 per cent, the rate during 1964 reaching the phenomenal level of about 10 per cent.

Estimates of gross fixed-investment expenditures for the years 1960–1963 indicate that between 14.0 and 15.2 per cent of gross national product was devoted to capital formation, more or less in line with the record established during the 1950s. The share accounted for by the public sector increased to around 50 per cent in 1961 and continued at this level through 1963. In 1964, however, private investment revived, and the record-breaking performance of the economy during 1964 is largely attributable to the full-scale investment boom which developed in the private sector—although unusually favorable agricultural yields and continuation of large-scale public investment expenditures were also important contributing factors.

Gross domestic savings are estimated to have averaged about 93

per cent of gross fixed-investment expenditures during the years 1960–1963. The share of total domestic savings accounted for by the public sector was approximately 30 per cent in each of 1960, 1961, and 1962, but in 1963 it increased to 37.4 per cent. Public sector savings were sufficient to finance a varying proportion of public sector investment expenditures (ranging from 55.2 per cent in 1961 to 66.7 per cent in 1963), the balance being financed by means of private sector and foreign savings. As already indicated, during 1964 the public sector depended to a greater extent than in previous years on foreign borrowing to satisfy deficit financing requirements—this in association with private sector absorption of a larger share of private savings.

Significant Trends and Fundamental Problems

Throughout the period since 1940 and especially in recent years there has occurred remarkable diversification of the Mexican economy, accompanied by a parallel diversification of the financial system. Financial intermediation has become increasingly important in the operation of the economy as the number and diversity of economic units participating in savings and investment decisions has increased. Along with this development financial institutions and instruments have evolved as means of facilitating and controlling the flow of credit resources to deficit spending units. At the same time the authorities have evidenced increased determination and ability to maintain domestic monetary stability and external financial equilibrium, and for this purpose—as well as for the purpose of influencing the allocation of resources—novel control techniques of both a quantitative and qualitative variety have been devised.

During the course of this development numerous trends became apparent which had special significance for the course of Mexican financial development. Likewise many problems were encountered which had great contemporary importance. Most of these significant trends and fundamental problems were discussed in previous chapters of this book. However, some of those trends and problems which were of importance during earlier stages of financial development have since become less significant (even though, in most instances, continuing to be quite relevant to understanding of the contemporary Mexican monetary and financial system). It seems appropriate,

fore, to briefly summarize what we view as the most significant
~~~us and most fundamental problems evidenced by the operation
of the Mexican financial system in the mid-1960s.

SIGNIFICANT TRENDS

The most significant contemporary trends in Mexican financial development, in addition to those growing out of the continuing process of diversification of both financial institutions and instruments,
are related to the stabilization program carried out during the last
half of the 1950s and the early 1960s. As already indicated, in addition to maintaining price stability, an impressive rate of output
growth has been achieved during the past several years along with
replenishment of the country's foreign exchange reserves. This has
occurred in association with a decline in interest rates and a growing
volume of investment expenditures. In short, the obvious financial
indexes of present-day Mexican economic performance indicate not
only that the stabilization program initiated in the second half of the
1950s was successful in achieving its objectives but also that the
Mexican economy is well on its way to unprecedented stability and
progress during the decade of the 1960s.

However, there are two contemporary financial trends which are
not so favorable and which must ultimately be arrested if this optimistic prognosis is to prove accurate. The first and most obvious of
these is the growth of Mexican external indebtedness. It is difficult
to define the limits of Mexico's debt servicing capacity, but in the
mid-1960s most observers (Mexican and foreign alike) are agreed
that further heavy reliance on foreign borrowing cannot be continued indefinitely into the future and, indeed, that Mexico's total
external indebtedness (public and private) has already reached a
level which is burdensome and which could become extremely so
during a period of slackened growth or balance of payments stringency.

The second potentially troublesome contemporary development is
the sharp increase in the outstanding volume of liquid financial assets
which has occurred since 1962. The danger in this connection is, of
course, that the degree of liquidity will be permitted to become excessive and give rise to upward pressures on the domestic price level
and also to renewal of adverse speculation against the peso. As of
mid-1965, however, it does not appear that liquidity has reached excessive proportions, and furthermore there is ample evidence to indi-

cate that the authorities are aware of the problem and that measures
are being taken to cope with it not only by means of the established
system of controls but also by efforts to reduce the liquidity of outstanding financial claims. As already noted, the liquidity of various
of the fixed-interest securities included in our measure of quasi-money
has been reduced by curtailment of the practice of supporting market
values at par. Furthermore, during the past several years the Mexican
public has evidenced greater willingness than previously to hold a
relatively larger portion of its accumulated wealth in the form of financial claims. Nevertheless, the increase in liquid financial assets
relative to gross national product which has occurred during the past
several years must be included along with the growth of external indebtedness as a potential source of future difficulty.

A third apparent trend which threatens to cause trouble for Mexico is that of an increasing capital-output ratio. Throughout most
of the period since 1940 additions to the country's capital stock yielded unusually large increments in output, but the available statistical
data (supported by a priori reasoning) suggest that during the past
ten years or so there has been a tendency for the capital-output ratio
to increase. As the process of industrialization has proceeded, production techniques have become increasingly capital intensive, and
also depreciation and obsolescence of existing capital has tended to
become a greater burden, so that a growing proportion of total capital
formation has been required to compensate for capital consumption.
It seems likely that this tendency will continue in the future not only
for the above reasons but also because policies required to bring
about the much needed stimulus to agricultural productivity will require heavy investment in irrigation and mechanization in the years
ahead, with a resulting higher capital-output ratio in the agricultural
sector. In short, it appears that in order to achieve the rates of output
growth which have been set as targets for the coming years, a significantly higher rate of capital formation will be necessary.

FUNDAMENTAL PROBLEMS

Along with these contemporary trends in Mexican financial development various fundamental problems have emerged which now
are commanding the attention of those responsible for policy formulation and which promise to continue to do so during the coming
years. These problems may be divided into three main groupings
for purposes of discussion: the problem of increasing domestic sav-

ings, the problem of rationalizing the allocation of investable resources, and the problem of improving financial markets and the structure of indebtedness.

Problem of domestic savings.—Enough savings must be generated in the domestic economy to permit, along with the aid of available
external financing, an adequate rate of capital formation and output
growth. In the past, two favorable circumstances—the prevalence of
a relatively low capital-output ratio and an ability to command foreign financing on relatively favorable terms—have worked to prevent the relatively low ratio of savings to current output from seriously inhibiting economic growth. However, as just argued, these circumstances cannot be expected to prevail in the future to the same
degree, and consequently a fundamental problem facing the country
is that of raising the proportion of domestic production available for
supporting capital formation, i.e., is that of increasing the savings-
output ratio.

The problem presented by the need for a higher rate of domestic
saving is compounded by the fact that in recent years the proportion
of total savings accounted for by the federal government has declined. Governmental expenditures for such things as education, public health, and other current operations have increased relative to tax
revenues, with the result that the ability of the government to finance
public investment expenditures from current revenues has been reduced. Given the necessity for progressively increasing expenditures
in support of social welfare programs and a variety of public works,
it is essential that federal tax revenues be increased as a percentage
of gross national product if public sector deficits are not to become
an excessive drain on the financial resources of the private sector—as
well as a potential source of renewed monetary instability. There
exists some scope for alleviating the situation by curtailing certain
government consumption subsidies, and by adjusting prices for publicly produced goods and services to reflect more adequately the
costs and requirements for investable funds of the various decentralized producing agencies, but aggressive action on these fronts may
be unlikely for political reasons. In any case, the really urgent need
is for a more productive and rational tax system which will permit
an increased volume of publicly financed capital formation without
unduly reducing savings and investment incentives in the private
sector.

It is evident that Mexican authorities are alerted to the potential

Recent Experience and Future Development

danger of excessive external indebtedness, and actions hav/ taken recently to control foreign borrowing and to refund (indebtedness in such a way as to make required repayment schea- ules more manageable. Of course the principal factor governing Mex- ico's debt servicing capacity is the ability to command foreign ex- change through exports, tourism, and other such commercial trans- actions, but an additional important determinant is the profitability of direct private foreign investment and the practices followed by foreign investors with regard to profit remittance. Clearly there is a close relation between this latter factor and profits taxation, and fu- ture fiscal reforms will need to be tailored to permit increased reve- nues without affecting adversely either the inflow of direct private investment or decisions regarding reinvestment of the profits of for- eign-owned enterprises.

Closely related to the problem of foreign indebtedness generally and to the question of private foreign investment in particular is the recently instituted policy of Mexicanization, i.e., the policy of re- quiring foreign-owned enterprises to offer opportunities for equity participation to Mexican investors. This policy is intended to have a threefold financial effect (as distinct from the obvious political ef- fects): increased profitable opportunities for domestic investors, with a related increase in the propensity to save and a decrease in the propensity to transfer investable funds abroad; greater partici- pation by domestic investors in earnings derived from the operations of foreign enterprises as well as in the prerogatives of management, and a consequent reduction in the risk of excessive profit remittan- ces abroad; increased supply of equity securities available to do- mestic investors, thereby stimulating the development of the capital market. While the success of the Mexicanization policy in bringing about these desirable financial effects remains to be established, it is apparent that financial considerations were important in motivat- ing the policy. Also apparent is the close relationship between this policy and certain dimensions of the fundamental problem of sav- ings—especially those aspects of the problem bearing on the need for substituting domestic savings for foreign savings and the need to gain greater protection from untimely conversions of peso earnings into other currencies.

The basic problem is that of increasing the domestic savings rate without giving rise to undesirable side effects. The solution to the problem lies mainly in the area of fiscal reform. There now exist in Mexico the necessary productive capacity, material standard of living, and institutional structure for effectively mobilizing a substantially larger proportion of current output into savings and capital formation. What is needed to bring this about is a system of taxation which not only appropriately limits luxury consumption and increases the ability of the federal government to finance an expanded volume of investment expenditures from current revenues but one which is also calculated to be sufficiently progressive (in the sense of producing a proportionately greater yield as output grows) so that consumption will not increase at the same rate as future output growth and the rate of domestically financed capital formation can be augmented.

Problem of investment priorities.—We have pointed out that if, as appears to be the case, the ratio of incremental capital formation to marginal product is increasing, the corollary proposition is that capital formation must increase relative to output in order to maintain satisfactory rates of economic growth. Clearly the attainment of a higher level of investment expenditure and the concomitant higher rate of saving is dependent upon effective operation of the financial system. Another approach to the problem, however, is that of promoting greater efficiency in the allocation of investable resources as between competing applications—and again the financial system must play a crucial role.

In a dynamic economy such as that of Mexico, investment priorities are subject to constant change. Changes in productive techniques and consumer preferences, as well as advances from one stage of economic growth to another (with associated changes is developmental policies or strategies), inevitably require shifts in the allocation of investable resources and loanable funds. The financial system, along with the fiscal system and the price system, must be sufficiently sensitive to detect these requirements as they arise and sufficiently flexible to permit necessary adjustments. More specifically, the financial system must constantly approximate an optimal allocation of investable resources such that those applications with the highest real net productivity are accorded priority.

The fact that large integrated financial groups tend to dominate industrial and commercial activity may be an important barrier to achievement of greater rationality in the application of available investable resources. Financial institutions belonging to these groupings are employed to facilitate the flow of credits to favored enterprises and in so doing serve to limit the availability of funds to other potential borrowers outside the group whose activities, if suitably financed, may be capable of greater productivity. Whether or not the predominance of closed financial groupings does result in inefficient allocation of investable resources cannot be established on the basis of available evidence, but clearly there exists the danger that misallocation will occur on this account, and certainly the danger can be hedged by policies which reduce monopolistic practices on the part of private credit institutions and which thereby increase the ability of all borrowers to compete on an equal footing for loan funds in the money and capital market.

Of particular importance is the need for greater access to the country's credit resources on the part of new, small enterprises since these must be depended upon as a principal source of product innovations as well as innovations in productive and distributive techniques. Measures recently taken to increase the flow of credits to small and medium-sized industries clearly indicate awareness of the problem, but further efforts to increase the availability of credits (particularly medium- and long-term credits) to this class of borrowers will be necessary in the future.

Similarly, it is evident that one of the principal factors restricting the growth and efficiency of the agricultural sector of the economy is the limited availability of suitable credits on reasonable terms. As in the case of small businesses, numerous measures have recently been taken with the purpose of augmenting the flow of credits to agricultural ventures. Clearly, however, more attention to the problem of inadequate agricultural credit will be necessary in connection with the government's program of promoting modernization in the agricultural sector.

Some further comments on the problem of inadequate agricultural credit may be in order. The basic difficulty in providing a suitable flow of credit resources into agricultural ventures is attributable to two things, the system of land tenure which limits the development of mortgage lending and the fact that the vast majority of persons whose living comes from agriculture is simply not creditworthy according to traditional banking standards. Yet, clearly, continued rapid economic development in Mexico is dependent upon radical upgrading of the productivity of agricultural land and labor—which, in turn, must depend upon the introduction and/or extension of the use of irrigation, fertilizers, insecticides, and machinery. While an increased flow of credits into the agricultural sector will serve to assist further modernization in those units which are already commercially successful, improvements in traditional, subsistence-type operations are necessarily dependent upon large-scale government assistance. A much larger volume of public funds, whether or not channeled through the established official agricultural lending agencies, is a prime requisite for needed improvement in the performance of the agricultural sector. If the increased flow of public funds into agriculture is not to be at the expense of continued large-scale public expenditures in other sectors, either government revenues must be raised through higher taxation or foreign borrowing must be further increased for this purpose.

Other areas in which the availability of credit continues to be unduly restricted are low-cost housing and basic municipal services. As already mentioned, the housing credit situation has recently been improved as a result of various measures calculated to induce greater interest on the part of domestic lending institutions in mortgage instruments based on small residences and multifamily dwellings. Potable water systems, sewerage, and similar public welfare projects carried out at the municipal level continue to be largely dependent upon federal funds (principally those at the disposal of Banco Nacional Hipotecario Urbano y de Obras Públicas), since voluntary credits from private financial institutions are virtually unobtainable for these purposes. Progress toward provision of more adequate public services at the local level would be accelerated if a market for municipal securities could be developed. For this to occur, more rational systems of charges for these services are needed, so that public works would be self-liquidating, and also needed perhaps is some fiscal inducement such as exemption from taxation of interest paid to holders of municipal securities.

Another line of activity which currently suffers from insufficient credit is export trade. While efforts have recently been made to increase the support afforded by private banking institutions, export financing has become progressively less adequate as the composition of exports has shifted to more highly processed products and as international competition has come to depend more on the relative attractiveness of the terms of payment offered by exporting countries. Development of institutions and instruments permitting better export financing would be helpful not only from a balance of payments point of view but also as a means of promoting further export diversification. While greater amounts of private domestic financing of exports will be necessary in the future, a further possibility is that arrangements can be made to increase the volume of foreign funds available for this purpose.

The really basic problem in so far as the need to achieve greater rationality in the allocation of investable resources is concerned is that of devising public policies which are consistent with this objective. Given the dynamism of the Mexican economy and constantly changing technology and conditions in international markets, there is the great danger that public policies appropriately designed to achieve desired results during a past period will continue to be rigidly followed and thereby become a source of inefficiency in resource allocation under different conditions. There is need for constant scrutiny of the selective credit control program to assure that the priorities underlying the requirements imposed on lending institutions are appropriate, and the same continuous reappraisal should be made in the case of criteria guiding public investment expenditures. The merit of most public investment projects is based on calculations of external economies or contributions to social welfare, and while appropriate priorities based on these calculations are exceedingly difficult to establish, the effort to do so must be determined and continuous. Other examples of public policies which require constant review if inefficiency is to be minimized are those of international trade and investment regulations and governmental tax and subsidy programs. Given the large proportion of the country's investable resources controlled in one way or another by the federal government and its agencies, and given the infeasibility of relying on the test of profitability in most cases, there is a real danger that very serious wastage of these resources will result from ill-advised public policies.

Clearly what is required for rationality in the operation of the affairs of the public sector—in addition to honest and efficient administration—is application of the best available techniques of economic planning. Fortunately Mexico is favored with both the necessary technical skills and the political stability required to permit effective planning. What is needed to reap the benefits of these favorable circumstances is commitment on the part of those in positions of decision-making responsibility in the public sector to be guided in their actions by the criteria of economic efficiency (including ample concern for social welfare) and to eschew in so far as possible the temptation to base decisions on noneconomic, political considerations.

Problem of debt and interest-rate structure.—The main problems of a strictly financial sort confronting the Mexican economy are a propensity toward excessive liquidity, inadequacy of both debt and equity financing of a long-term variety, an inappropriate level and structure of interest rates, and the threat of an unduly burdensome volume of foreign indebtedness.

Excessive liquidity and inadequacy of long-term financing are, of course, closely related. The high degree of liquidity results from the preference on the part of savers for liquid financial instruments and maintenance at virtually constant levels of the market values of a wide range of fixed-yield securities. Given the liquidity of their obligations, it is difficult for banking system institutions to grant credits of sufficiently long term to permit enterprises to finance capital expenditures with borrowed funds. And, under present circumstances, it is usually not possible for borrowers to go directly to the market for large amounts of long-term financing because of the preference of ultimate savers for claims on financial institutions rather than industrial or other sorts of primary securities. The consequence is, of course, that an unduly high proportion of investment expenditures in the private sector must be financed by means of funds generated by the activities of investing enterprises, presumably causing many worthy projects (especially those open to new and small enterprises) to be foregone for lack of adequate financing.

Solution to the problem must be sought along several lines. First, in order to permit banking system institutions to increase the length of term of their lending, it will be necessary to induce these institutions (or at least certain types of them) to employ less liquid instruments as means of mobilizing funds in the money and capital market. Recent actions designed to force the private financieras to rely more heavily on the issuance of bonds are an example of what might be done on a broader scale in the future. Second, in order to make nominally long-term instruments serve their appropriate function in the market, it will be necessary to take further steps (gradually, and in a manner calculated not to be disruptive to orderly market conditions) toward discontinuance of the practice of supporting the market values of these instruments at par. The third change which will be necessary in association with the two already mentioned is in the structure of interest rates. Further efforts must be made to induce lowering of the overall rate structure to the fullest extent consistent with maintenance of domestic price stability and external financial equilibrium and also to establish more appropriate differentials as between long- and short-term instruments and as between different types of instruments with the same maturities. Progress along these lines is already evident, but what will be required in the future is a much sharper distinction between the money market and the capital market.

The achievement of domestic monetary stability and external financial equilibrium which has been so laboriously pursued throughout the latter half of the 1950s and the first half of the 1960s has provided the necessary prerequisite for successfully revamping the domestic indebtedness and interest-rate structure. With the diminution of the risk of inflation and devaluation, both savers and investors, as well as the financial intermediaries providing the linkage between them, are now able to respond rationally to the real factors governing domestic market conditions. Given these circumstances, it is now appropriate that market forces be given broader scope for determining the allocation of loanable funds and investable resources. By so doing, not only will greater efficiency be achieved but also new opportunities for the effective application of monetary controls of a quantitative sort be afforded policy-making authorities.

Given the prospective need for greatly expanded investment expenditures in the private sector, more encouragement to the development of a broad market for equity securities will be necessary. The growth of many enterprises would be accelerated by access to long-term financing of the sort which equity issues afford, and furthermore the development of a more active market for these issues might well contribute to achievement of a higher rate of saving and greater efficiency in the process of financial intermediation. By providing a readily accessible avenue for widespread participation in the profits of industrial and commercial enterprises and by permitting savers to accumulate claims which are well protected from loss in value due to inflation, a broad, liquid market for equity securities seems likely to offer an attractive alternative to luxury consumption, real estate speculation, and the movement of capital to foreign financial markets.

In summary, Mexican financial development in the years ahead as we foresee it will be characterized by progressive improvement of the debt and interest-rate structure such that the rate of domestic savings and capital formation and the efficiency in resource allocation will be improved, and also such that resistance to destabilizing forces eman-

ating from the domestic money and capital market and from abroad
will be increased. What is required for the fulfillment of this optimistic prediction is greater enterprise and spirit of innovation on the
part of lenders in the private financial sector and more progressive
and enlightened policies on the part of the monetary and financial
authorities. The establishment of additional types of intermediary
institutions seems not to be necessary, and in fact it may be necessary to guard against overexpansion of the institutional framework
of the financial system. It is essential that the real costs of finance
be minimized and that resources, both human and material, not be
absorbed into the financial sector when they are capable of greater
contribution to the economic development of the country in alternative employments.

Toward a More Efficient Financial System

Throughout this chapter we have repeatedly appealed
to the criterion of efficiency as a guide to future policy in the financial
sphere. However, we have not defined what is meant by the term
"efficiency" when used in this context, and it is appropriate, therefore,
to state as explicitly as possible what constitutes an efficient financial
system.

Gurley and Shaw, in a provocative paper presented in Buenos
Aires in August of 1964 at the conference on financial aspects of development sponsored by Instituto Di Tella, defined as "optimal" a
financial structure that employs real factors of production up to the
point at which their marginal social cost is equal to the marginal
social benefit of their employment, and one in which these factors of
production are combined so that at all levels of financial activity marginal costs are minimized. On the basis of this application of traditional marginal analysis, they argue that a country's financial
structure may be suboptimal because social benefits are not adequately reflected in the demand for services of the financial sector, or
because real inputs are not employed up to that point at which their
marginal cost is equal to their true marginal value product, or because
marginal cost is unnecessarily high and marginal value product unnecessarily low.

Stated in less abstract terms, the three general reasons that a country's financial structure may be suboptimal, according to Gurley and
Shaw, are as follows. First, private financial entrepreneurs and public financial authorities may be either unable or unwilling to take

into proper account the external benefits and costs of their activities. Operation of the financial system strictly on the basis of either profit and loss calculations or political considerations may result in an institutional structure which is too large or too small in terms of the real resources required to support it. Second, the financial structure may be suboptimal because it is unable adequately to accommodate to changes in the pattern of saving and investment associated with different stages in the process of economic growth. The financial structure may be insufficiently flexible because of impediments to adjustment in degree of specialization and scale of operations of financial intermediaries attributable to monopolistic practices or other market imperfections, or because of public policies and regulations which prevent adaptation to changing circumstances. The third general reason for suboptimal financial structures, according to Gurley and Shaw's analysis, is existence of unnecessary risks and uncertainties for financial institutions and market participants resulting from such things as unreliable or otherwise inadequate information and communication systems, unstandardized and cumbersome financial instruments and legal procedures, highly variable real incomes of debtors, and capricious public policies, including, especially erratic inflation.

While it is not possible to specify what would constitute an optimal or perfectly efficient financial system for Mexico, it does seem both feasible and worthwhile for private financial entrepreneurs and public financial authorities alike to attempt a continuing appraisal of the efficiency of the Mexican financial system based on the theoretical principles outlined above. The immediate objective should be that of isolating existing inefficiencies and of indicating opportunities for productive, profitable, and socially beneficial innovations in financial practices and policies. The ultimate objective, however, should be that of facilitating continuous adaptation of the financial system to changing circumstances, thereby preventing any unnecessary restriction of saving and capital formation and any avoidable misallocation of investable resources as between alternative investment opportunities.

While correction of existing inefficiencies in both the public and private subsectors of the financial sector should be encouraged, clearly the public sector has special responsibilities in this connection. Numerous opportunities exist for assisting in the establishment of standards and procedures conducive to greater operating efficiency as well as in the reduction of unnecessary risks and uncertainties, for permitting recognition of external costs and benefits in the activities of both public and private financial institutions, for limiting undesirable monopolistic elements in the financial system, and, in general, for facilitating adjustment of the system to changes in the pattern of saving, investment, and the overall economic growth of the country. A wide variety of public policies might be devised for the purpose of promoting a more efficient financial system, ranging from requirement of improved accounting methods and financial reporting procedures to establishment of appropriate insurance and guarantee programs and to removal of unwarranted or outdated restrictions on the activities of financial institutions and the operation of financial markets.

The consequences of a more efficient financial system would be an enlarged volume of financial flows and probably also a higher level of saving and investment. Furthermore, a more efficient financial system would result in a better allocation of saving as between investment opportunities and, thereby, in an improved relationship between capital formation and output growth. In addition, as Gurley and Shaw point out, the more effective the financial system in supporting higher levels of saving and investment, and in bringing about a higher marginal productivity of investment, the less is the need for the government to attempt to supplement domestic savings with foreign savings or to force a higher level of domestic saving through the process of inflation. Also, where an efficient financial system exists, it is possible to pursue the objectives of financial stability and rapid economic growth within an institutional framework in which economic decision making in both the public and private sectors is less centralized than otherwise would be desirable and in which greater reliance can be placed on the free choices of individuals and private business firms regarding savings out of current income and regarding transfers of funds as between surplus and deficit spending units.

As a final note in this connection it should be re-emphasized that the finance function is itself costly in terms of real resources. The manpower required to operate a sophisticated financial system is generally of the sort capable of making important contributions to the effective operation of the economy by serving in alternative capacities. Therefore, care should be exercised not to pull an inordinate amount of the limited supply of administrative and technical talent into financial activities, thereby reducing the supply available to nonfinancial sectors such as industry, government, and education. Furthermore, care should be taken to assure that finance does not afford an avenue for introducing further inequality in income distribution. Finally, with greater financial sophistication will come increased opportunity for speculative abuses as well as increased danger of inflation and financial crises, and appropriate safeguards against these undesirable potentialities must be devised.

Conclusion

One of the most pressing and difficult contemporary problems in the financial sphere is that of achieving greater efficiency: efficiency in mobilizing potentially available savings, efficiency in the allocation of available credit resources as between application in the public and private sectors as well as within each of these sectors, and efficiency in the utilization of available credit resources in support of investment expenditures and in support of consumption expenditures and in decisions regarding the degree to which each of these warrants credit support. In the past public policies directed toward the promotion of a high rate of capital formation and output growth, the establishment of a variety of financial institutions, and the maintenance of a reasonable degree of financial stability have placed relatively little emphasis on financial efficiency as such. Likewise, because most private financial activities have been highly profitable, talent and other resources have been drawn into these activities without much regard to cost considerations. Consequently, there now exist numerous opportunities for adjustments in established financial practices which will lead to greater efficiency and, thereby, promote the overall growth of the Mexican economy.

Progress along this line will probably be difficult however, depending as it does on improved public administration and coordination of financial controls and of public revenue and expenditure policies as well as on the development of more vigorous competition and a heightened sense of cost consciousness and willingness to assume the risks inherent in exploitation of the numerous opportunities for financial innovation in the private sector. Clearly many of the obvious potential improvements in financial efficiency can be achieved only after substantial political resistance and inertia is overcome. Furthermore, difficulty will be encountered because there exist neither the well-defined economic principles nor sufficient statistical information upon which to base planning for improved financial efficiency. To some extent, of course, increased efficiency can be achieved by greater reliance on market forces, and by removal of barriers to the effective operation of these forces, but for the most part improvements are dependent upon a greater emphasis on financial efficiency in the conduct of public affairs. Assuming that financial stability can be sustained, it seems a safe prediction that the problem of financial efficiency will become increasingly central to the activities of monetary and fiscal authorities during the stage of Mexican financial development just beginning.

GUIDE TO FURTHER READING

The selected bibliography which follows is intended as a guide to further reading on various aspects of Mexican financial development. The statistical sources and theoretical works upon which principal reliance has been placed in writing this book are referred to in the Preface and the notes to the tables, and these references are not repeated here.

For those wishing to keep abreast of current financial developments, in addition to the annual reports of Banco de México, Nacional Financiera, and Comisión Nacional de Valores, it will be useful to consult the following periodicals: *El Mercado de Valores*, published weekly by Nacional Financiera; *Comercio Exterior*, published monthly by Banco Nacional de Comercio Exterior; *Examen de la Situación Económica de México*, published monthly by Banco Nacional de México; and the monthly bulletins reporting developments in the securities markets issued by Comisión Nacional de Valores and by Bolsa de Valores de México.

Alcocer, Mariano.
Las instituciones privadas de crédito en México, de 1921 a 1950. Carta mensual, v. 6, núm. 64–65, ago./sep., 1951.

Alvarado, José.
El extraño caso de la Secretaría de Hacienda. Problemas agrícolas e industriales de México. v. V, núm. 1, ene./mar., 1953.

Astudillo y Ursua, Pedro.
Banco de México, S.A., Revista de Administración Publica, núm. 6, abr./may. 1957.

Banco de Comercio de Tampico, S.A.
El ahorro y el desarrollo económico de México. Revista Bancaria, v. VI. núm. 1, ene./feb., 1958.

Banco de Londres y México, S.A.
100 (Cien) años de banca en México; primer centenario de la banca de depósito en México, 1864–1964. México: Cía. Impresora y Litográfica "Juventud", S.A., 1964.

Banco de México.
Instructivo sobre el depósito obligatorio y sus inversiones autorizadas. México: Banco de México, 1950.
– Directorio de empresas industriales beneficiadas con exenciones fiscales, 1940–1960. México: Talleres Gráficos, 1961.
– Informe sobre la revisión preliminar de las estimaciones del producto nacional de México para los años de 1950 a 1962. Elaborado por el Departmento de Estudios Económicos, sep., 1963.

Banco Nacional de Crédito Agrícola y Ganadero.
Legislación sobre crédito agrícola. México:Banco Nacional de Crédito Agrícola y Ganadero, 1951.
– Veinticinco años del Banco Nacional de Crédito Agrícola y Ganadero, S.A., 1926–1951. México: Oficina de Biblioteca y Publicaciones del Banco Nacional de Crédito Agrícola y Ganadero, 1951.

Barros Sierra, Manuel.
Banco Nacional Hipotecario Urbano y de Obras Públicas, S.A. Revista de Administración Pública, núm. 6, abr./jun., 1957.

Beers, John S. de
El peso mexicano, 1941–1949. Problemas Agrícolas e Industriales, v. V, núm. 1, ene./mar., 1953.

Bernal Molina, Julián.
El mercado de valores en México. El Trimestre Económico, v. 14, núm. 12, jul./sept., 1947.

Beteta, Mario Ramón.
El Banco Central como instrumento del desarrollo económico de México. Comercio Exterior, t. XI, núm. 6, jun., 1961.
– Tres aspectos del desarrollo económico de México: la revolución mexicana, marco institucional del desarrollo económico; el Banco Central, instrumento del desarrollo económico en México; las inversiones extranjeras, factor complementario del financiamiento del desarrollo. México: Publicaciones Especializadas S.A., 1963.
– (Con otros). I Foro mexicano sobre mercado de valores; sintesis de intervenciones. Actividad Económica en Latinoamérica. Año V, ago. 15, 1964.
– El sistema bancario mexicano y el Banco Central. México: Centro de Estudios Monetarios Latinoamericanos, 1964.

Bett, Virgil M.
Central Banking in Mexico; Monetary Policies and Financial Crises, 1864—1940. Ann Arbor: University of Michigan Press, 1957.

Bravo Aguilera, Luis.
El mercado de capitales en México. México: Impresores Unidos, 1958.

Brandenburg, Frank.
Organized Business in Mexico. Inter-American Economic Affairs, v. 12, no. 4. Winter, 1958.

Brothers, Dwight S.
Nexos entre la estabilidad monetaria y el desarrollo económico en América Latina: un escrito doctrinal y de política. El Trimestre Económico, v. XXIX, núm. 116, oct./dic., 1962.
– El financiamiento de la formación de capitales en México, 1950–1961. Supl. al Boletín Quincenal, Centro de Estudios Monetarios Latinoamericanos, núm. 9, sep., 1963.
– (Con Leopoldo Solís M.). Recent Financial Experience in Mexico. Economía Latinoamericana, v. II, no. 1, jul., 1965.

Bustani Hid, José.
Los gastos en inversión del Gobierno Federal. México: Ed. Logos, 1961.

Calderón, Antonio.
Resultados de la política monetaria. Revista de Economía, v. XIX, núm. 6, jun., 1956.

Campos Salas, Octaviano.
Nuestras reservas de oro y divisas. Revista de Economía, v. 7, núm. 4–6, jun., 1944.

Cárdenas, Felipe.
Comisión Nacional Bancaria. Revista de Administración Pública, núm. 6, abr./may., 1957.

Carrillo Flores, Antonio.
El sistema monetario mexicano. México: Editorial Cultura, 1946.
– Prácticas, métodos y problemas del financiamiento del desarrollo económico de México. Problemas Agrícolas e Industriales, v. II, núm. 1, ene./mar., 1949.

Castañeda, José H.
Proceso inflacionario durante la década de 1939–1948. Revista de Economía, v. XVI núm. 2, mar., 1953.

Cervantes, Manuel.
La moneda en México. Mexico: s.e., 1954.

Cervantes Delgado, Alejandro.
La política fiscal y las reformas impositivas de 1962. El Trimestre Económico, v. XXIX, núm. 115, jul./sep., 1962.

Chávez Hayhoe, Salvador.
El crédito agrícola en México. Ciencias Políticas y Sociales, año 2, núm. 4, abr./jun., 1956.

Comisión Nacional Bancaria.
Directorio de instituciones de crédito y organizaciones auxiliares. México: Secretaría de Hacienda y Crédito Público, 1961.

Connant, Charles A.
The Banking System of Mexico. U. S. Senate Document no. 493, 61st. Congress, 2nd session. Washington: National Monetary Commission, 1910.

Cornejo Flores, Gregorio Adolfo.
Las fuentes internas de financiamiento de las empresas. México, s.e., 1964.

Cosio Villegas, Daniel.
Historia moderna de México: El Porfiriato, la vida económica. México: Editorial Hermes, 1965. Especially, Fernando Rosenzweig, "Moneda y Bancos" pp. 785–885.

Cossio, Luis, and Izquiedo, Rafael.
Estimación de la relación producto-capital de México, 1940–1960. El Trimestre Económico, v. XXIX, húm. 116, oct./dic., 1962.

Cueto, Héctor Hugo del.
Cuando el peso valía más que el dólar. Ensayo histórico de las devaluaciones monetarias en México. México: Talls. de la Impresora Juan Pablos, 1959.

Dávila Gómez Palacio, Roberto.
Concentración financiera privada en México. Investigación Económica, v. XV, núm. 2, abr./jun., 1955.

Dueñes, Heliodoro.
Los bancos y la revolución. México: Editorial Cultura, 1945.

Fernández Hurtado, Ernesto y Villaseñor, Eduardo.
La expérience monétaire du Mexique. Paris: Presses Universitaires de France, 1956.

Fernández Moreno, Hector.
Intervención estatal en el crédito agrícola y ejidal. Revista de Economía, v. XXIII, núm. 11, nov., 1960.

Fernández y Fernández, Ramón.
El crédito ejidal. El Trimestre Económico, v. 25, núm. 2, abr./jun., 1958.
– El difícil problema del crédito ejidal. Revista de Economía, v. 17, núm. 8, ago., 1954.

Ferreiro, Elena.
Medidas de política monetaria y de créditos. Revista de Economía, v. XIX, núm. 6, jun., 1956.

Flores de la Peña, Horacio.
La mecánica de la inflación. Investigación Económica, v. XIII, núm. 4, oct./dic., 1953.
– (Con otros). Problemas del desarrollo económico mexicano. México: Universidad Nacional Autónoma de México, Escuela Nacional de Economía, 1958.

Fraustro, Oscar.
Nacional Financiera, S.A. Revista de Administración Pública, núm. 5, ene./mar., 1957.

García Maldonado, Edmundo.
El mercado nacional de valores; El mecanismo de inversión en México. México: Editorial libros de México, S.A., 1964.

García Muñoz, Lorenzo.
Función de las sociedades de inversión. Actividad Económica en Latinoamérica, núm. 54, ene., 1965.

García Reynoso, Plácido.
Growth with stability. Statist, Jan., 1965.

Glade, William P., Jr.
Las empresas gubernamentales descentralizadas. Problemas Agrícolas e Industriales de México, v. XI, núm. 1, ene./mar., 1959.
– and Anderson, Charles W.
The Political Economy of Mexico. Madison: University of Wisconsin Press, 1963.

Gómez Gordoa, José.
El sector privado ante los problemas del comercio exterior y del desarrollo económico de México. Comercio Exterior, t. XV, núm. 1, ene., 1965.

Gómez, Rodrigo
La evolución de México y las bases fundamentales de la política monetaria. (Discurso pronunciado ante la XXX Convención Nacional Bancaria). El Mercado de Valores, año XXIV, núm. 11, mar., 1964.

Gurza, Jaime.
Funciones monetarias del Banco de México, S.A. México: s.e., 1941.

Hernández Delgado, José.
La Nacional Financiera, S.A., como impulsora del mercado de valores mobiliarios. Revista Bancaria, v. VI, núm. 6, nov./dic., 1958.
– Nacional Financiera como coadyuvante de la industrialización. México: Nacional Financiera, 1961.

Herrera, Mario.
Obligaciones convertibles en acciones; doctrina, protección de los inversionistas, acuerdos de la Comisión Nacional Bancaria. México: Talls. de la Editorial Cultura, 1964.

Himes, James R.
La formación de capital en México. El Trimestre Económico, v. XXXII, núm. 125, ene./mar., 1965.

Iturbide, Anibal de.
La devaluación del peso mexicano y sus antecedentes. Revista de Economía, v. XI, núm. 8, ago., 1948.

Kemmerer, Edwin Walter.
Inflación y revolución: La experiencia mexicana de 1912–1917. Problemas Agrícolas e Industriales, v. V, núm. 1, 1953.

Lagunilla Iñarritu, Alfredo.
La tasa del dinero en México. El Trimestre Económico, v. XIII, núm. 4, ene./mar., 1947.

Legorreta, Agustín.
Financiamiento industrial. Examen de la Situación Económica de México, año XXXVIII, núm. 440, jul., 1962.

Limón, Gral. Gilberto R.
Banco Nacional del Ejército y de la Armada, S.A. de C.V. Revista de Administración Pública, núm. 6, abr./jun., 1957.

Lobato López, Ernesto.
El crédito en México, esbozo histórico hasta 1925. México: Fondo de Cultura Económica, 1945.
– La política monetaria mexicana. Investigación Económica, v. XVIII, núm. 72, oct./dic., 1958.

López Rosado, Diego.
Los bancos hipotecarios durante el porfirismo. Bancos, v. XVIII, núm. 72, oct./dic. 1958.
– Ensayos sobre historia económica de México. México: s.e., 1957.
– Banca Central: Cursos de mejoramiento del personal del Banco de México, S.A. México: Banco de México, 1954.
– Banco del Pequeño Comercio del Distrito Federal, S.A. Revista de Administración Pública, núm. 6, abr./jun., 1957.

Loss, Louis.
El papel del Gobierno en la protección de los inversionistas. México: Comisión Nacional de Valores, 1957.

Luna Olmedo, Agustín.
Banco Nacional de Crédito Ejidal, S.A. de C.V. Revista de Administración Pública, núm. 6, abr./jun., 1957.

Manero, Antonio.
La revolución bancaria en México, 1865–1955; una contribución a la historia de las instituciones de crédito en México. México: Talls. Gráfs. de la Nación, 1957.
– La reforma bancaria en la revolución constitucionalista. México: Talleres Gráficos de la Nación, 1958.

Martínez Domínguez, Guillermo.
Crédito al pequeño comercio; Banco sobre ruedas. Investigación Económica, v. XIV, núm. 3, jul./ago., 1954.

Martínez Le Clainche, Roberto.
La politique monétaire et bancaire du Mexique. Paris: Institut des Hautes Etudes de l'Amerique Latine, 1957.

Martínez Ostos, Raúl.
Algunos aspectos de la política monetaria del Banco de México. El Trimestre Económico, v. XI, núm. 2, jul./sep., 1944.

Mayobre, José Antonio.
El capital y el desarrollo económico. Investigación Económica, v. XII, núm. 2, abr./jun., 1952.

McCaleb, Walter F.
Present and Past Banking in Mexico. New York: Harper and Brothers, 1920.

Méndez, Oscar E.
Las deudas nacionales incluídas en los convenios de 1942 y 1946; pláticas al personal del Banco de México, S.A. México: Banco de México, 1957.

Montes de Oca, Luis.
Cinco artículos sobre la devaluación monetaria. México, s.e., 1954.

Mora Ortiz, Gonzalo.
El Banco Nacional de Comercio Exterior. México: Editorial Ruta, 1950.

Moreno Castañeda, Gilberto.
La Moneda y la banca en México. Guadalajara: Imprenta Universitaria, 1955.

Mosk, Sanford.
The Industrial Revolution in Mexico. Berkeley: University of California Press, 1950.

Nacional Financiera, S.A.
La Nacional Financiera, S.A., en el progreso económico de México; Documentos para la historia de un gobierno. México: Editorial la Justicia, 1959.
– Quince años de vida, 1934–1949. México: Nacional Financiera, 1949.
– Un sexenio de trabajo, 1952–1958. México: Nacional Financiera, 1958.

– Fondo de garantía y fomento de la industria mediana y pequeña. México: Editorial Cultura, 1958.
– Fondo de garantía y fomento del turismo. México: Editorial Cultura, 1958.

Navarrete, Alfredo.
El mercado de valores como instrumento de canalización del ahorro popular. El mercado de valores, año XXIV, núm. 30, jul., 1964.
– El desarrollo económico y el control del gasto público. Comercio Exterior, t. XII, núm. 7, jul., 1962.
– Instrumentos de política financiera mexicana. México: Publicaciones Especializadas, 1964.
– (Con otros). Financiamiento del desarrollo económico de México. México: Universidad Nacional Autónoma de México, Escuela Nacional de Economía, 1958.

Navarrete, Ifigenia M. de.
The tax structure and the economic development of Mexico. Public Finance, v. XIX, no. 2, may./jun., 1964.
– La distribución del ingreso y el desarrollo económico de México. México: Instituto de Investigaciones Económicas, Escuela Nacional de Economía, 1960.

Noriega, Alberto.
Las devaluaciones monetarias de México, 1938–1954. Investigación Economica, v. XV, no. 1, ene./mar., 1965.

Ortiz Mena, Raúl.
La moneda mexicana: Análisis histórico de sus fluctuaciones, las depreciaciones, y sus causas. México: Banco de México, S.A., 1955.
– (Con Victor L. Urquidi y otros). El desarrollo económico de México y su capacidad para absorber capital del exterior. México: Fondo de Cultura Económica, 1953.

Ortiz Rocha, Quirino.
Las sociedades financieras mexicanas. Actividad Económica en Latinoamérica, año 5, núm. 51, oct., 1964.

Padilla, Enrique.
La dinámica de la economía mexicana y el equilibrio monetario. El Trimestre Económico, v. 25, núm. 37, jul./sep., 1958.

- La devaluación del peso mexicano: cuatro conferencias. El Trimestre Económico, v. 15, núm. 3–4, oct./dic., 1948.

Pani, Alberto J.
Los orígenes de la política crediticia; con la réplica y las contrarréplicas suscitadas. México: Ed. Atlante, 1951.
- El problema supremo de México. México: Imp. de Manuel Casas, 1955.

Pérez López, Enrique.
El Mercado de Valores. México: Nacional Financiera, 1947.

Potash, Robert A.
El Banco de Avío de México: El fomento de la industria 1821–1846. México: Fondo de Cultura Económica, 1959.

Ramírez Solano, Ernesto.
Un ensayo teórico sobre la expansión monetaria en México. México: Impresores Salinas, 1957.

Ramos Uriarte, Alfredo.
El desarrollo económico y la bolsa de valores. México: s.e., 1963.

Reina Hermosillo, Práxedes.
Comisión Nacional de Valores. Revista de Administración Pública, núm. 2, abr./jun., 1956.

Ross, Stanford G., and Christensen, John B.
Tax Incentives for Industry in Mexico. Cambridge: Law School of Harvard University, 1959.

Ruiz Equihua, Arturo.
El encaje legal; instrumento fundamental de la política monetaria mexicana contemporánea. México: Ed. Cultura, 1963.

Salas Villagomez, Manuel.
Problemas financieros de la industrialización de México. Revista de Economía, v. 14, núm. 1, ene., 1951.

Salera, Virgil.
The depreciation of the Mexican peso. Inter-American Economic Affairs, v. III, no. 2, Autumn, 1949.

Sánchez Cuen, Manuel.
El crédito a largo plazo en México; reseña histórica. El Banco Nacional
Hipotecario Urbano y de Obras Públicas, S.A. México: Gráfica Panameri-
cana, 1958.

Secretaría de Hacienda y Crédito Público.
Discursos pronunciados por los CC. Secretarios de Hacienda y Crédito
Público en las convenciones bancarias celebradas del año 1934 a 1958.
México: Sría. de Hacienda y Crédito Público, 1958.
– Legislación bancaria. México: Sría. de Hacienda y Crédito Público,
1957.
– Legislación sobre el Banco de México. México: Sría. de Hacienda y Cré-
dito Público, 1958.

Sedwitz, Walter J.
La devaluación; su génesis y consecuencias. Revista Fiscal y Financiera,
v. XVII, núm. 118, abr., 1957.

Siegel, Barry N.
Inflación y desarrollo; las experiencias de México. México: Centro de
Estudios Monetarios Latinoamericanos, 1960.

Silva Ramírez, Enrique.
Captación de recursos en relación al capital de cada institución bancaria.
Actividad Económica en Latinoamérica, núm. 56, mar., 1965.

Simpson, Eyler N.
Recent Developments in Mexico in the Field of Money and Banking.
Mexico City: Institute of Current World Affairs, 1932.

Solana y Gutiérrez, Mateo.
Devaluaciones en México. México: Libro Mexicano, 1958.

Solís M., Leopoldo.
Intermediación financiera y desarrollo económico. El Trimestre Económ-
ico, v. XXXII, núm. 126, abr./jun., 1965.
– Controles selectivos del crédito: Un nuevo enfoque. El Trimestre Eco-
nómico, v. XXVIII, núm. 102, oct./dic., 1961.
– (Con Dwight S. Brothers). El mercado de dinero y capitales en México.
El Trimestre Económico, v. XXXI, núm. 124, oct./dic., 1964.

Sturmthal, Adolf.
Economic development, income distribution and capital formation in Mexico. Journal of Political Economy, v. LXIII, no. 3, June, 1955.

Szekely, Luis M.
Sobre la aplicación de modelos cuantitativos de decisiones para una política financiera a plazo corto y medio en México. México: Imprenta de "Pavia", 1963.

Tanner, Elaine.
The devaluation of the Mexican peso. Inter-American Economic Affairs, v. III, no. 1, Summer, 1949.

Tamagna, Frank.
La banca central en América Latina. México: Centro de Estudios Monetarios Latinoamericanos, 1963.

Tirado de Ruiz, Rosa Ma.
La Hacienda Pública y sus funciones económicas. Revista de Administración Pública, núm. 11, ene./mar., 1959.

Torres Gaitán, Ricardo.
La política financiera en la revolución. México, v. I, núm. 2, feb., 1956.
– Política monetaria mexicana. México: Lib. Ariel, 1944.

Urquidi, Victor L.
Tres lustros de experiencia monetaria en México: algunas enseñanzas. Meoria del Segundo Congreso Mexicano de Ciencias Sociales. México: Artes Gráficas del Estado, 1946.
– El papel de la política fiscal y monetaria en el desarrollo económico, México: El Trimestre Económico, v. XVIII, núm. 4, oct./dic., 1951.

Vernon, Raymond.
The Dilemma of Mexico's Development: The Roles of the Private and Public Sectors. Cambridge: Harvard University Press, 1963.
– Public Policy and Private Enterprise in Mexico: Studies by Miguel S. Wionczek, David H. Shelton, Calvin P. Blair, and Rafael Izquierdo. Cambridge: Harvard University Press, 1964.

Villaseñor, Eduardo.
La estructura bancaria y el desarrollo económico de México. El Trimestre Económico, v. XX, núm. 2, abr./jun., 1953.

Wionczek, Miguel S.
Incomplete Formal Planning: Mexico, ed. Everett E. Hagen, Planning Economic Development. Center for International Studies, Massachusetts Institute of Technology. Homewood, Illinois: Irwin, 1963.

Zumpano Ortiz, María Luisa.
Los bonos del ahorro nacional como una forma de ahorro popular. México: s.e., 1963.